PRAISE FOR *BREAKING CHA*

"Rich with historical fact, fascinating cha
personal narratives, Breaking Chains is ar
convoluted flirtation with 'our peculiar institution.'" —*The Oregonian*

"The truth is we all are hurt when our understanding of history is distorted or substantially incomplete. We need to know history to see clearly the present shaped by it. Nokes' book clears away some of the fog." —*The Seattle Times*

"In his post-journalism career as an author, R. Gregory Nokes is working on setting history straight .... Nokes' book ... captures a dark shard of Northwest history that might have been swept under the rug." —*Lewiston Tribune*

"This is how history should be written... it is a page-turner... Breaking Chains is a fine read and one that will be well-underlined in my collection of great historical works. I highly recommend it." —Jane Kirkpatrick, *New York Times* bestselling author of *One Glorious Ambition*

"Greg Nokes' fascinating and well-written book shines a welcome bright light on the dark side of Oregon's past by exposing the history of slavery and anti-black prejudice in Oregon." —Phillip Margolin, *New York Times* bestselling author of *Sleight of Hand*

"Greg is peeling off the blinders on aspects of Oregon history (American history) that have been hidden in shame for far too long. These are the stories that must be shared in order to understand how we've become who we are today—and perhaps have a chance to heal some historic wounds." —Tom DeWolf, author of *Gather at the Table: The Healing Journey of a Daughter of Slavery and a Son of the Slave Trade*

"Nokes brings Oregonians the fuller story of our relationship to slavery and exploitation... This is a history book that every school and family should have and use." —Rae Richen, author of *Uncharted Territory.*

* *An Oregon Writers Colony Book Club Selection* *

Breaking Chains

SLAVERY ON TRIAL IN THE OREGON TERRITORY

R. GREGORY NOKES

Oregon State University Press

Corvallis

The paper in this book meets the guidelines for permanence and durability of the Committee on Production Guidelines for Book Longevity of the Council on Library Resources and the minimum requirements of the American National Standard for Permanence of Paper for Printed Library Materials Z39.48-1984.

Library of Congress Cataloging-in-Publication Data
Nokes, R. Gregory.
  Breaking chains : slavery on trial in the Oregon Territory / R. Gregory Nokes.
    p. cm.
  Includes bibliographical references and index.
  ISBN 978-0-87071-712-3 (alk. paper) -- ISBN 978-0-87071-713-0 (e-book)
  1. Slavery--Law and legislation--Oregon. 2. Slaves--Legal status, laws, etc.--Oregon. 3. Slaveholders--Legal status, laws, etc.--Oregon. 4. Oregon--Social conditions--19th century. I. Title.
  KFO2801.6.S55N65 2013
  342.79508'7--dc23

                                                            2012044623

Oregon State University Press
121 The Valley Library
Corvallis OR 97331-4501
541-737-3166 • fax 541-737-3170
www.osupress.oregonstate.edu

To my late grandparents, Minnie and Will Junkin of Tigard, Oregon, whose mention of a slave in a family genealogy brought me to this story.

Reuben Shipley, a negro boy, residing a few miles south of here on Marys river, died on Wednesday.

(*Benton Democrat*, Corvallis, Oregon; July 26, 1872)

Table of Contents

Prologue

I owe an apology to Billy Taylor. It's not his real name, of course. Too much time has gone by for me to remember that. I believe he came from Virginia. But I'm not sure of that either. It was some place in the South.

Billy had come to Portland to spend a summer with his grandparents. They lived on the corner of Everett Street and Thirty-Second Avenue, a half-block down Everett from where I lived. Billy was a friendly kid—lanky, sandy hair, a big grin, twelve or so, same as me. We became instant friends for a time, not best friends, but friends.

However, in the year just ended at Laurelhurst Grade School, I'd been taught a brief history of slavery and the Civil War, an over-simplified narrative I interpreted as follows: North good, South bad; North fighting to free slaves, South fighting to keep slaves.

Of course, in my all-white neighborhood in virtually all-white Portland, there was but a single African American in our school. I had no idea how the North treated blacks. I do recall my sole black classmate, whom I didn't get to know very well, would occasionally come to school in a sweater with holes in it. A kid who didn't have holes in his sweaters remembers things like that.

But back to Billy. For some reason, which I don't recall, another neighborhood chum and I turned on Billy one day, and he became for us a contrived enemy. We used his southern background as a weapon, accusing him of supporting slavery and the Confederacy. We began calling him a Reb, which wasn't so bad. But the name-calling soon got uglier.

We taunted him. We refused to play with him. I hate to think we might even have thrown dirt clods at him once. There was one particularly sad afternoon, possibly the last time I saw Billy, when he left us in tears, head down, walking along Thirty-Second Avenue, back toward his grandparents' home, with us yelling and laughingly calling him names.

Kids can be cruel. No news there. But no excuse either. I'd guess that was one kid who never wanted to return to our City of Roses.

What I didn't know then, but I know now, is that we in Oregon had no reason to be smug about our attitudes and policies toward African Americans and other minorities. Indeed, our own history is shameful.

Witness:

- Many of our early leaders were pro-slavery.
- Serious debate was given to whether Oregon should become a slave state.

- There were slaves in Oregon and no one seemed to care much.
- Most of those who opposed slavery in the early years did so largely for economic reasons—moral issues were an afterthought.

Consider also the great shame of our black exclusion laws. Bad enough that a black exclusion clause was written into Oregon's constitution in 1857. Worse that it wasn't removed until 1926.

Moreover, I've faced personal regret on recently learning that a distant ancestor brought a slave to Oregon.

Darrell Millner, professor of black studies at Portland State University, said we shouldn't necessarily apply today's standards to events of the past. He is correct, of course. But we shouldn't hide our past either. And we have done this in Oregon. Our history books may boast that we had anti-slavery laws on our books from the earliest days of white settlement, but they overlook that slave owners were initially given three years to free their slaves. Three years! Turn this around. It meant that for individual slaves and slaveholders, slavery might be lawful for three years.

Ask any school teacher about our past sympathies and flirtations with slavery. You are likely to get a blank stare. Ask residents of liberal Lane County if they know of the pro-slavery background of one of Oregon's first U.S. senators, Joseph Lane, for whom the county was named in 1851. Who remembers today that members of the Oregon delegation to the 1860 Democratic National Convention walked out in solidarity with delegates from slave states? Few may know that Joseph Lane ran for vice president in 1860 on a secessionist ticket with John Breckinridge of Kentucky—against Abraham Lincoln.

Author Barry Lopez wrote that after moving to Oregon from New York in 1968, he was quickly disabused of any preconceptions about Oregon as a bastion of liberal orthodoxy. Behind the stories of courageous white settlers, he discovered "the fuller story of settlement that every state seeks to diminish or manipulate in presenting itself."[1]

In Oregon, this disconcerting history included the plundering of Indian lands, the rescinding, in 1868, of the state's 1866 ratification of the Fourteenth Amendment (guaranteeing citizenship and basic civil rights for African Americans); the formation of violent anti-Chinese leagues in Portland in the 1880s; and, later, the state's collusion in the development of a reckless system of commercial exploitation of the region's natural resources, especially timber. This uncomplimentary account tended to undermine the twentieth century image of western Oregon as a modern American Eden, an idyll many young people invested in and believed would unfold there in the years following Woodstock and the Summer of Love.[2]

·⁀ ⌣·

If I were in school again, I would want to understand the real history of our state, not a sanitized version that misleads us into myths and misplaced self-satisfaction. We can learn from our past. We should.

My intention with this book is to penetrate some of the myths we have about our heritage as it relates to slavery and our attitudes toward—and treatment of—people of color. We were not untainted by everything that slavery represented. Yes, we declared ourselves early on as opposed to slavery. But we also declared ourselves early on as opposed to having African Americans among us. This book will try to explain how these two positions were related, and to show that we in the Pacific Northwest were very much a part of the national turmoil and debate over slavery.

We had our own serious flirtation with the dark side of our nation's history. We were part of the problem.

·⁀ ⌣·

Billy, if you ever chance to read this, you will remember the pain I caused on those summer afternoons. Kids don't forget things like that.

R. Gregory Nokes
January 1, 2013

Columbia River

Oregon City   The Dalles

Philomath   Rickreall

Oregon Territory

Snake River

Fort Hall

Great Salt Lake

Sacramento

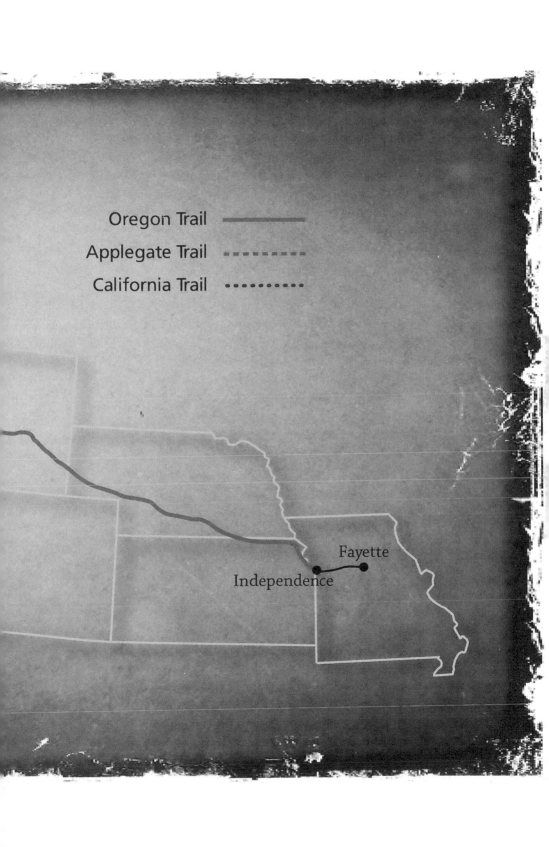

Oregon Trail

Applegate Trail

California Trail

Fayette

Independence

DATES AND EVENTS

July 13, 1787—Congress enacts the Northwest Ordinance, which prohibits slavery in the new Northwest Territory north of the Ohio River and east of the Mississippi River, effectively establishing the Ohio as the boundary between slave states and non-slave states.

Treaty of 1818—Provides for joint British and American occupation and settlement of the Oregon Country.

Missouri Compromise of 1820—Prohibits slavery in new territories north of a theoretical line drawn from the southern boundary of Missouri, except within Missouri.

May 2, 1843—Early inhabitants of Oregon Country meet at Champoeg to establish a provisional government.

July 5, 1843—Early settlers and others approve an organic act for the provisional government, which includes a prohibition against slavery.

December 25, 1843—The first major emigrant wagon train from Missouri, initially led by Peter Burnett, arrives at The Dalles.

June 18, 1844—The provisional government enacts the region's first exclusion law against blacks, with "lash law" punishment.

December 7, 1844—Nathaniel Ford's wagon train from Missouri arrives in Oregon City with slaves Robin and Polly Holmes, the Holmeses' three children, and another adult slave named Scott.

December 19, 1844—The exclusion law is modified to eliminate corporal punishment, but with a new forced-labor penalty for free blacks who refuse to leave.

July 25, 1845—Voters approve a new organic act with an anti-slavery provision, but no exclusion law, effectively abolishing the 1844 law before it takes effect.

June 15, 1846—The Oregon Treaty with Great Britain is approved, giving the United States jurisdiction over the Oregon Country south of the 49th parallel.

May 30, 1848—United States and Mexico ratify the Treaty of Guadalupe Hidalgo ending the war with Mexico and conceding to the United States present-day California, Nevada, and Utah, most of New Mexico and Arizona, and parts of Wyoming and Colorado.

August 14, 1848—Congress establishes the Oregon Territory with the provisional government's anti-slavery law intact. The new territory embraces all of the Pacific Northwest south of the 49th parallel and east to the Rocky Mountains.

September 21, 1849—The new Oregon Territorial Legislature enacts a second exclusion law against blacks, although it doesn't apply to existing residents.

Sometime in 1849—The Ford family undertakes its gold-mining expedition to California, taking along the slaves Robin Holmes and Scott.

Sometime in 1850—Nathaniel Ford gives Robin and Polly Holmes their freedom, but keeps three of their children.

September 18, 1850—Congress enacts the Compromise of 1850—with a new Fugitive Slave Act—that clears the way for California statehood.

September 27, 1850—The Donation Land Act for Oregon is enacted, providing up to a square mile of free land for the earliest settlers.

September 2, 1851—Oregon's 1849 exclusion law is enforced against Jacob Vanderpool, the only instance of an African American being expelled under one of Oregon's exclusion laws.

April 16, 1852—Former slave Robin Holmes files a custody suit against Nathaniel Ford, seeking freedom for his children.

March 2, 1853—Congress establishes the Washington Territory north of the Columbia River.

July 13, 1853—Judge George Williams rules in favor of Robin Holmes in his custody case, returning his children. It is the only slave case adjudicated in Oregon courts.

September 1, 1853—Robert Shipley arrives in Oregon from Missouri with his slave Reuben Shipley.

May 1, 1854—Oregon's 1849 exclusion law is repealed.

May 30, 1854—The Kansas-Nebraska Act is enacted by Congress, repealing the Missouri Compromise of 1820.

March 6, 1857—U.S. Supreme Court issues Dred Scott decision denying citizenship and constitutional protections to African Americans, whether slave or free.

July 28, 1857—Judge Williams' Free State Letter, arguing slavery won't work in Oregon, is published in the *Oregon Statesman*.

August 18, 1857—The Oregon Constitutional Convention convenes in Salem.

November 9, 1857—Voters approve Oregon's constitution with both a prohibition against slavery and an exclusion clause barring African Americans.

July 18, 1857—Former slave Reuben Shipley marries Mary Jane Holmes.

February 14, 1859—Oregon gains statehood, the only free state admitted into the union with an exclusion clause in its constitution.

November 6, 1860—Abraham Lincoln is elected President.

April 12, 1861—The Civil War opens with a Confederate attack on Fort Sumter in South Carolina.

May 11, 1861—Reuben and Mary Jane Holmes Shipley donate three acres of farmland in Benton County for the Mt. Union Cemetery, stipulating it be open to burials of both blacks and whites.

January 1, 1863—President Lincoln's Emancipation Proclamation takes effect, freeing slaves in the Confederate states.

April 9, 1865—General Robert E. Lee surrenders at Appomattox, bringing the Civil War to a close.

December 5, 1865—Oregon ratifies the Thirteenth Amendment to the U.S. Constitution, abolishing slavery.

September 19, 1866—Oregon ratifies the Fourteenth Amendment, guaranteeing citizenship and equal protection of laws to African Americans. The amendment renders Oregon's exclusion clause irrelevant, although it remains in the state constitution until 1926.

October 15, 1868—The Oregon legislature repeals its ratification of the Fourteenth Amendment, although its action has no effect because the amendment has been ratified by enough other states.

July 1872—Reuben Shipley dies of smallpox.

August 15, 1875—Mary Jane Holmes Shipley marries Alfred Drake.

November 2, 1900—Oregon voters reject a proposal to repeal the exclusion clause in the constitution.

January 13, 1926—Mary Jane Holmes Shipley Drake dies.

November 2, 1926—Oregon voters finally repeal the constitution's exclusion clause.

March 13, 1946—Edward Ficklin, the last surviving child of Reuben Shipley and Mary Jane Holmes Shipley, dies in Portland.

February 15, 1959—The Oregon State Legislature ratifies the Fifteenth Amendment granting voting rights to African Americans, eighty years after it became law. Notwithstanding Oregon's inaction, the Oregon Supreme Court had ruled in 1870 that African Americans could vote because the amendment was the law of the land.

May 21, 1973—The Oregon legislature re-ratifies the Fourteenth Amendment.

May 30, 1981—A granite memorial is dedicated at the entrance to the Mt. Union Cemetery in honor of Reuben Shipley and Mary Jane Holmes Shipley Drake.

First Slaves

There are two versions of how Robin and Polly Holmes, both Missouri slaves, came to Oregon. One, told by Robin Holmes, is that his owner, Nathaniel Ford, persuaded him to come in exchange for his freedom. The other, told by Ford descendants, is that Holmes begged to come and Ford brought Holmes—and Holmes' wife and children—against his better judgment.

Whichever version is correct, and Holmes' version is certainly the most believable, the family of slaves joined a wagon train of fifty-four wagons in 1844 for an eight-month journey along the Oregon Trail from Independence, Missouri. It was among the first emigrant wagon trains to leave for Oregon, and Robin and Polly Holmes would be among the first African Americans to live in Oregon.[1] They brought their three small children, and settled with the Ford family in what is now Polk County.

Years later, Holmes and Ford would face each other in a landmark court case that would help shape Oregon's policy toward slavery and slaves. The case was a *habeas corpus* suit brought by Holmes against Ford in 1852 seeking custody of his children, whom Ford tried to keep. A remarkable feature of the case is that it provides a rare written record of the relationship between a slave owner and a slave—from the slave's point of view.

Just as remarkable is the fact that a former slave managed to hold his own in a fourteen-month legal battle, which no judge seemed to want to decide. Holmes patiently stood his ground as the proceedings plodded through several Oregon courts before four different judges, at least one of whom appeared biased in favor of Ford. Holmes would demonstrate during the court battle—and also in his later life in Salem—a determination to struggle for personal justice in the face of overwhelming odds.

Like most slaves, Holmes was unable to read or write—it was against public policy in Missouri and throughout the South to educate a slave.[2] Nevertheless, aided by sympathetic attorneys, Holmes mounted a credible case against Ford, who was prominent in Oregon politics. Ford served in the territorial legislature and was appointed the region's chief judge in 1845, although he declined the office. Moreover, Holmes faced the added burden of taking on a slave owner in a farming community known to be sympathetic to slavery, and at a time when Oregon's own position on slavery, while technically outlawed, was still in flux.

To say Oregon came close to becoming a slave state would be an exaggeration. But not a wild one. There were influential leaders who wanted Oregon open to slavery. And there were those like Ford who wanted to, and did, keep slaves.

An early nineteenth century historian, Walter Carleton Woodward, concluded that slavery posed "an actual menace to Oregon" prior to the Civil War. Writing in a 1911 issue of *Oregon Historical Quarterly,* Woodward said:

> *At this distance it may seem almost inconceivable that there was any basis for such agitation [for slavery]; that there was any danger of Oregon's (sic) becoming a slave state. Whatever may be the mature conclusions on this point after the lapse of a half century, the fact remains that there was apparently very serious danger at the time.[3]*

The writer of a 1970 thesis, citing newspaper coverage, was led to remark: "The pro-slavery element was sufficiently vocal that the impression was gained in the territory and throughout the nation that Oregon was about to apply for admission to the Union as a slave state."[4]

There were probably never more than fifty slaves in Oregon, a number that pales in comparison with Missouri's total of 114,965 slaves in 1860, and the national total of 3,949,557.[5] And, in Oregon, slaves had an opportunity to gain their freedom, an opportunity denied them in slave states. Still, many may be surprised to learn that there were slaves in Oregon at all.

Trading in slaves was practiced in the Oregon Country long before the first wagon trains arrived. The earliest slaveholders and slaves were Native Americans. Some tribes captured members of other tribes for slaves, traded slaves among themselves, and, in later years, sold slaves to whites. "Hereditary slavery" was common among tribes around Puget Sound.[6]

A brief article in the *Oregon Journal* newspaper on January 8, 1920, said, "the principal slave market of the West was on the bank of the Willamette River at Oregon City near what is now the foot of Eleventh Street."

> *Here in the '40s and early '50s the Klamaths brought Indian slaves for sale, usually children captured in their frequent forays against the Shasta and Rogue Indians. The Klamaths traded these Indian slaves for blankets or other Hudson's Bay wares owned by the Willamette Valley Indians. Scores of these Indian slaves were purchased from their Indian owners by the white residents of Oregon City. In most cases they were liberated. Occasionally they were adopted and educated.[7]*

·–·–

I learned of the Holmes family while researching the background of another Missouri slave, known as Reuben Shipley. I had recently discovered in a long-unread family genealogy that I am a shirttail descendant of the man who owned Shipley and brought him to Oregon.[8] I was less than pleased to learn of this, and sought to know more. I was soon to discover that Reuben Shipley put his own important stamp on race relations in present-day Benton County, where, after receiving his freedom, he owned a farm near the small town of Philomath.

The lives of Reuben Shipley and Robin Holmes would intersect in later years, another of the several compelling stories involving these two former slaves, both unschooled, both of whom signed their names with X's.

The Good Life in Missouri

How the Holmes family became Ford's slaves in the first place is a story in itself. It begins in Howard County, Missouri.

Howard County is part of a central Missouri region that was known for years as "Little Dixie," a name befitting its similarity to the slave-based economies of the Deep South. Established in 1816, the county was named for Benjamin Howard, Missouri's first territorial governor. The Missouri River borders it on the south and west. Howard County had 4,890 slaves in 1850, one-third of its population of 13,969, making it the second largest slave-holding county in the state.[1] Slaves worked primarily in the hemp fields, cutting and crushing the tall, woody plant whose fiber was used for rope and textiles.

As told by Holmes, he and his wife had been owned for a dozen years by a Major Whitman, or Whitmore, a U.S. Army paymaster stationed in Missouri. The Holmeses were both born in Virginia about the year 1810. Polly was a house servant, Robin most likely a field hand.[2] In 1841, or possibly earlier, their ownership changed. The major had fallen deeply into debt and was unable to pay his creditors. Holmes said Nathaniel Ford, the sheriff of Howard County, seized the Holmeses under what was known as a writ of execution for an unpaid lien. He said Ford sold them at a sheriff's auction in Fayette, the county seat, with the proceeds helping pay the major's debts.[3]

Holmes said they were purchased by a local merchant—he didn't remember the man's name. But he did remember that Ford directed him to go to the buyer's home and request a wagon to transport his wife and their children—they then had four—and return them to the new owner's home. However, on arrival, Holmes said the buyer was absent and the man's wife declared she knew nothing about the purchase, and sent them away. Holmes reported back to Ford, who next informed him he had made a separate arrangement to keep Holmes and his family. The Holmeses went to work as Ford's slaves.[4]

Holmes was mistaken on one important point. Ford was not sheriff of Howard County in 1841. The sheriff at that time was Lewis Crigler, who seems to have been a rival of Ford's.[5] Ford did serve four two-year terms as the elected sheriff from 1828 to 1832 and from 1836 to 1840, when Crigler succeeded him. Crigler would have conducted the sheriff's auction in 1841.

It is possible Crigler awarded Holmes to Ford when the original purchaser backed out. But it is more likely Holmes—or the person who transcribed his recollection of events—mixed up the date, putting down 1841 instead of the more logical year of 1831, when Ford was still sheriff. However, it is curious Ford failed to correct Holmes' version of events when he easily—in court, in Oregon—could have done so.

Holmes would later say that because of the confusion surrounding the outcome of the auction, he couldn't be certain he and his wife were ever legally Ford's slaves, even though Ford claimed them, and, in later years in Oregon, considered trying to return the entire Holmes family to Missouri to be sold back into slavery.

·⸦·

Nathaniel Ford evidently was not an outwardly cruel man—the Holmeses did not complain he beat them, although beatings were commonplace in slave states. One historian of the slave experience wrote of "the helpless feeling" of slave parents on seeing children whipped, unable to intervene, or, the terror of slave children watching their parents being beaten.[6]

Ford was someone with a firm belief in what was right for himself and his family, to the exclusion of the rights of others. He was careless about his debts, insensitive to his slaves, and he once manipulated the outcome of an election to Oregon's territorial legislature to make himself the winner. A grandson, John Thorp Ford, said Ford was of "forceful character" with "black hair and blue eyes, which looked out from under heavy, bushy eyebrows." He was short and stocky—five-foot-nine, and two hundred pounds.[7] Photographs of Ford bear out the description. He is seen in one photograph as unsmiling, with unkempt hair and beard, mouth clenched tightly in what might best be described as a

Nathaniel Ford and his wife, Lucinda. The Fords brought six slaves from Missouri to Oregon in 1844 and established a farm near present-day Rickreall in Polk County. Ford was sued by his former slave, Robin Holmes, seeking freedom for his children. (Oregon Historical Society)

sneer. Ford's descendants said he treated his slaves well. Holmes would say, not so well.

More is known about Ford's life in Oregon than his earlier years in Missouri. But it is possible to piece together his background from family histories, newspaper clippings, and court records, of which there are many. During Howard County's boom years in the 1820s, caravans of slave owners arrived daily from the tobacco and hemp-growing areas of Virginia, Tennessee, and Kentucky, lured by cheap land and fertile soil, much as Missouri emigrants would be lured to Oregon a quarter-century later. Those with wealth and large numbers of slaves—slaves equaled wealth—became gentlemen farmers, with plenty of time to involve themselves in local and state politics. This seemed to be Ford's path as well.

Ford was well known and evidently respected during most of the two decades he lived in Missouri—he was a sheriff, state legislator, and major landholder. However, in the last few years before he departed for Oregon, his reputation seemed to nosedive under a cloud of debt.

Ford was born in Buckingham County, Virginia, in 1795, the son of a soldier in the Revolutionary War. He arrived in Missouri in 1822 and married Lucinda Embree that same year in Fayette. The couple had ten children, eight daughters and two sons, although four children died in infancy or early childhood. Ford would bring his six surviving children, five daughters and one son, with him to Oregon.[8]

Ford had both land and slaves in Missouri. The 1830 Census listed him with one slave, a female. By 1840, he had nine slaves: two adult or adolescent males, three adult or adolescent females, and four children—three girls and a boy.[9] Over time, he may have had as many as thirteen different slaves, including the Holmeses. He frequently mortgaged his slaves as collateral for loans, and forfeited several, including three of the Holmeses' children. The transactions involving Ford's slaves were typical of many slave owners, who bought, sold, and mortgaged slaves, with little or no regard for their family situations. Some slaveholders tried to keep families together, but others did not, either because it didn't matter to them, or they felt compelled to break up families for financial reasons. Children were sold away from their parents; parents were sold away from one another. Such upheavals in their lives might occur without warning. The complexity and suddenness of these transactions led to the near constant uncertainty that most slaves, including the Holmeses, had about their future. It's perfectly understandable that Robin and Polly Holmes might confuse the dates they were sold or purchased in a particular transaction.

Among Ford's Missouri land holdings were eight hundred and thirty-two acres in Howard County and nearby Chariton County that he owned from 1841 to 1843. Family records say he had two other properties, one of eighteen hundred acres and another of four hundred acres. His Oregon descendants called these properties farms, although in Missouri they were large enough to classify as plantations. Ford most likely grew tobacco and hemp—especially hemp—as these were the major crops in the region's fertile soils. The chief market for hemp was in the cotton-growing regions of the Deep South where hemp rope was needed to wrap bales of cotton. Holmes, Scott, and Ford's other male slaves would mostly likely have helped cut and harvest hemp, as nearly every male slave in the region was involved with hemp at some point. A 1914 study of slavery in Missouri said the hemp culture made slave labor profitable.[10]

Ford listed his home in census records as Richmond Township, east of Fayette. Descendants said the Fords divided their time between a farm home and a Fayette town home.

In addition to four terms as the sheriff of Howard County, Ford was elected a state representative in 1832, serving a single term in the Missouri Legislature at Jefferson City. He was Fayette postmaster in 1841 and county clerk in 1842.[11] Some of these positions he may have held simultaneously. He also worked as a surveyor, a skill that would serve him well in Oregon.

One oddity is an article in the *Missouri Intelligencer* of Fayette, reporting Ford's death. The one-sentence article on July 14, 1832, said: "Died—recently at New Orleans, Nathaniel Ford, Esq., sheriff of Howard County, Mo."[12] The same newspaper two months later, on September 29, 1832, reported Ford's election to the legislature. The newspaper offered no explanation for its earlier erroneous report. Ford did frequently travel to New Orleans, ferrying produce on a flatboat from his farm, and possibly the farms of others, down the Mississippi River.[13]

·-~·

Ford was referred to throughout his life in Oregon—less so in Missouri—as "Colonel Ford," a rank said to have been attained during a skirmish in the so-named Mormon War of 1838.[14] There is no record of Ford serving in the U.S. military. A Ford granddaughter, Caroline Burch, recalled in later years the family's prestige and active social life in Missouri. She listed several prominent people whom members of the family knew, including Mary Todd, the future wife of Abraham Lincoln, and Thomas Hart Benton, the Missouri senator.

Two Ford daughters, Josephine and Mary Ann, attended the Columbia Female Academy—now Stephens College—in Columbia, Missouri. They were said to have participated in a ceremony for the laying of the cornerstone at Columbia University on July 4, 1840, with their names placed inside the stone. Caroline Burch, who died in 1952, described in detail a ball attended by the two Ford daughters, with Ford as their escort.

> *That evening grandfather took them to the ball. They were dressed in white dresses, with long tight waists, very short sleeves, long white silk gloves, and blue ribbon sashes . . . white hose, black slippers with long ribbons that wrapped around their ankles and tied in a bow.*[15]

The Fords' prominence couldn't save them financially, however. During the three years—or thirteen—after Ford claimed the Holmeses as his slaves to settle another man's debts, Ford himself fell into debt from which he could not extricate himself. Robin Holmes would later tell an Oregon court that Ford at the time was "very much embarrassed in his pecuniary circumstances."[16] Court records in Howard County reveal that Ford was in debt to a James Ferguson for "about twenty four hundred dollars" in 1842. Some of his property was seized to pay his debts, including three parcels totaling four hundred and eighty acres sold at a sheriff's auction—presumably by Sheriff Lewis Crigler—in Fayette on September 23, 1843.[17]

The auctioned lands were properties Ford and his wife, Lucinda, purchased in the New Madrid area in 1827 and 1828. They were described in a court document as "being the place where said Ford now lives on," although this conflicts with other records that had Ford living near Fayette. Ford sold or mortgaged his remaining property in 1843, as by this time he may have decided his economic situation was hopeless and was eager to try his luck in Oregon. He no doubt was aware of Peter Burnett's preparations to lead the first major wagon train from Missouri to the Oregon Country that same year.

Nothing underscores the instability and uncertainty in the lives of Robin and Polly Holmes as much as Ford's transactions in this period. During his final year in Missouri, Ford also sold, mortgaged, or forfeited, several of his slaves to satisfy his debts, including three of the six Holmes children—there were then six—and a slave named Harrison. The three Holmes children taken from their parents were Eliza, born in 1831; Clarisa, born in 1832; and William, also born in 1832. Their names and birth years are listed in the Ford family Bible under "Birth of Blacks." Harrison is also listed in the Bible as being born on January 10, 1824. The recording of specific birth dates suggest the slaves were born into Ford's ownership.[18]

Ford had used Harrison as collateral on at least two previous occasions, the first to secure a loan of $600 from Samuel Major on October 10, 1842. He gave Harrison's age as about twenty-two and affirmed he was "sound and healthy . . . in mind and body." He reclaimed Harrison on that occasion.[19] The last mention of Ford's ownership of Harrison and the three Holmes children—Elisa, Clarisa, and William—was in a loan agreement dated May 20, 1843, in which Ford mortgaged Robin and Polly Holmes and five of their children, plus eight hundred and forty acres of land, as collateral for four loans totaling nearly $1,600, most of it owed to the Fayette Branch Bank of the State of Missouri. At least one of the loans was overdue. In the mortgage document, Ford declared the children were "sound and healthy and slaves for life."[20] Terms of the agreement provided that if Ford repaid the loans, plus interest, his ownership of the slaves and land was to be restored. He managed to regain Robin and Polly Holmes and two of their children—but apparently not Harrison and the other three children. Or if he regained them, he sold them soon after, as there was no further mention of them.[21]

Ford had also mortgaged Scott, another "slave for life," on June 17, 1843, as collateral for a loan of $500 from a woman named Polly Davis. Ford had four months to repay, or Scott would be sold at auction. As Ford also took Scott to Oregon, he must have repaid Davis, or walked out on the debt. In the court documents, Ford gave Scott's age as twenty, and said he does "hereby warrant the said negro boy sound and healthy both in mind and body."[22]

Additionally, Ford borrowed against his personal property, listing as collateral for a package of loans on May 17, 1843: "3 beds and bedding, 3 bedsteds (sic), 2 bureaus, 1 bookcase, 6 rattan chairs, 1 four-year-old mare, 4 cows and calves, 6 head of young cattle, 2 yoke of steers." It seems likely Ford had no intention of paying off these and other loans, and was, in effect, cashing out his property before departing for Oregon.[23]

Ford's debts—some paid, some unpaid—may explain why in later years he complained that he was poorly regarded in Missouri. In a letter from Oregon to a Missouri acquaintance, James Shirley, in 1852, Ford wrote, "I have long since come to the conclusion that I have no friends in that 'country' even amongst my relatives."[24]

Ford was not alone in his financial distress. The nation was mired in depression in the 1840s, which reached deep into rural Howard County and the Mississippi Valley. The region depended on sales of farm products for its economic health, and prices had plunged to well below the cost of production. Wheat was selling for twenty-five cents a bushel, half of what was required for a profit. Hog prices fell from four dollars and twenty cents per hundredweight to under a dollar.[25]

⌐∽

Slaveholding in Missouri was on a smaller scale than in the slave states of the Deep South. There were few large plantations. The average number of slaves held by an individual slaveholder in Howard County in 1850 was under seven.[26] Many households employed a single slave as a house servant and a few slaves to assist with farm work.[27]

A 2010 study challenged the notion, popular in Missouri, that slavery in Missouri was somehow less onerous than in other slave states. The author wrote that this misconception grew out of the prevalence of smaller slave-holdings. However, there was little, if any, difference in how a slave was treated. "Missouri was just as cruel and exploitative as anywhere in the South."[28]

Howard County—and Missouri generally—played a major role in the interstate slave trade, supplying slaves for plantations in the Deep South. The price for a healthy male slave in the 1860s averaged about $1,300, and for

Renovated slave quarters on the Redstone plantation near Roanoke in Howard County, Missouri. It was owned by agriculturalist and Baptist Minister Younger R. Pitts. Built in the 1830s the structure is about 18 by 43 feet and served as a summer kitchen and housing for some of the plantation slaves. (Courtesy of Gary Fuenfhausen)

Renovated slave quarters belonging to Abiel Leonard at the Oakwood plantation near Fayette, Missouri. Built about 1830, the cabin measures about 16 by 17 feet. Leonard, an attorney, owned 60,000 acres and fifteen slaves and three slave houses. He was the Missouri State Supreme Court Justice prior to the Civil War, but was removed during the war. (Courtesy of Gary Fuenfhausen)

a female, $1,000.²⁹ A slave in the hemp fields was expected to "break"—or thrash—at least one hundred pounds of hemp a day, after which he typically was paid an additional penny for every pound over that amount. The process separated the fibers—used for rope—from the woody stems.

Whipping was not an uncommon punishment for slaves who failed to produce the minimum. Typical, apparently, was this recollection by a Lafayette County resident of a slave's work:

> *I can remember how twenty or thirty negroes would work in line cutting hemp with sickles. It was then left to rot til January. Then it was broken and the pith removed by means of a heavy crusher which the slave swung up and down. He often received the lash if not breaking his one hundred pounds.³⁰*

Howard County produced 904 tons of hemp in 1850, and 655 tons in 1860, after which production dropped precipitously because of the Civil War and the loss of slave labor.³¹ Howard County today remains rural, and, as with many other rural counties nationwide, it has lost residents, with a population of 10,204 in 2011, down from 17,233 in 1870.³² African Americans constituted less than 4 percent of the total, down from one-third in 1850. Fayette, still the county seat, is now a college town, home to Central Methodist University, with an enrollment of nearly twenty-five hundred students. Hemp and tobacco are no longer major crops. Without slaves, there was little profit left in hemp. The last tobacco warehouse closed in the mid-1990s.

Slave quarters are still found throughout central Missouri. Some are in ruins; others have been renovated by their owners. They are curiosities, attractions for tourists, a reminder of what was, and should never be again.

The Lure of Oregon

Beginning in the 1840s, Oregon became a magnet for many distressed Missourians. Interest was piqued partly by news that Congress was giving serious consideration to a bill offering free land in the Oregon Country to settlers willing to farm it. The bill was approved by the Senate in 1843, although it wouldn't be enacted into law until 1850. Hundreds of families from Missouri and elsewhere prepared to emigrate, despite knowing little about their destination, or the two thousand-mile ordeal required to get there. Some of the stories circulating about Oregon were far too incredible to be believed. An Iowa pioneer who settled in Benton County recalled years later one of the more impossible exaggerations:

> [H]earing of the great wealth of Oregon, west of the Rockies, and especially the Willamette River which wended its way to the great Pacific, and the great Willamette Valley beyond the Cascades, where it was believed only necessary to sow a crop of wheat once in ten years, and the cattle were so fat that tallow candles actually grew out of the ends of their horns.[1]

Wrote the nineteenth century historians Hubert Bancroft and Frances Fuller Victor in 1886, "Many . . . imagined that all they had to do after reaching [the] Snake River was to embark upon its waters and float down to the mouth of the Columbia."[2] But even though emigrants in the early wagon trains would confront perils they were not told to expect and could not have imagined, the remarkable outcome was that nearly all of them made it. They survived to build a prosperous new society, one that worked very well for the new white population, but not so well for minorities or the native people they displaced.

The first of the major emigrant wagon trains set out from Independence, Missouri, on May 21, 1843—one hundred and twenty wagons and nearly nine hundred people, including at least a few slaves.[3] The emigrants were headed for an unknown region with few non-Native American inhabitants. One estimate put the "American population" of the Oregon Country at slightly less than two hundred and fifty.[4] Another estimate attributed to Catholic missionaries put the white population in 1841 at two hundred and ten—of whom one hundred and forty were Americans and sixty were Canadians.[5] Most of the Canadians were in the employ of the Hudson's Bay Company.

The arrival of the emigrants in the fall of 1843 quadrupled the Euro-American population.[6] Three more wagon trains would leave the following year, and more in the years after that. Nearly fifty-three thousand emigrants traveled to the Oregon Country along the Oregon Trail from 1840 to 1861. Of these, more than ten thousand emigrated during the five years from 1843 to 1849; most were farm families from the Mississippi and Ohio River valleys.[7]

⌁

The settlers arriving from Missouri in the 1843 wagons would provide leadership in the American West for decades to come. They would rise to influence not just in the Oregon Country, which embraced the entire Pacific Northwest, but also in California, then still a province of Mexico. They would become governors, senators, legislators, and judges. They would frame the laws and constitutions of the region as it organized into provisional, territorial, and, finally, statehood status. They would decide, often after harsh and appallingly ugly debate, the region's policies toward slavery, African Americans, and other minorities. By their very presence, they would seal the United States' claim to the region.

Among the 1843 emigrants were two men who would play dominant roles virtually from the day they arrived. They were Jesse Applegate, thirty-two, a farmer from St. Clair County, Missouri, and Peter Burnett, thirty-five, a storekeeper and lawyer in the Missouri River port of Weston in Platte County.

Burnett was one of the defense attorneys in the 1839 Missouri treason case against Mormon leader Joseph Smith.[8] He would serve in Oregon's provisional legislature and as the region's first judge, and, after moving to California in search of gold, would be elected that state's first governor in 1849.[9] He would also have an outsized, and negative, influence on racial policies in both Oregon and California.

Applegate would also serve in Oregon's provisional legislature, as well as the territorial legislature and the 1857 Constitutional Convention. Among other achievements, he would help establish a new trail into Oregon known as the Applegate Trail. Another settler in this first group was James Nesmith from New Hampshire, who would be one of Oregon's first U.S. senators.

The influence of Burnett and Applegate would extend well beyond politics. John Minto, who traveled to Oregon in 1844, credited Burnett with organizing the emigration of new settlers through a series of speeches he gave across Missouri

Estimated immigration on the Oregon Trail, 1840-1860		
Year	to Oregon	to California
1840	13	0
1841	24	34
1842	125	0
1843	875	38
1844	1,475	53
1845	2,500	260
1846	1,200	1,500
1847	4,000	450
1848	1,300	400
1849	450	25,000
1850	6,000	44,000
1851	3,600	1,100
1852	10,000	50,000
1853	7,500	20,000
1854	6,000	12,000
1855	500	1,500
1856	1,000	8,000
1857	1,500	4,000
1858	1,500	6,000
1859	2,000	17,000
1860	1,500	9,000
Totals	53,062	200,335

Source: John D. Unruh, *The Plains Across: The Overland Emigrants and the Trans-Mississippi West, 1840-1860*

in 1842.[10] Of Applegate, Minto would write he was "the natural leader upon the highest plane of thought for the future of Oregon as an American community."[11]

The opportunity for free land drew Burnett, who was elected captain of the wagon train. Like many other emigrants, Burnett was, by his own admission, deeply in debt. He calculated that if the proposed land law was approved, he might be able to pay off his Missouri debts.[12] When the law, known as the Donation Land Act, was eventually approved for Oregon in 1850—it allowed six hundred and forty acres for a married couple if they were among the first settlers, with half in the wife's name. It was an enormous amount of free land, a full square mile. Previously, settlers were allowed one hundred and sixty acres of public land under the Preemption Act of 1841.[13]

Applegate wrote more generally of what led people to leave homes and possessions behind and figuratively roll the dice for a new opportunity:

This state of things [the depression] created much discontent and restlessness among a people who had for many generations been nomadic, and had been taught by the example of their ancestors to see a home in 'new country' as a sure way of bettering their condition.[14]

In addition to their individual reasons for journeying to an unknown land, emigrants were influenced by the promotional publicity coming from zealous enthusiasts and other boosters of emigration. So-called emigrating societies for Oregon were organized throughout the country.

Once underway, Burnett was the leader of his wagon train for only a short time, although it is still known by his name. Burnett, always impatient, resigned after just ten days, blaming "ten thousand little vexations." Among them, he complained: "At one time an ox would be missing, at another time a mule, and then a struggle for the best encampment, and for a supply of wood and water; and, in these struggles, the worst traits of human nature were displayed, and there was no remedy but patient endurance."[15] A persistent complaint was that the wagon train was slowed by the livestock of some emigrants.[16]

Jesse Applegate and William Martin afterward shared the leadership, with Applegate taking charge of the slower half of the wagon train bringing the settlers' livestock, which he called "the cow column." Jesse and his two brothers, Lindsay and Charles, and another settler, Daniel Waldo, together set out with more than a thousand head of cattle.[17] According to John Minto, the Applegate brothers planned to go into the cattle business in Oregon, and were joined by Waldo, a forty-three-year-old neighbor. Waldo and Jesse Applegate had been partners in a St. Louis sawmill.[18] The Applegates would lose half their cattle during the journey, with the biggest loss at Fort Walla Walla where they left the herd for the winter.[19]

⌐⌐

The Missouri influence in the development of Oregon cannot be overstated. By 1850, one-quarter of Oregon's population, or 2,291 people, were from Missouri, more than from any other state.[20] Two Missouri senators, Lewis Linn and Thomas Hart Benton, played leading roles in promoting settlement of the Oregon Country to support America's claim to the region.

Senator Linn proposed the donation land bill that eventually would be enacted. Senator Benton, in strong support, argued that "nobody will go three thousand miles to settle a new country unless he gets land by it."[21] Oregon's Linn and Benton counties are named for the two senators, neither of whom apparently ever visited Oregon. Linn also introduced a bill in the Senate in 1844 calling on the United States "to occupy and create a territorial government" in Oregon. It was defeated, but not without consequences. Disappointment over the bill's defeat was especially acute in the Mississippi Valley, prompting even more emigrants to head West, intent on settling the Oregon Country for the United States.[22] As many as a thousand new settlers would leave from Missouri in 1845.

⌐⌐

The settlers' wagon journey over the two thousand miles from Independence, Missouri, to Oregon, across lands they had never seen, posed a daunting prospect, especially for families with children. While most made it, lives were lost. Burnett would write years later that the wagon train started with two hundred and ninety three men over age sixteen. Of these, two hundred and sixty-seven made it to Oregon, six died on the way, five turned back, and fifteen continued on to California.[23]

One tragedy struck the extended Applegate family. Two of their children drowned on November 6, 1843, when a boat capsized in the Columbia River rapids above The Dalles—probably at or near Celilo Falls.[24] One of Lindsay's sons, also named Jesse, witnessed the tragedy from a second boat in which he rode with the Applegate fathers, their wives, and a Native American guide. The fathers were at the oars. The doomed boat was across the river. Jesse, just age seven, recalled in later years the terror and helplessness on the faces of the two fathers as they watched the boat begin to founder, with their children aboard.

This boat now near the south shore, it would seem, should have followed our boat as the pilot was with us, and this was a dangerous part of the river. But there was little time to consider mistakes, or to be troubled about what might be the consequences, for presently there was a wail of anguish, a shriek, and a scene of confusion in one boat that no language can describe. The boat we were watching disappeared and we saw the men and boys struggling in the water. Father and Uncle Jesse, seeing their children drowning, were seized with frenzy, and dropping their oars spring up from their seats and were about to leap from the boat to make a desperate attempt to swim to them, when Mother and Aunt Cynthia, in voices that were distinctly heard above the roar of the rushing waters, by commands and entreaties brought them to a realization of our own perilous situation, and the madness of an attempt to reach the other side of the river by swimming. . . . The men returned to the oars just in time to avoid, by great exertion, a rock against which the current dashed with such fury that the foam and froth upon its apex was as white as milk.[25]

Those lost were nine-year-old Warren Applegate, one of Jesse's sons, and Warren Applegate, also nine, Lindsay's son. Also drowned was seventy-year-old Alexander "Mac" McClellan, who was steering the raft. Another son of Lindsay's, eleven-year-old Elisha, swam to safety. A man identified as William Doke also survived.[26] The Applegates learned later that the boat had foundered in a whirlpool. The bodies of the boys were not recovered. The tragedy haunted the Applegate brothers for years, and, in 1846, led them to mount an expedition to search for a safer trail into Oregon, a search that would also involve Nathaniel Ford.

It wasn't the only loss in the Columbia River that day. The night of the tragedy, the Burnett party lost another child near The Dalles, said to be an African American girl about age five. Recalled young Applegate:

During the late evening, a man from Peter Burnett's camp came to ours and said that a little Negro girl was lost. She had been sent to the river where the boats were to get a bucket of water. The storm had continued and the boats on the beach were wildly rocked and tossed by the waves. Some thought the girl had entered one of the boats to dip up the water, and had been thrown into the river and was never found.[27]

In a separate accident, another of the Applegate children, Lisbon, suffered serious injuries from which he would never fully recover. Lisbon was the son of Charles, the third Applegate brother. The accident occurred when an emigrant named George Beale lost control of his wagon in which Lisbon was riding. In 1865, Beale would be convicted with a second man of murdering another member of the wagon train, Daniel Delaney Sr.[28]

Several slaves came with their owners. While young Applegate didn't mention the name of the girl who drowned, she possibly was a slave girl belonging to one of the settlers. A recollection by another member of the Burnett party, Nineveh Ford, said the victim was a slave woman, who was a "servant" of Burnett's wife, or of a relative.[29] Given Burnett's hostility toward slavery, this might seem improbable. However, owning a slave to help around the house may well have been perfectly acceptable to Burnett—his objections to slavery were economic, not moral.

There has long been published speculation that Daniel Waldo brought several slaves, including a black slave woman and her daughter, America Waldo, of whom he was said to be the father. America became America Bogle when she married a free black, Richard A. Bogle, in 1863. A Bogle family spokeswoman and descendant of America, Renita Bogle-Byrd of Decatur, Georgia, told the author that the Bogle "family tradition" is that Daniel Waldo

Missouri-born America Waldo Bogle, third from right, was brought to Oregon as a small child in the mid 1840s along with her mother, both believed to be slaves to the Waldo family. America was raised near Salem by Daniel Waldo, thought for many years to be her father. Recent research points to Daniel's brother, Joseph Waldo, as her father. She married Richard Bogle, a free black from Jamaica, in 1863. The couple is seen with five of their eight children about 1884. (Oregon Historical Society)

was America's father.[30] However, a descendant of Daniel Waldo disputes this version of events. Brian Waldo Johnson of Monmouth, Oregon, said America's date of birth is listed on her headstone, and in census records, as June 1844, more than a year after Daniel Waldo left Missouri, so he could not have been the father. He said Daniel's brother, Joseph Waldo, who emigrated in 1846 and apparently did bring slaves, was the more likely candidate to be her father.[31]

There was at least one identified slave in the party: a woman named Rachel Belden, the property of Daniel Delaney Sr., a former plantation owner from Tennessee.[32] Accounts of Delaney's slaves differ. One said he sold all his slaves before leaving Tennessee; another said he brought "a few slaves" to Oregon and later sold them. Delaney settled on a farm at Turner, near Salem. John Minto, who knew Delaney, thought him lazy, spending his time hunting and reading his Bible while his three sons and his slave did the farm work. Added Minto, "He seemed to read his Bible chiefly to find in it support for his dominion over the soul and body of his female slave."[33]

Delaney was shot and killed in 1865 during a robbery at his home. The killers fled with $1,400. The crime was witnessed by one of Rachel Belden's children, seven-year-old Jack, or Jackson, hiding in a woodpile. Even though Oregon's 1857 constitution prohibited blacks from testifying against whites, the boy nevertheless was allowed to testify and helped convict the two accused killers, George Beale and George Baker, a Salem tavern owner. They were hanged May 17, 1865.[34] Beale had traveled to Oregon with the Burnett wagon train in 1843. Rachel was said to have witnessed the hanging.

·-· ·-·

There were reasons other than the economic difficulties for risking the long journey to Oregon. These included the spirit of adventure, patriotism, the goal of a healthier climate, and, important to some, escape from the worsening conflicts engendered by slavery. Settlers from Missouri, Kentucky, Tennessee, and Arkansas, all slave states, were the majority of the early pioneers in Oregon. Most were not slaveholders, and many wished to leave behind the slave-based economies. Many also didn't want to live among blacks. They—in the words of one historian—wished "to rid themselves of the blight that broods over the land where involuntary servitude prevails."[35]

One emigrant who sought to leave slavery behind was Wilson Morrison, a farmer at St. Joseph, Missouri, who came to Oregon with a wagon train headed by Cornelius Gilliam in 1844. Minto, who worked for Morrison, quoted him as saying:

Unless a man keeps niggers (and I won't) he has no even chance; he cannot compete with the man who does. There is Dick Owens my neighbor, he has a few field hands, and a few house niggers. They raise and make all that the family and themselves eat and wear, and some hemp and tobacco besides. If markets are good, Dick will sell; if not, he can hold over, while I am compelled to sell all I can make every year in order to make ends meet. I'm going to Oregon, where there'll be no slaves, and we'll all start even.[36]

However, opposition to slavery didn't mean the welcome mat was out for blacks in Oregon. It wasn't. Hostility toward slavery was nearly equally matched by hostility toward blacks, accounting for Oregon's long flirtation with exclusion laws. And not all the emigrants opposed slavery. Nathaniel Ford certainly didn't.

⁓ ⁓

The issue of slavery—where it would be legal; where it would not—once again had a firm grip on the nation's throat. The patchwork of decades of past compromises was unraveling. These compromises included the Northwest Ordinance of 1787, which established the Ohio River as the boundary between free and slave territory in the territories east of the Mississippi River—territories south of the Ohio could become slave states, those to the north, could not.[37] The Northwest Ordinance was followed in 1820 by the Missouri Compromise, which banned slavery north of the thirty-sixth parallel for most lands acquired as part of the Louisiana Purchase. The exception was Missouri, where slavery was allowed.

As settlers expanded the white man's reach into the Midwest, West, and Southwest, Congress and the courts struggled with the increasingly difficult challenge of balancing anti-slave and pro-slave interests. A new Fugitive Slave Act would be passed as part of the Compromise of 1850, with draconian enforcement provisions. It required so little proof that a free African American might be entrapped in a free state and claimed by a bogus owner in a slave state.[38] The Compromise of 1850, which also cleared the way for California statehood, was a consequence of the war with Mexico, from 1846 to 1848, which gained the United States an additional five hundred thousand square miles of territory in the West and Southwest. The enormous new territory embroiled Congress in yet another divisive debate over how and where to extend, or not extend, slavery.

Next would come the Kansas-Nebraska Act of 1854, effectively repealing the Missouri Compromise and potentially opening more of the West to slavery, bringing near-civil war to Kansas. That act would be followed by the Supreme Court's Dred Scott decision of 1857—denying constitutional protections and citizenship to all African Americans, both free and slaves, and their descendants, and holding that Congress lacked the authority to prohibit slavery in the territories.[39]

Each of these measures and compromises constituted another tear in the fabric of the Union that would culminate in Civil War in 1861. Whether they wanted it or not—and most didn't—the controversy over slavery traveled with the emigrants on their westward journey.

On the Trail

Nathaniel Ford's fifty-four wagons set out from Independence, Missouri, on May 14, 1844. It was the second, or third, of the major emigrant trains to strike out across the prairie, headed for Oregon. Departing wagon trains were a national event, much like astronauts headed for the moon. Newspapers throughout the country ran accounts of Ford's progress. In an article under the headline "The Oregon Expedition," the *Maine Cultivator* told its readers in nearly breathless prose on July 8, 1844, that:

> *the Oregon emigrants started from their place of general rendezvous at the 'Lone Elm,' on the 14th, and that although they had been gone upward of two weeks, they had, in consequence of the high waters, only travelled almost one hundred miles. . . . There are several small parties on the route, which have not yet reached Col. Ford's company.*[1]

In Ford's wagon train were fifty-five married couples, one hundred sixty-eight children, and eighty single men, a total of three hundred and fifty-eight pioneers. They brought with them five hundred head of cattle, sixty horses, and twenty-eight mules.[2] No separate breakdown was given for slaves, although there were at least seven. Ford brought six. There was also a woman slave belonging to William M. Case, who settled in Marion County.[3]

The group hired as its guide, Moses "Black" Harris, an experienced mountain man, said by some to be African American, by others to be white. He was believed to have been born in Union County, South Carolina, but no birth certificate has been found to verify his race. What is certain is that, if white, he had an unusually dark skin. Harris was a former fur trapper who guided several of the early wagon trains; he also served as guide to missionary Marcus Whitman, and his wife, Narcissa, on their journey to the Oregon Country in 1836.[4] Accounts of Harris' life said "he was generally liked by whites"[5] and advocated "the freedom of equal rights."[6] Harris had urged a popular Missouri military leader, Colonel Thornton Grimsley, to mount a military expedition in 1841 to help "clear" the Oregon Country of "British and Indians" and secure it for the United States. In a letter to Grimsley on June 4, 1841, Harris wrote, "[I] will be with you if you can get the Government of the United States to authorize the occupancy of the Origon (sic) Country." He also voiced disgust that the British had taken over Fort Hall, a former trading post of American fur trappers in present-day Idaho. "[The British] are repairing it and putting it into military customs (sic). Why our government suffers these things I know not."[7]

Harris would later help rescue the ill-fated "lost" wagon train led by Stephen Meek into Oregon's high desert in 1845.[8] He also would join the Applegate brothers in their 1846 expedition to map the Applegate Trail and lead a rescue of some of the stranded emigrants.

·⟩ ⟨·

Ford was chosen leader of his wagon train. Five days earlier, another party of seventy-four wagons, with three hundred and twenty-three emigrants, left from St. Joseph, Missouri, led by Cornelius Gilliam.[9] Gilliam was described as a former bounty hunter of slaves, a Missouri sheriff, a member of the Missouri legislature, captain in the Seminole war, an ordained minister, and "instrumental in running Mormons out of Missouri."[10] Harris served as guide to both Gilliam and Ford, and the two wagon trains traveled near one another. The newspaper account said "Col. Ford's company, it is thought, will reach Gen. Gilliam's in about two weeks; the latter having crossed the river near Fort Leavenworth, and is now encamped on the Nimahaw River, waiting for Col. Ford's company."[11] Combined, they were a single train of one hundred and thirty-six wagons and nearly seven hundred emigrants.

The historians Bancroft and Victor contrasted the settlers in the Ford-Gilliam train of 1844 with the Burnett wagon train of 1843. They said the Burnett party was composed of people "of pronounced character, rudely arrogant and aggressive, rather than tame and submissive." When they arrived in Oregon, they were determined to shape a government that "suited them."[12] On the other hand, members of the Gilliam-Ford train "were hardly equal to those of the previous year," followers rather than leaders. They were "brave, loyal, earnest, but better fitted to execute than to command; to be loyal to a government than to construct one." Moreover, "their tendencies were more toward military glory than pride of statesmanship."[13] The critique seemed aimed more at Gilliam than Ford, who, at a later point in the Bancroft-Fuller history, was called "a man of character and influence."[14]

There's no record of any slaves in Gilliam's party. However, it included one free black, George Washington Bush, his white wife, and their five sons.[15]

Ford remained in charge of his wagon train from start to finish. Gilliam, however, was forced to resign leadership of his wagon train because of his peculiar behavior—a spontaneous decision to stage what turned out to be a disorderly buffalo hunt proved the final straw.[16]

Ford brought three wagons of his own, plus a specially constructed carriage to transport his family and possessions. Pulled by four mules, the carriage was large enough to accommodate a bed for his ailing wife.[17] Ford family members said the poor health of Lucinda Ford was a major reason for the family's decision to emigrate.[18] The Fords were far from penniless. They carried $1,000 in gold coin, stashed by Mrs. Ford in the bottom drawer of a dresser.[19] The gold possibly was proceeds from the sale of the Ford properties. The six Ford children who made the trip were a son, Marcus—a grown man at age twenty-one—and five daughters: Mary Ann, sixteen; Josephine Pauline, fourteen; Lavina Caroline, twelve; Sarah Elizabeth, seven; and Lucinda Miller, five. Also in the party were two Ford brothers-in-law, Carey Embree and David Goff.

According to family histories, Ford left behind his house, possessions, and "several negro slaves" to satisfy his debts.[20] The six slaves he brought with him were Robin and Polly Holmes, three of the Holmeses children—Harriett, seven; Celi Ann, five; and Mary Jane, three—and the male slave named Scott. The other three Holmes children were left behind, property of new owners and all described by Ford in a court document months earlier as "slaves for life."[21]

·⌣·⌣·

When the Ford wagon train left Missouri, Oregon's policy toward slavery was unresolved. The slaves in the party could only guess at their future. The Oregon Country, which then encompassed the entire Pacific Northwest, was still under joint occupation by the British and the Americans, as provided under the Treaty of 1818.

Robin Holmes would later tell an Oregon court that Ford promised him and his wife, Polly, their freedom if Holmes would help him settle in Oregon.[22] With that understanding, Holmes said he accepted. Robin and Polly were each about age twenty-four. A Ford family account written in 1953 by another Ford descendant, Pauline Burch, said Nathaniel Ford hadn't wanted to bring the Holmes family to Oregon at all.[23] She wrote that Ford intended to bring just one slave, Scott, to drive the team of oxen pulling the family's supply wagon. But Burch said just before the wagon train was to leave from Independence, Holmes and his family showed up in a horse-drawn wagon. She said, "Robin said he did not want to be left behind, but wanted to stay with the family. Nathaniel Ford consented, and out of his own meager funds added the required supplies for one more family."[24]

Caroline Burch offered a different version—her undated account would have been written earlier than Pauline's. Caroline was Ford's granddaughter; her mother was Sarah Elizabeth Ford, who was born in Missouri and married Samuel T. Burch in Oregon in 1856. Pauline Burch was Sarah's niece. Caroline wrote that Ford gave the Holmeses their freedom before departing.

Grandfather objected to bringing the negroes. One young darkey (Scott) begged to come. He drove one of the teams. He came with the understanding that if negroes were free in Oregon he was to have his freedom, if slave, he was to keep his old place. Old Uncle Robbin (sic), his wife Polly and family he gave their freedom. They wanted to come, but Grandfather refused to bring them. Just as they were settled for the first night's camp they saw a small black speck away in the distance. It was interesting to the whole camp. They all watched until it came near and saw it was old Uncle Robb, Aunt Polly and the family. They had, in some way, got hold of an old wagon and oxen. Grandfather tried, next morning, to get them to go back, but they would not, so the only way left for Grandfather was to bring them along and look after them the best he could.[25]

There may be elements of truth in these two family versions. However, both were written years later by descendants who may well have heard imprecise recollections, filtered through rose-colored memories. Pauline Burch also made clear in her account she wanted to rebut the negative portrayal of Ford that grew out of the custody suit Robin Holmes would bring against him. But it is significant that during Ford's testimony in that same court case, he did not challenge Holmes' version of the circumstances of his coming to Oregon—trading work for freedom. Moreover, Ford's later acknowledgment that he once considered returning the Holmeses to Missouri to be sold as slaves, leaves little doubt that he had not given Robin and Polly Holmes their freedom in Missouri.

⌣

Travel in the Ford-Gilliam wagon train was made miserable by the weather—rain at the start, snow and cold near the end. There were at least five deaths. Gilliam's wagons were delayed seventeen days by high water before it could cross the Black Vermillion River in Kansas. Gilliam finally made the crossing by using two hollowed-out logs as pontoons for the wagons. Emigrant B. F. Nichols recalled how mothers went "splashing through the mud and slime to reach the pontoons that had started across."[26] Ford's wagons crossed the Black Vermillion four days later, although a separate account said Ford crossed the river with relative ease ahead of Gilliam, before the river rose.[27]

Once they made contact, Ford and Gilliam decided to travel no farther apart "than necessary for the good of their stock." Both leaders organized the men in their wagon trains into militias to defend against hostile tribes, although neither group encountered conflict.[28]

One of those who perished in the Ford wagon train was Joseph M. Barnette from Jackson County, Missouri, who died on August 26, 1844, of an unknown fever along the Sweetwater River in present-day Wyoming. Typical of deaths on wagon trains, there was little time for mourning. James Clyman, a former mountain man and friend of Black Harris, stayed behind with Harris and a few others to care for Barnette in his final hours—the other wagons had moved on. Clyman, who kept one of the few journals in the Ford party, said someone tossed a shovel out of a departing wagon "which looked rather ominous." Clyman later wrote in his journal:

> *He departed this life very easy . . . & all his troubles were in (sic) silent death. Having nothing better we cut a bed of green willows and laid him out on the cold ground & all of us seated ourselves around our camp fire & listened to the hair breadth escapes of Mr. Harris and other mountaineers.*[29]

Clyman also wrote of the challenge posed during the journey by the inclement weather. He said emigrants at one place struggled to move their wagons "over a steep rock bluff through mud knee deep and in the rain pouring in. . . . Men, women, and children were dripping in mud and water over 'shoe mouth' (sic) deep." He praised one unidentified young woman "worthy of the bravest undaunted pioneer of the west," as she sheltered a fire with an umbrella in one hand while baking bread in a skillet with the other. After two hours, she managed to bake "enough to give us a very plentiful supper."[30]

Minto, a member of Gilliam's group, said "the misery entailed upon the belated travelers by the change in winter weather was indescribable." Leaving the party near The Dalles, Minto went ahead to the Willamette Valley for help. On his return, he said he found "a panorama of suffering and destitution":

men in the prime of life lying among the rocks seeming ready to die. I found there mothers with their families, whose husbands were snow-bound in the Cascade Mountains, without provisions, and obliged to kill and eat their game dogs. Mrs. Morrison had traded her only dress except the one she wore for a bag of potatoes. There was scarcely a dry day, and the snow line was nearly down to the river.[31]

The Ford, Gilliam, and other wagon trains of 1844 increased the Oregon Country's population by an estimated eight hundred in that one year alone.

⌁ ⌁

Ford descendants provided details of the family's experiences on the Oregon Trail. Besides problems with rain and mud, the Ford histories mention widespread exhaustion and a serious shortage of food near the end of the journey. After the wagons crossed the Snake River into Oregon, Ford's son, Marcus, rode ahead to the Whitman's mission at Waiilaptu, near present-day Walla Walla, Washington, to acquire emergency provisions.

The only mention of the slaves during the journey was by Pauline Burch, who said the Holmeses' daughter, Harriett, was a playmate of the white children. There's no mention of how Robin and Polly Holmes were treated in the overwhelmingly white wagon train. However, as slaves they may have been positioned at, or near, the end of the long wagon train—on some occasions smothered in dust; on others mired in mud—their ordeal even more daunting than for the white settlers. When the wagons stopped for the night, they may have hurried forward to tend to the needs of the Ford family.

While the Holmeses are otherwise ignored in family accounts of the westward journey, a great deal is written about Ford, who is occasionally portrayed as heroic. One notable example, according to Pauline Burch, occurred at a portage around the Columbia River rapids near present-day Cascade Locks.

[T]he captain [Ford] having had experience in flat boating on the Mississippi River to New Orleans to market his produce, had the wagons

and all the personal belongings of the company loaded onto a flatboat
that he agreed to take down the river. Several men offered to assist
Nathaniel Ford on the flatboat through the rapids, but he insisted on going
alone, saying: "One life is enough to imperil in these mad and turbulent
waters."[32]

·~·

Ford's wagon train reached Oregon City on December 7, 1844, nearly eight
months after leaving Missouri—some later wagon trains would make the
journey in less than five months. Oregon City in 1844 was the gateway into
the Willamette Valley. It was a growing village of several dozen houses, shops,
and a sawmill, all clustered at the base of one hundred and twenty–foot cliffs
on the east side of the Willamette River below the falls from which it took
its first name, Willamette Falls. The town was established in 1829 by John
McLoughlin, chief factor of the Hudson's Bay Company, as a place for the
company's fur traders to live. Methodist missionaries, led by Jason Lee, arrived
in the region in 1834, bringing additional development, including the first
Protestant church west of the Rocky Mountains in 1843. Oregon City would
be designated capital of Oregon's fledgling provisional government in 1845,
and of the territorial government in 1848. The city's population, augmented
by emigrants, would reach five hundred by 1846 and nine hundred by 1849.

Pauline Burch wrote that all arrived in Oregon City "in fair health and
rejoicing that they had come to the beautiful valley that lay before them."[33]
She apparently referred only to Ford family members, or, if she referred to
everyone, she was overlooking the death of James Barnette and the deprivations
described by John Minto at The Dalles. Even so, if all but one member of the
Ford party reached Oregon safely, it was a major achievement. Loss of life
due to illness, accident, or childbirth, was common in most wagon trains. The
Gilliam party lost at least four people.

Many more emigrants would perish in years ahead. One estimate put the
death toll in 1850 alone at five thousand, many from cholera. Most were
emigrants bound for the California gold fields—the California Trail broke off
from the Oregon Trail near Fort Hall.[34]

Robin Holmes resurfaces in the family account once the settlers reach
Oregon City. Ford had gone ahead to scout for land for himself and his two
brothers-in-law in what is now Polk County. Marcus and "negro Scott" went
with Ford. "Negro Robin" stayed behind at Oregon City to look after Mrs.
Ford and their daughters.[35]

Ford claimed fertile land along Rickreall Creek. The men built three cabins, a two-room cabin for the Fords, another smaller cabin for the Holmes family, and a third for Scott. The Ford and Holmes cabins were fixed with fireplaces—two in the Ford home—one at each end—and one in the smaller Holmes cabin.[36] Scott's cabin was across the road from the Ford home on the south bank of Rickreall Creek. Robin and Polly's cabin was nearby, also on the creek side of the road.[37] When the cabins were finished, Ford returned to Oregon City to gather his family and the Holmeses. They traveled by boat up the Willamette River to be met by Scott, who took them by wagon to their new homes. Ford, with his slaves' help, went about establishing his farm. According to Pauline Burch:

> *In a short time a garden was planted, some fences built and wheat sown. The negroes, Robin and Scott, were given plots of ground on which to raise gardens of their own. They immediately had a ready sale for all the vegetables they could raise, as each company of pioneers arriving had suffered the usual hardship of shortage of food, particularly fresh vegetables. The negroes had a good income from the vegetables in the years 1845, 1846, 1847 and 1848. During all these years, Nathaniel Ford continued to furnish their living expenses.[38]*

It is at this point in the family history that the narrative appears especially saccharine with respect to Ford's treatment of his slaves. Wrote Pauline Burch: "The first years in the Oregon Country were happy ones for the Ford family,

Rickreall Creek flows through the southern portion of the former Ford property. (Photo by author.)

their associates and the negroes." She maintained that Ford was widely praised for his treatment of, and care for, his slaves, and wrote of his "unselfish kindness" toward the Holmeses in allowing them to accompany him to Oregon.[39]

·⌣ ⌣·

Ford gave over one room in his home in 1845 for use as the region's first school. Among the students were Jesse Applegate's children from nearby Salt Creek,[40] and three Ford daughters: Mary, Sarah, and Caroline. The school was moved the following year to a nearby cabin and named the Jefferson Institute. It laid claim to being the first "term" school in the Oregon Country—students paid eight dollars for a twenty-four week term. Ford was one of the school's "trustees."[41] Absent from the school, apparently, were the Holmes children— they were not on the list of enrollments—although they no doubt lived close enough to see the white children coming and going. Were they invited? Were they welcome to attend? The question surely answers itself.

The first teacher was John Lyle, who would recall an unusually comfortable pioneer life for the Fords, waited on by their slaves.

> *Lyle boarded with Colonel Ford and in so doing stepped into the niceties of living that he enjoyed. The Fords represented pioneering 'de luxe.' Not only were they charming and cultivated people, they had brought with them Negroes, Scott, Robbin (sic) and Polly, and their children, who had their own cabins and performed the farm and household labor. It was a happy winter for Lyle.*[42]

Lyle's description of life at the Fords suggests that Ford had managed in a very short period of time to recreate in Oregon a lifestyle similar to that which he and his family had enjoyed in Missouri. He almost certainly lived more comfortably than many of his fellow settlers—better than Peter Burnett, for example, who did not have slaves to help with the farm work, and who seems to have lacked the farming skills Ford had honed in Missouri.

Ford possibly built a second home in the early 1850s at what was then known as Nesmith Mills, a community built around a gristmill and boarding house, about five miles to the west. A photograph identified as the Ford house reveals a substantial building with a large front porch, and a cabin, or cabins, barely visible behind a large tree. A note on the back of the undated photograph identifies the cabin as "slave quarters."[43] However, there is no family reference to the Fords having lived at Nesmith Mills. The building is more likely the boarding house, where the Holmeses worked for a time after they gained their freedom. The Holmeses may have lived in the cabin behind the building, giving rise over time to the rumor it was "slave quarters." The boarding house provided lodging for gold miners headed for California.

A memo attributed to the Oregon Writers Project of the Works Progress Administration said the slaves' quarters—if they were slaves' quarters—were still standing as late as 1940.[44] But no longer.

Freedom Delayed

Robin Holmes said he was promised freedom for himself and his family if he helped Nathaniel Ford develop his farm. Holmes upheld his part of the bargain—within a few years, the Ford farm became well established and, apparently, quite profitable. But Ford proved in no hurry to fulfill his part of the agreement. One reason may have been that Oregon's new provisional government had changed its rules on slavery.

When the Ford wagon train left Missouri, slavery in Oregon was prohibited. A small group of Oregon Country inhabitants, including settlers, missionaries, trappers, and others, had met at Champoeg—then called Champooick— south of Portland on May 2, 1843, and voted to establish a provisional government. The vote was close, fifty-two to fifty, with British-oriented opponents suspecting—correctly—that the majority was trying to pave the way for American rule.[1] One account, written in 1911, said "opposition to the Hudson's Bay Company was the ruling passion with the men who were projecting the new government."[2]

At a follow-up meeting on July 5, 1843, those in attendance adopted a set of laws, known as the Organic Laws of Oregon, in effect, a constitution for their fledgling government. The organic laws were based on the laws of the Iowa Territory and incorporated a provision of the 1787 Northwest Ordinance, enacted by Congress to regulate slavery in the Northwest Territory east of the Mississippi River. Article 6 of the Northwest Ordinance declared: "There shall be neither slavery nor involuntary servitude in the said territory otherwise than in the punishment of crimes whereof the party shall have been duly convicted." This wording became Article 1, Section 4, of the organic laws, which also guaranteed "freedom of worship, trial by jury, *habeas corpus* and the sanctity of private contracts."[3]

The right to vote was limited to "every free male descendant of a white man" over the age of twenty-one. African American males would be denied the vote in Oregon until enactment of the Fifteenth Amendment following the Civil War. Women gained the right to vote in Oregon in 1912. The settlers also elected representatives to a nine-member legislative committee and named other officers to govern "until such time as the United States of America extends jurisdiction over us."[4] To these settlers, the organic laws applied to a region, extending to the Rocky Mountains.[5]

The prohibition on slavery conformed to the policy of the British, who shared jurisdiction over Oregon. Great Britain had abolished the slave trade in 1807 and banned slavery throughout the British Empire, including its Caribbean colonies, in 1833.[6] Oregon's ban on slavery existed in one form or another throughout its history—from the provisional government in 1843, to the territorial government in 1848, to statehood in 1859. However, there apparently was never any effort to enforce the provisional government's ban. Indeed, it may not have been enforceable. Oregon was not yet a part of the United States, and the provisional law "was not connected to a national legal or legislative structure or enforcement machinery," Darrell Millner, a professor of black studies at Portland State University, told the author. "Anyone who wanted to bring a slave to Oregon, and who could effectively keep that slave under their control, was not breaking any law of the United States."[7] Yet whatever the legal defects of the provisional law, it was nevertheless a firm statement that the early settlers opposed slavery. The influence of those more tolerant of slavery had not yet surfaced, but it soon would.

·~·

Ford, possibly aware of the decision made at Champoeg to ban slavery, and most certainly aware of the British prohibition against slavery, may have assumed that he would have to free his slaves upon his arrival. However, while the Ford wagon train was en route to Oregon, a new legislative committee modified the anti-slavery law at its June 1844 session in Oregon City. Peter Burnett, who had emerged as the leading member of the committee, advocated the change, which was ominous in its implications for blacks.

The flat prohibition against owning slaves had proved "unsatisfactory to many."[8] The new law maintained the overall prohibition against slavery, but allowed slaveholders a grace period of three years to free their slaves. It provided, in part:

Section 1. That slavery and involuntary servitude shall be forever prohibited in Oregon.

Section 2. That in all cases where slaves have been, or shall hereafter be brought into Oregon, the owner of such slaves shall have the term of three years from the introduction of such slaves to remove them out of the country.

Section 3. That if such owner of slaves shall neglect or refuse to remove such slaves from the country within the time specified in the preceding section, such slaves shall be free.[9]

The effect of the grace period was to make slavery temporarily legal for individual slaveholders—three years was not an inconsequential period of time for the slave. The modified slavery law passed the committee on June 26, 1844, by a vote of six to two. Voting with Burnett were two other members of his wagon train, Daniel Waldo and Morton McCarver.[10]

The legislative committee also voted to exclude blacks from the Oregon Country, and threatened severe punishment—whipping—if they refused to leave. It would not be the first such law. Exclusion laws in their various forms would be a major blemish on Oregon's history well into the twentieth century.

Oregon's Dixie

Rickreall today is an unincorporated farm community of fewer than a hundred inhabitants eleven miles west of Salem in Oregon's lush Willamette Valley. Modest homes and small businesses extend along both sides of busy Rickreall Road, which parallels the north bank of Rickreall Creek, known for years as La Creole Creek.[1] Towering oaks shade the homes and creek, giving the community a quaint charm. Looking west from the Highway 99 bridge over Rickreall Creek, one looks directly into the old Ford property. Across the bridge at the south end of town are the Polk County Fairgrounds, separated by the highway from the eastern boundary of the Ford land. Rickreall village was frequently referred to as Dixie "because of Southern sentiment in the community."[2] Surely, Ford's considerable influence in the region played into such sentiment. Ford was one of the region's first settlers when he arrived with family and slaves. Caroline Burch wrote that when the extended Ford family settled along Rickreall Creek, they were the southernmost white family in the Oregon Country.[3]

View of Rickreall today, looking east along Rickreall Road near the intersection with Oregon Route 223. The unincorporated town of fewer than 100 residents is eleven miles west of Salem in Polk County. Most of the town is on land that once belonged to Nathaniel Ford. (Photo by author)

In a letter Ford sent to a friend in Missouri on April 6, 1845, five months after arriving in Oregon, he is effusive in his praise of his new home, and predicts lush harvests. The letter was addressed to a Dr. John Lowery in Fayette, and reprinted in the *Jefferson City* [Missouri] *Inquirer* on July 25, 1845. Lowery, president of the Fayette bank, was one of several acquaintants who posted a $10,000 bond for Ford's second term as the sheriff of Howard County in 1830.

> *I have settled in the Wallamette (sic) Valley, some forty miles above Oregon City, on a little river called the Rickerall (sic) on the west side of the Wallamette in the prettiest country I have ever seen for farming and stock raising. I am now breaking prairie to put in spring wheat. I shall put in some forty acres, which will produce this season, some 20 bushels per acre. The second crop will produce 40 or 50 bushels per acre, when sewed (sic) in the fall.*[4]

Oregon's earliest settlers acquired land on a first-come, first-served basis, relying largely on agreements among themselves. It was no different for Ford. He paid a squatter named Billie Doak twenty-five dollars for land straddling Rickreall Creek. Doak had marked his claim by axing a chip out of an oak tree.[5] The fledgling provisional government decreed in 1844 that "in all cases where claims are already made, and in all cases where there are agreed lines between the parties occupying adjacent tracts, such claims shall be valid to the extent of six hundred and forty acres"—one square mile.[6] Ford and many other early arriving settlers claimed the maximum.

In those early years, settlers were few, so it shouldn't come as a surprise that Ford, with his experience in Missouri government, would step seamlessly into a leadership role in Oregon's governmental and civic affairs. He engaged in a wide variety of activities that enhanced his status, and probably his wealth. He was a landowner, farmer, postmaster, school administrator, California gold miner, and a legislator in the territorial government. He was also a skilled surveyor and conducted surveys for the government throughout Oregon and Northern California, including a section of the Oregon-California border in 1855.

The provisional legislature elected Ford on August 9, 1845, as the first supreme judge, the top judicial position in the new provisional government, which preceded the territorial government. However, Ford turned down the appointment, according to a letter dated August 18, 1845, from Governor George Abernethy to the legislature.[7] No reason was given. But Ford remains today on an official list of Oregon's provisional supreme court justices, with the notation he "declined service."[8] The second choice for supreme judge was Burnett, who accepted.[9] Ford did accept an appointment by Abernethy to the road commission on December 19, 1846. Why he accepted this less prestigious position is not explained.[10]

Ford's son, Marcus, seemed destined for his own leadership role. He was appointed to a two-year term as prosecuting attorney for the Oregon region in October 1845—although he resigned three months later—and was elected to the provisional legislature in 1847, representing Polk County.[11] He had a joint law practice in Rickreall with James Nesmith, a member of the Burnett wagon train and a future U.S. senator. However, as will be discussed later, Marcus' life was cut short in 1850 by a tragic incident.

Nathaniel Ford was among organizers in 1850 of Oregon's Democratic Party, which would dominate Oregon politics until the Civil War.[12] He was elected to five terms in the territorial legislative assembly representing Polk County—four times to the nine-member upper chamber, called the Council, in 1849, 1855, 1857, and 1858 (he was defeated in 1853).[13] He also served one term in the eighteen-member territorial House in 1851. As a leading Democrat, Ford appeared positioned for even higher office. Several writers have mistakenly written that Nathaniel Ford also served in the state senate in 1866 and 1868 after Oregon became a state in 1859. But they confuse Nathaniel Ford with Nineveh Ford of Umatilla County, who emigrated to Oregon with the Burnett wagon train in 1843.[14]

Nathaniel Ford's election to the Council in June 1855, representing Polk and Tillamook counties, was contested by another candidate, H. N. V. Holmes, who had served with Ford in the 1851-1852 House. Ford, running as an independent, beat Holmes, a Democrat, by a single vote in the initial count. Holmes, no relation to Robin Holmes, alleged improprieties among Ford voters, apparently with justification. Voting at the time was done orally, so voters were easily identified. Holmes cited two examples of unqualified voters who cast ballots for Ford.[15] However, it didn't alter the outcome. A family account explained how Ford maneuvered himself to victory. After Holmes successfully challenged the improper votes, Ford used his surveying skills "to have enough Holmes' voters surveyed out of the county to defeat his opponent."[16]

⋅⌣ ⌣

Ford's 1845 letter to John Lowery in Missouri reads like a promotional tract. Everything is wonderful: hogs are fat; views are great; wheat virtually explodes from the lush soil.

> [W]e are in the best country I have ever seen for farming and stock raising. The green grass, similar to the blue grass of the States, is now some six inches high. . . . From the best information I have of this country, it is large enough to make some 3 or 4 good states. The Indians are harmless, with the exception of stealing some little things, which they think all right. . . .
>
> Families wishing to move to this country should leave Independence [Missouri] by the 15th of April, if they possibly can, in consequence of the fall rains in Oregon. I believe the distance will be shortened by a new route, some 300 miles, and a better road obtained. . . .
>
> Our laws are few and simple. . . . A portion of the people go for an independent government; the larger portion of us adhere to the United States, and hope they will soon, if they have not already, done something for this fine country. Many of my acquaintances in that country would do well if they were here.
>
> . . . we enjoy the sea breeze all the summer season from the north west. . . . The land is well watered; all the springs and streams are cool and fine flavored. We have a fine view of the snow mountains [probably the Cascades]. We have the finest fish I ever saw.[17]

In promoting the ease of living and farming in Oregon, Ford left out the obvious downsides: loneliness, separation from extended families, and the everyday hardships of building new lives from scratch in an unfamiliar land. There were few roads, schools, and stores, no store-bought clothing or shoes—maybe no shoes at all—limited medical care, occasional hunger, distant neighbors, and, perhaps most notably, the frequent relentless rains. The settlers also lived amid Native Americans, many resenting the whites' claims to the tribes' traditional homelands.

However, Ford apparently was not far off when he wrote that the Native Americans in the Willamette Valley were largely "harmless." Missionaries calculated that nearly 70 percent of the Native American inhabitants, known as the Kalapuyans, had perished from a deadly fever—possibly malaria— between 1830 and 1833, well before the first settlers arrived.[18] Described as small in stature, dressed in skins and cedar caps worn over braided hair, with ornaments of teeth and bone, the Kalapuyans were dispersed in a dozen bands throughout the 110-mile-long valley. Some of the better-known bands were the Tualatin, Yamhill, Champoeg, Santiam, Luckiamute, and Yoncalla. The number of Kalapuyan language speakers was reduced from about two thousand in 1806—a figure reported by the Lewis and Clark expedition—to about three hundred in 1844, the year Ford arrived in the valley.[19]

By the time of settlement, the Kalapuyans were too few to offer resistance to the newcomers, who simply moved onto the land. Peter Burnett, who settled on two hundred and fifty acres in the Tualatin Valley, said Native Americans were shoved aside with little regard for their well-being.

We came not to establish trade with the Indians but to take and settle the country exclusively for ourselves. Consequently, we went anywhere we pleased, settled down without any treaty or consultation with the Indians, and occupied our claims without their consent and without compensation. . . . They instinctively saw annihilation before them.[20]

In 1844, the provisional government's legislative committee passed a law to protect Native Americans in their "free use of such places of vacant land as they now occupy with their villages and other improvements." However, the law was misleading, if not outright devious. It claimed that because the Native Americans weren't engaged in farming, "they have no use for land not actually occupied or use (sic) by them." Treaties, it said, were useless because the tribes lacked a responsible government with which to negotiate. Moreover, the Native Americans were "rapidly diminishing" and "mere remnants of once powerful tribes."[21] By 1845, wrote the late Terence O'Donnell, there were more whites in the valley, about two thousand, than Native Americans.[22]

One can only speculate whether the Kalapuyans might have offered resistance were they anywhere near full strength.[23] There was armed and bloody conflict with other tribes in the region, notably the Cayuse and Snakes east of the Cascades, and the Rogue River, Shasta, and Modocs in southern Oregon and northern California.

·, ⌣ ·.

Ford's fulsome praise of Oregon duplicates the sentiments in letters sent home by other early settlers, including Peter Burnett. Such boosterism, aimed at encouraging more settlers, was common in the sparsely settled West. In a letter published in the *Jefferson City Inquirer* on August 8, 1845—written the previous November 4—Burnett suggested Oregon's climate and fertile soils brought out the best in a man. "Our country is most beautiful, fertile and well-watered, with the most equable and pleasant climate. Our population is rapidly increasing, and the country is making great progress in wealth and refinement. I have never yet before seen a population so industrious, sober and honest as this."[23] Even earlier, on October 23, 1843—only months after he arrived—Burnett wrote of the ease of life in Oregon.

Perhaps, there is no country in the world where man can live so well, upon so little labor. The climate here is much milder than that of Missouri, and it is the highest and most pleasant climate I have ever seen—In the lower section, (Wallamette) (sic) the climate is still milder, but much damper. Provisions can be had to any amount, and emigrants need have no fear on that head. They could readily live on salmon alone, any quantity of which can be had at the lowest price. Beef cattle and hogs are plenty.[24]

Burnett ignored in these letters his own family's plight after they arrived in Oregon. Years later in his memoirs, he provided this more truthful account: "For the first two years after our arrival in Oregon we were frequently without any meat for weeks at a time, and sometimes without bread, and occasionally without both bread and meat at the same time. On these occasions, if we had milk, butter, and potatoes, we were well content."[25] Burnett wrote about going shoeless, and of winter rains that "were far worse than driving snow, as they wet and chilled the rider through." Still, he said, the rain made "Oregon one of the loveliest and most fertile spots on earth."[26]

Influenced by boosters to come to Oregon, the early settlers became boosters themselves. They had a compelling interest in rapidly expanding their ranks. They wanted buyers for their land, crops, and other goods. They needed help to develop the roads, markets, and trade required for a vibrant economy. They also believed, correctly, that a growing American population would strengthen the American claim to the Oregon Country, still officially under joint occupation with Great Britain.

Ford's advice on when and how to travel, and what to bring, echoes advice given by Burnett: small groups of settlers were easier to manage than large companies; smaller herds of livestock were easier to feed than large herds; tension and conflicts over leadership were less likely to erupt in a smaller group of wagons.

⸱⸱ ⸱

Not mentioned in Ford's letter were his slaves, who by this time were no doubt plowing his land, sowing his wheat, feeding his hogs, and preparing his meals.

Aided by his slaves, Ford evidently prospered as a wheat grower. A letter from Charles Pickett (an early emigrant who moved from Oregon to California and back again) of Sacramento in 1847, addressed jointly to Ford, Burnett, Daniel Waldo, and Morton McCarver, urged them to grow as much wheat as possible for the California market: "California wants 20,000 barrels of flour from Oregon the present year, if not more, and also several thousand bushels of white wheat for sowing next fall, if the next immigration be of any size." However, Pickett cautioned that a recent shipment of Oregon wheat "is slightly musty," the discovery of which "is to give your flour a bad name in every market."[27] But Oregon wheat growers and farmers would soon turn their attention to California for another reason: *gold*. Ford and Burnett would be among them.

Land and More Land

The American strategy of gaining Oregon by occupying Oregon succeeded. Great Britain relinquished its claim under terms of the Oregon Treaty of 1846, which established the boundary between British and American jurisdiction at the forty-ninth parallel, today's border with Canada. The American flag could now fly uncontested over the Oregon Country. Congress gave Oregon territorial status on August 14, 1848. The new territory covered a land mass that extended east to the Rocky Mountains, and included present-day Washington and Idaho, and portions of western Montana and Wyoming. Washington would be established as a separate territory in 1853; Idaho in 1863.

Near the end of his administration, President James Polk appointed North Carolina-born Joseph Lane as the first governor of the Oregon Territory. At the time of his appointment, the forty-eight-year-old Lane lived in Indiana with his wife and eight children. He had been a member of the Indiana General Assembly and served with distinction in the Mexican War. Polk's successor, Zachary Taylor, nominated Abraham Lincoln to succeed Lane, but Lincoln turned him down. Lincoln gave no reason, although his political ambitions may have been directed toward the East, rather than the West. His letter of refusal was sent to Interior Secretary Thomas Ewing on September 23, 1849. In a letter to a friend four days later, Lincoln thanked his supporters for encouraging him, "but on as much reflection as I have had time to give the subject, I cannot consent to accept it."[1] Lane remained governor until 1850, when he resigned to successfully run for election as Oregon's territorial delegate to Congress, following the death of Oregon's first delegate, Samuel Thurston.

At the time Oregon gained territorial status, the white population was soaring, relatively speaking. The trickle of emigrants along the Oregon Trail was now a steady stream. Additional settlers came by ship. There were farmers, merchants, lawyers, journalists, bankers, tradesmen, seafarers, and speculators, all constituting the human material necessary to build a viable society. The 1850 U.S. Census put the territory's population at 12,093, most residing south of the Columbia River around Oregon City and in the Willamette Valley. Included in the count were an estimated fifty-four African Americans.[2]

After granting territorial status to Oregon, Congress followed up on September 27, 1850, by enacting the Donation Land Act that offered free land in Oregon to white settlers and so-called "half-breeds," persons with mixed blood at least 50 percent white. It excluded blacks, Hawaiians, Native Americans, and Asians. The vote to exclude blacks was contentious, passing the House by a vote of sixty-eight to fifty-one.[3] When Representative William Sackett of New York questioned why blacks should be denied the same land rights as whites, he was told by Oregon's delegate, Samuel Thurston, that the African Americans in Oregon "preferred to rove with the Indians, encouraging them to acts of hostility against the whites, instead of settling down and laboring like the settlers."[4]

The act had the effect of upholding Nathaniel Ford's claim to six hundred and forty acres—one square mile—as well as the land claims of other early white settlers. They included Ford's brother-in-law David Goff, whose claim bordered Ford's. Married couples who arrived in Oregon prior to December 1, 1850, such as the Fords, were entitled to the maximum six hundred and forty acres. Significantly, half of the property—or three hundred and twenty acres—

was to be in the wife's name, making the law notable as one of the first in the nation allowing married women to own property. Unmarried white males eighteen and older could claim three hundred and twenty acres. Later-arriving pioneers, who settled in Oregon between December 1850 and December 1854, were entitled to half the amount of the earlier settlers. Settlers were required to live on the land and cultivate it for four years before they could own it outright.[5]

Gus Quiring said the old Nathaniel Ford property "has some of the best soil in Polk County." Quiring farmed a portion of the property for some of the owners who followed Ford. (Photo by author)

The law created an incentive for quickie weddings. A man and wife could jointly claim six hundred and forty acres if they married within a year of the 1850 deadline. "Brief courtships and early weddings became the rule, and many brides were in their early teens when the knots were tied."[6] The purpose of the law, of course, was to reward early settlers and encourage other emigrants. However, a major criticism was that the law gave settlers more land than they could possibly cultivate themselves.[7] Help was difficult to find, and some farmers began to agitate for the cheap labor that would come with slavery.

In approving the land claim act, Congress was giving away Indian lands without treaties or compensation. Congress did create the office of Superintendent of Indian Affairs for the Oregon Territory in 1851, as well as a Treaty Commission to begin the long, inconclusive, and painful—for the tribes—process that would eventually remove the Native Americans to out-of-the-way reservations.

The Kalapuyan bands formally yielded their Willamette Valley lands in treaties signed with Joel Palmer, superintendent of Oregon Indian Affairs, in 1854 and 1855. Typical was the treaty signed with the Tualatins on March 25, 1854, in which the band surrendered their claim to nearly fifteen hundred square miles in exchange for farming equipment and other goods and services—but no money—plus the promise of forty acres of land on a future reservation.[8] The Tualatins initially resisted selling their land, but Palmer warned them in writing they had no real choice. "The whites are determined to settle on your land. We cannot prevent them and in a few years there will be no place left for you. Then what will you do? Will you live in the mountains like wolves?"[9]

The Kalapuyans were eventually sent to what became the Grand Ronde Reservation in western Oregon, lumped together with survivors of other much-depleted tribes and bands, among them the Clackamas, Mollala, Upper Umpqua, Takelma, and Shasta.[10] It is of no little irony that it was the openness of the Willamette Valley that helped make it attractive to Ford and other settlers, and this was due in part to the land policies of the Kalapuyans. At the end of each summer, they burned sections of the valley floor to maintain open pasture for hunting deer and elk, and also to facilitate the harvest of tarweed seeds and encourage growth of the camas root, major components of their diet.[11]

The best land went quickly. When the land law expired in 1856, some seventy-five hundred claims had been filed totaling more than 2.5 million acres, accounting for virtually all of the best land in the Willamette Valley.[12]

The Fords were assigned Donation Land Claim No. 44. The Fords gained formal title to their land in 1858, half in Nathaniel Ford's name and half in Lucinda's. A map of the original claim shows it to be in a bulky J-shape. A narrow strip of land separates the top two-thirds of Nathaniel Ford's property from his wife's, with the properties joined at the southern end of the tract.[13] The reason for the odd configuration isn't known with any certainty. However, because the strip of land extends north from Rickreall Creek, it quite possibly was the same "narrow strip of land" mentioned in county records that the Fords sold in 1865. Two neighbors, J. Dempsey and J. C. Thorp, bought the land for one hundred dollars to accommodate a mill-race for a flour mill.[14]

A Ford granddaughter, Aurelia Burch, who died in 1971 at age ninety-one, offered a brief history of her family's claim to water from Rickreall Creek. Her recollection may have been used to adjudicate a water rights dispute.

> *My family and my grandparents family used the waters of Rickreall Creek since about 1845, and the waters of Rickreall Creek have been used continually by the Samuel T. Burch family, and thus pertain to the property of Alma O. Dempsey and Ralph W. Dempsey.*[15]

The Donation Land Act served its purpose of drawing thousands of additional land-hungry pioneers to Oregon, helping bring about the development sought by the earliest settlers. Oregon's population more than quadrupled between

1850 and 1860 to a total of 52,465. But there were few African Americans, a mere one hundred and twenty-four counted in the 1860 Census.[16] Denied the same access to land as whites, and with Oregon's exclusion law in place for much of the decade, a free black would be hard-pressed to find a reason to come.

The Applegate Trail

Ford's mention to John Lowery of a new and shorter trail to Oregon referred to plans already under way to find an alternative route for emigrants. Ford would play a role in developing what would later be known as the Applegate Trail, although it's not clear how much of a role. Pauline Burch said Ford left home for six months in 1846 to help locate a new trail, leaving his farm in the care of his son, Marcus, and the slaves, Robin and Scott.[1]

The Applegate Trail was the vision of Jesse and Lindsay Applegate, who sought a southern route into Oregon's Willamette Valley that would enable emigrants to avoid the perilous trip down the Columbia River where the brothers each lost a son in 1843. It would also diminish the influence of the Hudson's Bay Company, which controlled the route along the Columbia River through its ownership of Fort Hall and other forts.

The British company, with its fur trade and other business operations, had dominated commerce in the region since the 1820s. Fort Vancouver, its Northwest headquarters, was established in 1825 by Dr. John McLoughlin as a replacement for Fort George near Astoria.[2] McLoughlin had been sent to the Northwest as the company's chief factor in 1824, for the two-fold purpose of preserving the company's monopoly over the fur trade and "to prevent the Oregon Country from being settled by Americans."[3] However, instead of discouraging settlers, McLoughlin provided them with valuable assistance. According to one account, "He furnished boats to carry them from the Cascades to Vancouver. He sold supplies to those who were able to pay, and gave credit to all who were in want. By his orders, the sick were nursed and cared for in the company's hospital at the Fort."[4]

The joint claim to the Oregon Country had not yet been resolved, and relations between Britain and the United States had soured. There was saber rattling on both sides. The Americans wanted all of the Pacific Northwest, including most of present-day British Columbia, a position reflected in the battle cry "fifty-four forty or fight!" Britain effectively conceded that the area south of the Columbia River was under de facto control of the Americans, but it maintained a tenuous hold on the region north of the river. And it appeared ready to fight over British Columbia.

Britain sent a fleet of sixteen vessels to the region in a show of military muscle. Among these was the eighteen-gun sloop-of-war *Modeste*, which anchored at Fort Vancouver on November 29, 1845, to protect the Hudson's Bay Company from a possible attack.[5] These "obvious warlike preparations" provided another incentive to find a road into Oregon free of threat from the British. U.S. troops, should they be required, might gain access to the territory by a more practicable overland route than had previously been discovered.[6]

An earlier attempt to find a new route into Oregon had ended in tragedy. As many as two hundred wagons and a thousand settlers became lost in 1845 while following the so-called "Meek Cutoff." Trail guide Stephen Meek had convinced the settlers he knew of a shorter road, circling south from Fort Boise, near the present Oregon-Idaho border, around eastern Oregon's Blue Mountains. Saying his cutoff was two hundred miles shorter than the Columbia River route, Meek convinced emigrants to follow him for a fee of five dollars per wagon. One settler, a teenager, recalled years later that Meek told them "we could save six weeks."[7] However, Meek didn't know the route well enough, and the settlers became lost in southeastern Oregon's high desert in present-day Harney and Malheur counties. Short on supplies and water, as many as fifty would eventually die.[8] One of those in the Meek wagon train, Richard Watson Helm, said in a 1924 interview that some of the angry emigrants planned to kill Meek, but that Meek had already gone for help. Helm said it was Moses "Black" Harris who rescued the settlers:

> *Meek reached The Dalles and sent Black Harris, who knew the country, to guide our party to The Dalles. He brought some food on pack horses and met us not far from where Tygh Creek enters the Deschutes.*[9]

What Helm may not have known, however, was that Harris stepped in to help after the local Methodist mission rejected Meek's request for aid.[10] Meek turned to Harris, who secured relief supplies from area tribes and led the rescue mission.

⸱⁓⸱

The project to develop the Applegate Trail followed a year later. However, it proved not to be a significant improvement over the Meek Cutoff, at least for the first settlers who followed it. Ford helped organize an initial effort. Settlers in Polk County—Ford among them—raised the money and other support to develop the southern route, a project endorsed by the new provisional government. Ford took out an ad in the *Oregon Spectator* on April 15, 1846, seeking volunteers. Under the headline, "Over the Mountains," the ad read:

> *The company to examine for a practicable wagon route from the Willamette valley to Snake river, will rendezvous at the residence of Nat. Ford on the Rickreal (sic) so as to be ready to start on the trip on the first day of next May. The contemplated route will be up the Willamette valley, crossing the Cascade mountains south of the three snowy buttes [the Three Sisters]. A portion of the company will return after crossing the Cascade mountains. It is hoped that several young men will be prepared to go on to meet the emigration. Those agreed to start at the time above mentioned, are Solomon Tetherow, Nathaniel Ford, Gen. C[ornelius] Gilliam, Stephen H. L. Meek, and Moses Harris, and many others, it is expected, will be ready by the time above specified.*[11]

All were hardened pioneers. Cornelius Gilliam led the wagon train that traveled with Ford's train in 1844. Moses Harris guided both trains. Meek was guide for the lost wagon train, and Solomon Tetherow was a captain of the wagon train that followed Meek. The first expedition, however, was a flop. Led by Levi Scott, the expedition set out in May 1846 from Rickreall to cross the Calapooya Range at the southern end of the Willamette Valley. But when some members became wary of the Native American tribes further south, several decided to turn back. The expedition was then too small to accomplish its goal and returned to Rickreall.

Ford strongly objected to a characterization in the *Oregon Spectator* that they had returned "unsuccessful and discouraged." In a letter to editor Henry A. G. Lee, published on June 25, 1846, Ford argued, "It is true they returned, but not discouraged." He wrote that they had found "nothing in the way of a practicable wagon road, and they were prevented from going on by the hardships of having to stand guard every night."[12] Ford said the party returned to gather reinforcements—"energetic and persevering men"—to renew their effort. Among the new members, he listed Jesse and Lindsay Applegate, and his own brother-in-law, David Goff. Carryovers from the first group were Levi Scott and Moses Harris. Notable in Ford's letter is that despite his flowery rhetoric, he ended by questioning whether Applegate and the others would find the hoped-for southern route.

> *By the addition of these men, the party is sufficiently strong to insure safety against the attacks of Indians, and to greatly lessen the hardships of the trip.*
>
> *The party left the Rickreall on the 22nd in fine spirits and high hopes of bringing our next emigration in at the head of the Willamette Valley. They left with a firm determination never to retrace their steps—never to abandon the noble and philanthropic enterprise, until they have found a good wagon road, if such a thing is possible.*[13]

Ford did not leave with this second expedition of fifteen men, known to history as the Applegate party. Ford's letter to the Oregon City newspaper was dated three days after the group set out. Nor is his name included on Lindsay Applegate's list of its members. Possibly, Ford joined them later. More likely, he opted out. Perhaps he was among the wary ones from the first expedition.

The Applegate party succeeded in finding a route through the several mountain ranges of central and southern Oregon and northern California, and out across Nevada's Black Rock Desert. Once Jesse Applegate had convinced himself the route was good for wagons, he rode ahead to Fort Hall where he persuaded several parties of settlers to give it a try. The trail led south from Fort Hall, starting down the established California Trail as far as the Humboldt River in Nevada. At the Humboldt, the new trail left the California Trail to turn northwest across the Black Rock Desert toward the Klamath Basin. It crossed the Siskiyou Mountains to present-day Ashland and the Rogue Valley. From the Rogue Valley, the trail turned north through the Umpqua and Calapooya Mountains to reach the Willamette Valley near present-day Eugene. That was the plan. Jesse Applegate extolled the advantages of the new trail—overstated as it turned out—in a letter to a Missouri newspaper, *The Independence Expositor*. The letter was dated September 10, 1846, from Fort Hall and addressed to "the future Emigrants to Oregon Territory."

> *The advantages given to the emigrants by this route is of the greatest importance. The distance is considerably shortened, the grass and water plenty, the sterile regions and dangerous crossings of the Snake and Columbia Rivers avoided, as well as the Cascade Mts.—he may reach his destination with his wagons and property in time to build a cabin and sow wheat before the rainy season. This road has been explored and will be*

opened at the expense of the citizens of Oregon and nothing whatever is demanded of the emigrants.[14]

However, Applegate failed to make clear to the initial party of settlers that once they had crossed the Nevada desert and reached the Oregon mountain ranges, they would need to help build the rest of the road. Moreover, while Applegate seemed to believe that the trail was shorter than the route down the Columbia River, it wasn't—it was about two hundred miles longer. Applegate either was a poor judge of distance or he wanted so badly to believe his road was shorter that he fooled himself. According to one writer, "Applegate was an honest man, painfully so. He would not have deliberately lied to the pioneers."[15]

Between ninety and one hundred wagons took to the new trail, a procession that extended over many miles, with the first wagons as much as three weeks travel time ahead of the last. Ford's brother-in-law, Goff, remained at the cutoff point in Nevada to direct the wagons to Oregon.[16] As happened with the lost Meek party a year earlier, food stocks wouldn't stretch for a much-longer-than-promised journey. And that wasn't the only problem. The emigrants faced thirst in the desert, inadequate forage for livestock, harassment by Native Americans, and winter rains three weeks earlier than usual, all of which slowed the travelers to a crawl in Oregon's Umpqua Valley. Of the estimated one hundred and sixty adults, plus children, who started from Fort Hall, twelve adults would die, along with an unknown number of children. Typhoid fever claimed the largest number. Oxen and cattle perished along the way, or were killed or stolen by the Modocs and other tribes. One settler lost his entire flock of fifty or so sheep—stolen apparently—on a single night in the Rogue River Valley near present-day Gold Hill.[17]

The Applegate Trail proved to be little more than a footpath in places, no doubt an unwelcome and discouraging surprise to the emigrants. In the rugged Umpqua Valley, especially, there was no track that could be considered a wagon road. For a time, members of the Applegate expedition worked at road building ahead of the wagons. However, most of the crew, including Jesse Applegate, abandoned the work before it was completed, leaving it for the exhausted settlers to finish the road. One member of the expedition, Levi Scott, remained with the settlers during the entire journey and saw them through to the Willamette Valley, although much later than anyone had intended.

The first settlers passed through the Calapooya Mountains into the Willamette Valley in mid-November. Among these first was J. Quinn Thornton, who wrote the *Spectator* from Rickreall on November 30, 1846, seeking help for those still struggling on the trail.

I have just arrived in the settlements of the valley from the Kanyon (sic) in the Umpqua mountains. I left the people suffering beyond any thing you have ever known. They must perish with hunger unless the people of the settlements go to their relief with pack horses and provisions, and bring them in. . . . I implore the people of this valley, in the name of humanity, and in behalf of my starving and perishing fellow travelers to hasten to their relief.[18]

The newspaper added a paragraph to Thornton's letter, saying a party of rescuers with "a considerable band of horses" had already left to help the remaining emigrants. The last of the emigrants reached the Willamette Valley in late January, with snow falling, some having endured further privations. Most had abandoned their wagons.[19] Thornton became so relentless in his criticism of the Applegates—claiming incompetence—that James Nesmith, a close friend of the Applegates, challenged him to a duel, although violence was avoided.[20] Thornton, an abolitionist, became a judge of Oregon's Territorial Supreme Court in 1847. He later served in the Oregon House of Representatives, representing Benton County.

⌣

The experience of the first group of settlers on the Applegate Trail caused Peter Burnett to pronounce the southern route both unfinished and unsafe. In a letter printed in the *Liberty* [Missouri] *Weekly Tribune* on August 21, 1847, Burnett recommended that Oregon-bound settlers continue to follow the established route down the Columbia River. He predicted that the Applegate Trail would eventually prove of "great importance," which it did. But not yet. Burnett told the newspaper:

The southern route was surveyed by Jesse Applegate, Moses Harris and others, prompted no doubt by the most laudable motives; and cost them much labor and expense, and subjected them to much censure. . . . Those who came that way certainly suffered very much, losing most of their cattle and reached the settlements in November and December, half starved and half naked.[21]

Lindsay Applegate blamed much of the criticism on agitators for the Hudson's Bay Company, which had a commercial interest in maintaining the Columbia River route as the preferred route. He did acknowledge "many of the immigrants who followed us had a hard time, although not as hard as they would likely have experienced on the other route."[22]

As for Nathaniel Ford's involvement, Pauline Burch said Ford and others had gone to present-day Winnemucca, Nevada, "to assist a wagon train of emigrants coming over the Oregon Trail." But she said it proved to be "a wasted six months, as the emigrant train was late and the men were forced to return home at once on account of heavy rains."[23]

If Burch's account is correct—and there's no reason to think otherwise—it means Ford probably at some point joined Applegate's crew to help guide the settlers. Perhaps he worked with Goff at the cutoff point in Nevada.

Burch may have overstated the length of Ford's absence when she said he was gone for six months—the Applegates were gone about four months. However long Ford was gone, Burch wrote that while he was away, "the son Mark, with the help of Scott and Robin, looked after the farm."[24]

Oregon's "Lash Law"

Peter Burnett was a major proponent of Oregon's 1844 exclusion law, the first of several such laws. Along with many others, he wanted to leave behind not just the culture of slavery, but also African Americans, whether free or not. He cited this as a major motive for his coming to Oregon:

The object is to keep clear of that most troublesome class of population [blacks]. We are in a new world, under the most favorable circumstances, and we wish to avoid most of those evils that have so much afflicted the United States and other countries.[1]

Oregon's exclusion law required that "any free Negro or mulatto" over age eighteen must leave within two years, and females within three years. This included slaves freed by their owners. Violators were to be severely whipped. The penalty gave the law the name by which it became known in Oregon history: "The Lash Law," or, "Peter Burnett's Lash Law." It provided:

Section 6. That if any such free negro or mulatto shall fail to quit the country as required by this act, he or she may be arrested upon a warrant issued by some justice of the peace, and if guilty upon trial before such

*justice, shall receive upon his or her bare back not less than twenty, nor
more than thirty-nine stripes, to be inflicted by the constable of the proper
county.*[2]

However, the harshness of the lash law evidently shocked more thoughtful
members of the community. An executive committee of the provisional
government formally recommended to the legislative committee on December
17, 1844, that the law "be so amended as to exclude corporal punishment,
and require bonds for good behavior in its stead."[3] The legislative committee
responded by modifying the law the following day, December 19, 1844—
before it could take effect, and before anyone was whipped. Even though the
executive committee compelled him to make the change, Burnett would later
say he recognized that whipping was too severe. As the author of the lash law,
he lamely said, "the second sober thought of the member [Burnett] was better
than the first hasty thought."[4]

In place of whipping, the committee approved another punishment that
seemed to condemn a free black who refused to leave the Oregon Country to
a potential outcome not unlike slavery. The new penalty provided that if the
"free negro or mulatto" failed to leave the region, he or she would be arrested
and tried. And if found guilty, a court representative "will publicly hire out
such free negro or mulatto to the lowest bidder" who " will obligate himself to
remove such free negro or mulatto out of the country within six months after
the term of service shall expire."[5]

⸱⸱ ⸱⸱

Exclusion laws weren't unique to Oregon. The states of the Old Northwest—
Ohio, Indiana, and Illinois—had, or soon would have, exclusion laws of their
own, along with other discriminatory measures.[6] In California, the legislature
on several occasions debated an exclusion law, although declining to enact
one. Oregon's exclusion laws reflected racial attitudes that the early settlers
had acquired long before they set out on the Oregon Trail and "were a part of
the baggage they brought with them along with their plows, guns and rocking
chairs."[7] Many western farmers "equated the Negro with slavery, and if slavery
was to be prohibited, then the Negro was also to be excluded."[8] Some of the
resistance to free blacks in the Old Northwest stemmed from a concern these
states would be overwhelmed by freed slaves from the South. The reasons were
also economic—whites wanted to secure the available jobs, and wealth, for
themselves.[9] Oregon was not unique in considering whipping as a penalty. The
Illinois Territorial Legislature in 1813 imposed a penalty of thirty-nine lashes
for newly arriving free blacks who refused to leave—repeated every fifteen

days until the individual left.[10] As in Oregon, exclusion laws were generally not enforced, and did not apply to existing residents.

The two thousand-mile crossing on the Oregon Trail both hardened and emboldened the early settlers, giving them what Gordon Dodds called "a sense of power" that reinforced already deep-seated prejudices, as well as a conservative outlook on life. "They not only chose to leave home, but they also selected their jumping off places, their traveling companions, their officers and guides. They made their own rules and regulations for the journey and enforced them. They made their government responsive to their needs. They fought the Indians and nature. They were courted when they arrived at their destination . . . what challenge would be too strong for those who had mastered the trail?"[11]

The amended 1844 exclusion law was not enforced, and soon changed. A new and larger legislative committee, with Jesse Applegate among the members—and without Burnett, who did not seek reelection—voted on July 3, 1845, to repeal "the several actions relating to slavery in Oregon."[12] The action amounted to a repudiation of Burnett, although it was by no means the last time exclusion would dominate Oregon's racial debate. Applegate's influence was probably key to the outcome, as he seemed to be the one Oregon leader of stature who consistently spoke out for fair treatment of others.

The committee approved a new anti-slavery measure as an amendment to Oregon's organic laws. It declared, "this government can recognize the right of one person to the services of another only upon a 'bona fide' contract, made and entered into and equally binding on both parties." Applegate threw his full weight behind the amendment. The vote in favor was ten to three.[13] The committee also requested Congress to establish a territorial government and "legalize the previous acts of the people so far as these might be in accord with the federal constitution."[14]

The amended Organic Laws of Oregon was approved by voters on July 25, 1845, by a vote of 255 to 22.[15] The section on slavery retained the wording of the Northwest Ordinance that, "There shall be neither slavery nor involuntary servitude in said Territory, otherwise than for the punishment of crimes, whereof the party should have been duly convicted."[16] But the amended laws also retained the provision restricting voting to "free male descendants of a white man."[17]

Jesse Applegate is credited with playing a pivotal role in the decision to include the prohibition against slavery. He was quoted in later years as saying his unstated "political purpose" was "to settle the slavery question west of the Rocky Mountains [just] as the Ordinance had settled it in the Northwest states to the east of them."[18] Whether Applegate's motives were understood, the majority of the early Oregon inhabitants agreed with the outcome. "They were fully in sympathy with its prohibition of slavery, each of their subsequent frames of government containing the same provision."[19]

Voters elected George Abernethy governor, and the legislative committee was reconstituted into a provisional legislature. It was at this same election that Marcus Ford was selected as the region's prosecuting attorney. This meant young Ford was responsible for helping enforce the anti-slavery law. Whether he ever had a conversation with his father about his slaves isn't known. But what is known is that no serious attempt was made to force Nathaniel Ford to give up his slaves until Robin Holmes brought his custody suit seven years later. The requirement of a "bona fide" contract for services proved of no help to the Holmeses—and probably not to other slaves—if they even knew about it.

Nearly three thousand additional settlers, the largest number yet, would arrive in Oregon in 1845. Each arrival brought new leaders and new prejudices. Attitudes toward blacks would harden yet again.

·-~·

Oregon, of course, was not isolated from the national debate over slavery, which would explode into the Civil War in 1861. Congressional debate over whether slavery could, or should, be extended into the territories had delayed territorial status for Oregon. An often-heated debate over Oregon between anti-slave and pro-slave legislators lasted eighteen months, from December 1846 to the summer of 1848. Disagreement focused on whether Oregon's territorial bill would include a prohibition against slavery. Pro-slave interests weren't especially concerned over whether slavery would be extended to Oregon, but they were concerned lest a specific prohibition for Oregon would set an anti-slavery precedent for other western territories.[20] They also wanted to maintain a balance between slave and free states, which would keep the membership of the U.S. Senate in relative balance as well.

During the administration of President James Polk, from 1845 to 1849, sentiment was strong for annexing Texas, where slavery already was legal. Northern Democrats thought there was a deal to also admit Oregon as a free state, although not just the Oregon of today. They expected Polk to advocate for a territory that included all of the Oregon Country, including what is now British Columbia. Texas was annexed in February 1845, but no action was taken on Oregon, a major disappointment to northern Democrats.

An even greater disappointment was that Polk backed away from the larger territorial strategy for Oregon. In June 1846, he submitted for ratification the Oregon Treaty that divided Oregon equally between Britain and the United

States. An angry Senator Edward A. Hannegan of Indiana declared: "Texas and Oregon were born the same instant, nursed and cradled in the same cradle . . . [but once Texas was admitted] the peculiar friends of Texas turned, and were doing all they could to strangle Oregon."[21] The treaty was approved, albeit narrowly. However, in the words of one historian, the outcome "left many northern Democrats with a sense of betrayal [and] signaled the first open breach in Congress between southern and northern wings of the Democratic party."[22]

In the meantime, war with Mexico erupted in April 1846. When it ended in February 1848, Polk had achieved his hopes of acquiring significant new lands from the conflict. While the United States didn't gain everything Polk wanted—he coveted present-day northern Mexico—it acquired a huge area of the Southwest and West. With General Winfield Scott's forces occupying Mexico City, the Mexican government conceded in the Treaty of Guadalupe Hidalgo five hundred thousand square miles, including all of today's California, Nevada, and Utah, most of New Mexico and Arizona, and parts of Wyoming and Colorado.[23]

Congress faced the overarching challenge of how to apply slavery in these new lands, if at all—they had been free under Mexico. One major issue was whether the territories could decide slavery for themselves—a concept called popular sovereignty that would soon become especially important to Oregon.

An Oregon bill for territorial status that excluded slavery was presented to Congress in January 1847. But it could not get past the stumbling block of southern opposition. Oregon would become a bargaining chip.'[24] When a Senate committee removed the slavery restriction, the Senate majority tabled the bill.

Senator Benton of Missouri explained the last-minute delay to disappointed territorial advocates. In a "Letter to the People of Oregon" in March 1847, he said the U.S. House of Representatives had in January approved territorial status in a bill that "sanctioned and legalized your provisional organic act, one of the clauses of which forever prohibited the existence of slavery in Oregon." However, he said supporters could not in good conscience endorse the bill in the Senate after a Senate committee revoked the anti-slavery wording. He went on to say:

> *This will be a great disappointment to you, and a real calamity; already five years without law or legal institutions for the protection of life, liberty and property and now doomed to wait a year longer. This is a strange and anomalous condition, almost incredible to contemplate, and most*

critical to endure, a colony of free men 4,000 miles from the metropolitan
government and without law or government to preserve them. But do
not be alarmed or desperate. You will not be outlawed for not admitting
slavery. . . . Oregon is not the target. The most ardent propagandist of
slavery cannot expect to plant it on the shores of the Pacific.[25]

Benton blamed Senator John Calhoun of South Carolina for striking out the anti-slavery clause. He said Calhoun was playing to his home constituency. "A home agitation and disunion purposes is all that is intended by thrusting this firebrand question into your bill, and at the next session when it is thrust in again, we will scourge it out, and pass our bill as it ought to be."[26]

On August 11, 1848, when the Oregon bill came up again, a solution for Oregon that would have included allowing slavery in some of the new territories almost became law. Senator Stephen A. Douglas, an Illinois Democrat who chaired the important Committee on the Territories, introduced a bill that would have admitted slavery south of a line extending west from the southern border of Missouri. The bill passed the Senate, but was derailed in the House. On August 12, after an angry night of debate over the Douglas amendment, territorial status for Oregon was finally approved, with Oregon's anti-slavery stand intact. Territorial status became official on August 14, 1848.[27]

The final bill did not make specific mention of slavery. However, it incorporated Oregon's anti-slavery ban by reaffirming the application of the Northwest Ordinance to the Oregon Territory. Section 14 of "An Act to Establish the Territorial Government of Oregon" read:

the inhabitants of said Territory shall be entitled to enjoy all and singular,
the rights, privileges, and advantages granted and secured to the people
of the Territory of the United States northwest of the river Ohio, by the
articles of compact contained in the ordinance for the government of said
Territory on [January 13, 1787] and shall be subject to all the conditions,
and restrictions and prohibitions in said articles of compact imposed upon
the people of said Territory; and the existing laws now in force in the
Territory of Oregon, under the authority of the provisional government
established by the people thereof, shall continue to be valid and operative
therein so far as the same be not incompatible with the Constitution of the
United States.[28]

The process by which Oregon became a territory was ugly, but ultimately successful. The next battle for Oregon would be over statehood a decade later, and the slavery issue would again weasel its way into the debate, this time not just in Congress, but in Oregon as well.

The Cockstock Affair

Oregon's 1844 exclusion law was at least in part a knee-jerk response to a perceived threat of racial violence—how large a part is debatable. The threat allegedly came from a free black named James Saules, who had been arrested for his role in what became known as the Cockstock Affair. Saules had been a cook, or a cabin boy, on the *USS Peacock*, a sloop-of-war used as an exploration ship that broke up on the Columbia River bar near Astoria in July 1841.[1] The entire crew was saved. Saules chose to stay in Oregon where he subsequently married a Native American woman.

In 1844, Saules and a Native American named Cockstock—a member of the Wasco tribe—fell into an angry dispute over a horse. The horse allegedly had been promised to Cockstock by another free black, Winslow Anderson, as payment for work on Anderson's farm; Anderson was a former fur trapper who had lived in Oregon since 1834. However, Anderson sold his farm and horse to Saules, who declined to turn the horse over to Cockstock.[2] The dispute escalated into violence when Cockstock appeared near Oregon City with several tribal members on or about March 4, 1844, and a fight broke out, involving arrows and guns. Cockstock and two white men, Sterling Rogers and George LeBreton, were killed. LeBreton was clerk and recorder for the provisional government. According to one version, Cockstock may have been killed by Anderson.[3]

Local whites blamed Saules and Anderson for the incident and threatened Saules' life. Saules was taken into custody and both he and Anderson were "encouraged" to leave the area. They moved to Clatsop County in northwestern Oregon.[4] Yet another version—the facts are impossible to pin down—was that Saules threatened to incite his wife's people to "a great interracial war" unless he was released. That Saules on his own could rally Native Americans to such violence is, in retrospect, improbable. But improbability was beside the point. The incident "triggered further racist sentiment" among settlers already hostile toward blacks.[5]

The Cockstock affair and other incidents in which Saules was involved led the resident Indian agent, Elijah White, to recommend to his superiors in Washington, D.C., that African Americans be banned from Oregon as "dangerous subjects." Writing on May 1, 1844, to Secretary of War J. M. Porter, White noted that he had sent—in effect, banished—Saules to live in present-day Clatsop County following the Cockstock incident. White said that although Saules

> *remains in that vicinity with his Indian wife and family, conducting [behaving], as yet, in a quiet manner, but doubtless ought to be transported, together with every other negro, being in our condition dangerous subjects.*
>
> *Until we have some further means of protection their immigration ought to be prohibited. Can this be done?*[6]

One historian has written that while the Cockstock incident itself was the "immediate impetus" for the 1844 exclusion law, the greater influence was probably White's letter urging action to exclude blacks.[7] The law was enacted in June, three months after the incident. In the words of Quintard Taylor, a University of Washington historian, the significance of the exclusion law should be seen more "as a symbol of the evolving attitude toward future black migration, than as a measure that would immediately eliminate or reduce the 'troublesome' black population."[8] That Anderson and Saules could avoid punishment by moving to a less populated area illustrated the ineffectiveness of provisional laws.

⸺

Although the legislative committee abolished the 1844 exclusion law in 1845, the first territorial legislature enacted a new exclusion law in September 1849. Once again, fear of an alliance between blacks and the tribes was a contributing cause, or at least an excuse. Fear of the tribes was heightened by the massacre of Marcus and Narcissa Whitman, and eleven others, on November 29, 1847, by members of the Cayuse tribe at the Whitman mission near Walla Walla.

The preamble to the new law declared it would be "highly dangerous to allow free Negroes and mulattoes to reside in the Territory, or to intermix with Indians, instilling into their minds feelings of hostility toward the white race."[9] The law easily passed the House of Representatives by a vote of twelve to four on September 19, but it was challenged in the nine-member Council. Wilson Blain of the then-Tuality County objected to even considering the bill. However, it was narrowly approved by a vote of five to four on September 21, 1849. Nathaniel Ford cast one of the five votes in favor.[10]

The 1849 law did not apply to African Americans already in the territory, but newcomers would have to leave. Section one stipulated:

*it shall not be lawful for any negro or mulatto to enter into, or reside
within the limits of this Territory. Providing that nothing in this act shall
. . . apply to any negro or mulatto now resident in this Territory, nor shall
it apply to the offspring of any such as are residents.*

A first violation would result in arrest; a second violation could cause the
Negro or mulatto, if convicted, to "be fined and imprisoned at the discretion of
the court." Black seamen were singled out for special mention. Ships frequently
included African Americans as crewmen, and the framers of the law clearly
didn't want them jumping ship in Oregon. "Masters and owners of vessels"
were made responsible for the conduct of black seamen "and shall be liable
to any person aggrieved by such negro or mulatto." Masters and owners had
forty days to remove them from Oregon, or face possible imprisonment and
a fine of up to $500.[11] The provision aimed at black crewmen was probably
influenced by the behavior of the former seaman, James Saules, who continued
to pose problems. The *Oregon Spectator* reported on December 24, 1846, that
Saules had been charged with murdering his Native American wife, but "is at
large and likely to remain so," suggesting that authorities were reluctant, or
unable, to track him down.[12]

⸱⸱⸱⸱

There was one known expulsion of an African American under Oregon's
exclusion laws, although there may well have been others not recorded. The
expulsion was of Jacob Vanderpool, said to be a sailor from the West Indies
who arrived by ship in 1850 and took up residence in Oregon City, where he
apparently operated a boarding house.[13] Vanderpool was arrested and jailed in
August 1851 on a charge of violating "the statutes and laws of the territory,"
specifically the 1849 exclusion act. The complaint was brought by Theophilus
Magruder, who had served briefly as the territorial secretary of state in 1849,
and, at the time he brought his complaint, was proprietor of the Main Street
House, a well-known hostelry in Oregon City.[14] Magruder may have sought to
remove a business competitor.

The Vanderpool case went to trial in Oregon City on August 25, 1851,
before Judge Nelson, the same Territorial Supreme Court justice who, the
following year, would be the first to hear the suit brought by Robin Holmes
against Nathaniel Ford. Vanderpool's lawyer, A. Holbrook, mounted an
aggressive, but unsuccessful, defense. He argued that the 1849 exclusion law
violated several provisions of the U.S. Constitution, including Article 4, Section
2, which said, "The citizens of each state shall be entitled to all privileges and

immunities of citizens in the several states." He also contended enactment of the legislation was "not within the jurisdiction of the Legislative Assembly of Oregon" and, moreover, had been improperly executed.[15] Three witnesses spoke to Vanderpool's good character.

Judge Nelson issued his one paragraph ruling the following day, on August 26, finding Vanderpool guilty of violating the 1849 exclusion law, and ordering him "removed from the said territory within thirty days." Nelson didn't address any of Holbrook's arguments.[16] The outcome was reported in the *Spectator* on September 2, 1851, with the newspaper's explanation to readers that since the 1849 law was on the books, it should be enforced:

> *There is a statute prohibiting the introduction of negroes in Oregon. A misdemeanor committed by one Vanderpool was the cause of bringing this individual before his Honor Judge Nelson and a decision called for respecting the enforcement of that law; [Judge Nelson] decided that the statute should be immediately enforced, and the negro shall be banished forthwith from the Territory. There is no use of enacting laws if they are to remain a dead letter on our statute book. A notorious villain, who calls himself Winslow, has cursed this community with his presence for a number of years. All manner of crimes have been laid to his charge—we shall rejoice at his removal. Thirty days are allowed them to clear the Territory.*[17]

The reference to Winslow was no doubt to the same Winslow Anderson involved in the Cockstock incident. It is unlikely Anderson was threatened with expulsion—he was a resident of Oregon before enactment of the 1849 law, which was not retroactive. The newspaper's editor must have been expressing his wish that a way could be found to expel him. Instead, Anderson would meet with a violent death in July of 1853 in what a jury ruled was "death by violence . . . a blow to the side of the head."[18] Apparently, no one was held accountable. In its article on the Vanderpool case, the *Oregon Statesman* said Nelson ruled that the 1849 exclusion law was "constitutional" and "the reaffirmation of a well-settled doctrine."[19]

There was at least one other expulsion order, this one directed at O. B. Francis and probably also his brother, Abner Hunt Francis, a well-known abolitionist. Recently arrived in Oregon, the brothers, both free blacks, had opened a mercantile store in downtown Portland in 1851.

Abner Francis had been an anti-slavery activist in Buffalo, New York, before coming to Portland. He was also a friend of prominent black abolitionist Frederick Douglass and contributed articles to *Frederick Douglass' Paper*.[20]

Francis' background and connections to the abolitionist movement may have aroused concern among Portland's anti-black whites, or perhaps the new store alarmed a white competitor. Whatever the motivation, O. B. Francis was arrested while Abner was out of town, and charged with violating Oregon's exclusion law. A justice of the peace ordered O. B. to leave Oregon within six months.[21]

Judge O. C. Pratt of Oregon's Territorial Supreme Court upheld the order after hearing the case on appeal on September 16, 1851, even reducing the time Francis could remain in Oregon to four months. In a letter to Frederick Douglass on October 30, 1851, Abner Francis suggested the exclusion order also applied to him. He wrote that they had been expertly defended by Frank Tilford, a former San Francisco judge, who argued that under the U.S. Constitution "citizens of one state had a right to enjoy the same privileges that the same class of citizens enjoy in the state which they visit" and, moreover. that the law was unconstitutional because it lacked a provision for a trial by jury.

Judge Pratt disregarded these arguments, Francis said, and "we now stand condemned under his decision, which is to close up business and leave the territory within four months." In his letter, published in Douglass' newspaper on December 11, 1851, Francis said he wanted to alert people

> that even in the so-called free territory of Oregon, the colored American
> citizen, though he may possess all the qualities and qualifications which
> make a man a good citizen is driven out like a beast in the forest, made to
> sacrifice every interest dear to him, and forbidden the privilege to take the
> portion of the soil which the government says every citizen shall enjoy.[22]

The exclusion order brought an outpouring of support for the Francises. In December, a petition with two hundred and eleven signatures urged the territorial legislature to repeal or modify the law. It said, in part:

> There are frequently coming into the Territory a class of men to whom this
> law will apply. They have proved themselves to be moral, industrious, and
> civil. Having no knowledge of this law some of them have spent their all
> by purchasing property, or entering into business to gain an honest living.
> We see and feel this injustice done them, by more unworthy and designing
> men lodging complaint against them under this law, and they thus [were]
> ordered at great sacrifice to leave the Territory.[23]

The lengthy petition went on to say that the reason for the law, the alleged "dangers arising from a colored population instilling hostility into the minds of the Indians, has ceased." It urged "that a special act may be passed at the earliest period possible, permitting O. B. and A. H. Francis, citizens from the state of New York, located in business in Portland[,] to remain, having committed no crime."

Representative John Anderson of Clatsop County introduced a bill on December 9, 1851, to allow blacks to remain in Oregon if they posted a bond and pledged that the "Negro or mulatto will . . . conduct himself as a good and law-abiding citizen of the Territory." However, the Legislature declined to modify the law.

It's not clear that the legislature voted on the appeal for the Francises. However, they were allowed to stay. Abner Francis and his wife, Lynda, remained in Portland until 1860, when they moved to Victoria, British Columbia, where Abner was elected in 1865 as the city's first black city councilman. He died in 1872.[24]

Another attempt to enforce the law in 1854 was aimed at Morris Thomas of Portland and his family. Thomas, "a free man of color," was married to Jane Snowden, a servant in the household of Andrew Skidmore—the Skidmores were a prominent Portland family. A petition with one hundred and twenty-seven signatures was sent to the legislature seeking to give Thomas an exemption. It said Thomas was "an industrious, peaceable, well-disposed mulatto man" for whom the exemption "will be of no detriment to the welfare of the Territory or the interests of any citizen."

An exemption bill was introduced in the House on January 25, 1854. It passed the House by a vote of nineteen to three, but the Council deadlocked four to four, after which it was tabled, with no further action.[25] However, Thomas remained in Oregon—it isn't clear why. Perhaps authorities chose to look the other way. Another possibility is that the legislators anticipated that the 1849 exclusion law was about to be repealed in a new legal code.[26]

·–~ ~·

One African American emigrant deterred by Oregon's first exclusion law was George Washington Bush, a Pennsylvania-born free black who had been a prosperous farmer in Missouri. Bush and his family were among six families who were part of the Gilliam wagon train that left from St. Joseph, Missouri, in 1844. They called themselves "the Independent Colony" and were headed by William Simmons, a close Bush friend and second in command to Gilliam.[27] John Minto, who also traveled with the Gilliam party, became an admirer of Bush and his accomplishments: "Not many men of color left a slave state so well-to-do, and so generally respected," he wrote. "But it was not in the nature of things that he should be permitted to forget his color." Minto said Bush confided during the trip that "if he could not have a free man's rights" in Oregon, "he would seek the protection of the Mexican government in California or New Mexico."[28] After arriving in Oregon, Bush stayed the winter in The Dalles to take care of the emigrants' livestock, after which he turned north, not south in 1845, becoming one of the first American settlers, and probably the first black settler, north of the Columbia River.

Bush moved with Simmons and others to the south end of Puget Sound, near present-day Olympia. It placed Bush beyond the reach of the provisional exclusion law, as the region north of the Columbia was then under the nominal control of the British government. Bush may have been influenced in his choice of destination by Dr. John McLoughlin, chief factor of the Hudson's Bay Company.[29] Up to that point, the powerful British company had discouraged Americans from settling north of the Columbia. However, McLoughlin was said to be sympathetic to Bush's situation.

Bush became a successful farmer, homesteading six hundred and forty acres near present-day Tumwater. One account said he introduced the first mower and reaper to farmers in the region. By dint of his status as a leading citizen, he also inspired in others "a respect for color" that extended well beyond his own community.[30] He had helped several white families buy provisions and outfits for the journey west in 1844. And after they arrived, he continued to help some neighbors who became destitute.[31] Bush's widespread support in the white community became apparent when he was threatened with the loss of his land. After Washington was organized as a territory in 1853, Bush's homestead was in jeopardy, as the Donation Land Act of 1850 excluded blacks from obtaining the free land. However, fifty-five citizens signed a petition urging an exemption. The appeal was endorsed by the Washington Territorial Legislature and forwarded to Congress, which approved the exemption in 1855. Today's Bush Prairie is named for Bush.[32]

⌁

Blacks were marginally better off in California, if only because its legislature declined to impose an exclusion act, despite the urging of Peter Burnett, its new governor. Burnett had left Oregon to join the gold rush to California in 1848 and stayed. He was elected governor in 1849, and remained governor when California became a state in 1850. California, like Oregon, included an anti-slavery provision in its constitution, which Burnett supported.[33]

But in his initial speech to the legislature, Burnett urged enactment of an exclusion law, as he had in Oregon. Demonstrating anew his racial prejudice,

Burnett argued that the commercial and mineral attractions of California "would bring swarms of [Negroes] to our shores" and a destructive mixing of races. Banning blacks, he said, would produce "the greatest good for the greatest number."[34] The legislature rejected his appeal.

ᴗ ᴗ

California gained statehood as a result of the Compromise of 1850, hammered out by Senator Douglas after many false starts. The final bill, actually a collection of bills, admitted California as a free state, New Mexico and Utah as territories, and maintained slavery—while abolishing the slave trade—in the District of Columbia. While the North appeared to achieve most from the settlement, the South gained a new Fugitive Slave Law. The compromise was also seen as symbolically important for the South, in part because it supported the existence of slavery in the nation's capital and, probably even more important, defused the anti-slavery crusade for the time being "for lack of issues on which to feed."[35]

The compromise also didn't include the "Wilmot Proviso," first proposed by Representative David Wilmot of Pennsylvania in 1846, which would have extended the anti-slavery provision of the 1787 Northwest Ordinance to all of the region acquired from Mexico. The proviso had great appeal in the North, angered the South, and was an important piece of several seriously considered legislative proposals.

The compromise left open the question of slavery in the new territories—part of Douglas' strategy to get the votes he needed from both northern and southern legislators. The result was that each side offered its own interpretation of what this meant. To some in the North, it mean the territories themselves could decide to reject slavery—an affirmation of the concept of popular sovereignty—while Southern legislators took the view that slavery could not be excluded until the territories became states.[36] Of course, this ambiguity in the compromise didn't mean the issue would go away, and it didn't.

Until California determined its status as a free state, and rejected exclusion laws, the West held little appeal for free blacks in the North. Ohio, Indiana, Illinois, and the Oregon Territory had all enacted discriminatory laws.[37] Moreover, until October 1849, when California declared itself a free state, "abolition journalists" were almost certain it would also become a slave state.[38]

The Washington Territory was established in 1853 without a specific commitment to the anti-slavery clause in the 1787 Northwest Ordinance, leading the *Baltimore Sun* in Maryland to speculate the new territory could be open "to the reception of Southern immigrants with their slaves." The concern

African American Population in Far West, 1850-2010

Year	Oregon		California		Washington	
	Pop	Blacks	Pop	Blacks	Pop	Blacks
1850	12,093	55	92,597	962	n/a	n/a
1860	52,465	128	379,994	4,086	11,594	30
1870	90,923	346*	560,247	4,272	23.955	207
1880	174,768	487	864,694	6,018	75,116	325
1890	317,704	1,186	1,208,130	11,322	357,232	1,602
1900	413,536	1,105	1,485,053	11,045	518,103	2,514
1910	672,765	1.492	2,377,549	21,645	1,141,990	6,058
1920	783,389	2,144	3,426,861	38,763	1,356,621	6,883
1930	953,786	2,234	5,677,251	81,048	1,563,396	6,840
1940	1,089,684	2,565	6,907,387	124,306	1,736,191	7,424
1950	1,521,341	11,529	10,586,223	462,172	2,378,963	30,691
1960	1,768,687	18,133	15,717,204	883,861	2,853,214	48,738
1970	2,091,385	26,308	19,953,134	1,400,143	3,409,169	71,308
1980	2,633,105	37,060	23,667,902	1,819,281	4,132,156	105,574
1990	2,842,321	46,178	29,760,021	2,208,801	4,866,692	149,801
2000	3,831,074	55,662	33,871,648	2,263,882	6,724,540	190,267
2010	3,871,859	69,206	37,253,956	2,299,072	6,830,038	240,042

Source: U.S. Census Bureau. Historical Census Statistics on Population Totals by Race, 1790-1990, Table 52. U.S. Census 2000, 2010.

was without merit. Congress stipulated laws previously enacted in Oregon applied also in Washington, which, by implication, included Oregon's law prohibiting slavery.[39]

However, as in Oregon, there was support for the South. And there was at least one slave, a young boy in Olympia called Charles Mitchell, who belonged to surveyor-general James Tilton and escaped into Canada in 1860.[40] Among the territory's leaders, Isaac I. Stevens, the first territorial governor and the first congressional delegate, supported secessionist John Breckinridge of South Carolina for president and ran his campaign in 1860.[41] Another governor, Richard Dickerson Gholson, appointed by President Buchanan in 1859, owned slaves in Kentucky and Texas.[42]

Although California was hardly a paradise for blacks, it became a land of opportunity following the discovery of gold, with a magnetic pull for many free blacks, especially from New England.[43] It was also a lure to slaveholders, who brought slaves to help mine gold. California's black population, just a few dozen in 1848, totalled about two thousand by 1852.[44] By the 1860 U.S. Census, it was 4,086. By contrast, the census counted just 128 African Americans in Oregon, and 30 in the Washington Territory. Oregon's black population had increased by only about 73 during the decade.[45] Moreover, it seems safe to conclude that at least half of Oregon's total included slaves or former slaves, few of whom would have had any choice about where they lived.

·⌣·⌣·

The repeal of Oregon's 1849 exclusion law in 1854 has long been considered inadvertent, an omission made by mistake during a rewriting of Oregon's territorial laws by a three-member code commission. The territorial legislature repealed all laws not specifically included in the new code. One of those was the exclusion law. As later explained by House Speaker LaFayette Grover: "By inadvertence the act prohibiting the immigration of negroes was omitted in that repealing act." Once the error was discovered, Grover "immediately" moved to reinstate it, which passed the House, but failed in the Council.[46] While Grover's claim that the law was left out by accident has been widely accepted, there is reason to believe that the omission was not entirely inadvertent.

The fact that the Council rejected the attempt to reinstate the exclusion law suggests its omission met with some approval. Moreover, one of the members of the three-member code commission was Reuben P. Boise, a future chief justice of the Oregon Supreme Court, who, over time, would demonstrate support for African Americans. Boise was elected to the House, assigned to shepherd the new code through that body. Did he have a hand in the confusion that caused the exclusion law to be overlooked? It's worth speculating.

It is also noteworthy that the commission employed Joseph G. Wilson as a clerk to transcribe the drafts of the new code for presentation to the legislature. Wilson would later serve on the supreme court, and, with Chief Justice Boise, would invite controversy by attending a wedding of a black couple in Salem in 1863. Not without significance either is that the chairman of the commission, James K. Kelly, a future U.S. senator and future member of the Oregon Supreme Court, later wrote a history of the new code in which he made no mention of anything being inadvertently left out.[47]

Several subsequent attempts to enact a new exclusion law by the territorial legislature failed. The support wasn't there. The final attempt during the 1856-1857 session of the legislature was led by Grover, a future governor who, after the Civil War, would help torpedo Oregon's ratification of the Fifteenth Amendment granting voting rights to African Americans. He declared in an impassioned plea for exclusion: "I am one of those who believe that the government of the United States is a government of white men; that the Declaration of Independence was a declaration of the equality and natural free citizenship of white men."[48]

The bill "to prevent negroes and mulattoes entering and residing in Oregon" easily passed the Council, by a five to two vote—Nathaniel Ford cast one of the Council's two negative votes. At first glance, Ford's vote might appear to reflect a change of heart by the former slave owner. However, the reason for his vote became clear during the subsequent House debate. The bill made no distinction between free blacks and slaves, and pro-slavery legislators wanted to keep the door open to slavery—they favored exclusion for free blacks only. Representative William Allen, a pro-slavery legislator from Yamhill County, moved to amend the bill to specify only free blacks would be excluded, but the amendment failed.[49]

The House debate extended over two days, January 8 and 9, 1857. Reflecting the intense interest in the outcome, the *Oregon Statesman*, a weekly, devoted most of a full page to the debate in each of its January 13 and January 20 editions.

Asa L. Lovejoy, one of the founders of Portland, argued in the House that the proposal to prohibit slaves as well as free blacks was an attempt to expose pro-slavery legislators by forcing them into opposition. Said Lovejoy, who represented Clackamas County: "I believe this bill is an abolition measure, got up to sound the opinion of people on the question of slavery, and find out what ground gentlemen stand on."[50] He claimed that the 1854 Kansas-Nebraska Act had already opened a path to slavery in Oregon—by no means a majority view.

A leader of the opposition was *Oregonian* editor Thomas Dryer, an anti-slavery Whig who would later join Oregon's new Republican Party. Dryer cited the O. B. and Abner Francis case as an example of why the bill should be defeated.

> *There are some free negroes now in Oregon. Mr. Francis, living in the city of Portland, is a black man, and good citizen. A man of property, who attends to his own business and does as much for the country as any other man in the country. They [blacks] have committed no crime. . . . Why not make a law to exclude Irishmen, Chinamen, Italians, Englishmen and all other foreigners? Such a law would be just as republican [sic]. It strikes me that this law would be a disgrace to Oregon.*[51]

Among legislators joining Dryer in denouncing the bill was J. W. Moffit, who made the point, too seldom made, that "the negroes did not come here of their own accord. . . . Supposing a law was passed in every state driving them out . . . that there were laws excluding them from the entire continent, where would these unfortunate people go?" Such laws, he said, are "a disgrace to the human race."[52]

When the exclusion bill came to a vote on January 9, the bill failed in the House by a vote of twenty-three to three. The issue could not be put to rest, however. In November 1857, a new exclusion law—Oregon's third—was approved by Oregon voters, this time as a clause in Oregon's constitution. The debate in the Constitutional Convention that placed the exclusion measure before voters reflected a deep-seated hostility toward all minorities and at least symbolically marked a low point in Oregon history.

Gold Miners and Slaves

It was against the background of mixed messages on slavery that Robin Holmes pressed Nathaniel Ford in 1849 to deliver on his promise of freedom. The three-year grace period that began when Ford arrived in Oregon had run out. Ford had used every day of it, and more.[1]

Pauline Burch wrote that Ford gave Scott his freedom in 1847, and the Holmeses—Robin and Polly—their freedom in 1848 and 1849.[2] Assuming those years are correct, Robin and Polly were kept as slaves for four and five years, respectively. However, grace period aside, slaveholders like Ford didn't have to worry about Oregon's anti-slavery law. There's no record of it ever being enforced prior to 1853. Ford would tell a court in the suit brought against him by Holmes in 1852 that Robin and Polly Holmes were "his servants and slaves, and so continued till in or about the year 1849."[3] Once freed, Pauline Burch said, the Holmeses "could come and go as they pleased," although she said they chose to continue living in their cabin on the Ford property. As existing residents, the Holmeses were not subject to a threat of expulsion under the 1849 exclusion law.

·~·

Robin Holmes would offer a much different account than Ford of the circumstances under which he was finally freed. Holmes said when he asked

Ford in 1849 for the freedom he'd been promised, Ford insisted he first go to California to mine gold with Ford's son, Marcus, and the slave, Scott.[4] At some point, Nathaniel Ford also headed for the gold fields, as did a son-in-law, Carey Embree, and Embree's son.[5] Holmes said he agreed to go because he felt it was his best chance of obtaining his family's freedom.[6] He said Ford also promised him some of the gold.

The Fords were part of a flood of Oregon settlers who headed south after gold was discovered on January 24, 1848, at Sutter's Mill in present-day El Dorado County. There were possibly exaggerated estimates that "three-quarters of the male population of Oregon went south looking for gold."[7] Seven members of Oregon's provisional legislative assembly, Peter Burnett among them, resigned in the fall of 1848, to join the exodus.[8]

Nathaniel Ford wasn't alone in taking slaves to California during this period. Southern slaveholders—primarily from Missouri, Kentucky, Tennessee, and North Carolina—brought slaves, either to help search for gold, or to hire them out to others. One estimate was that a thousand slaves were in California during the gold rush, although there was no accurate count.[9] Most slaveholders stayed only a few years, returning home with their earnings and their slaves.[10]

Slaveholders were undeterred by California's constitutional prohibition against slavery. Some intended to soon free their slaves; others planned only to remain long enough to find gold, and still others acted out of a belief that California eventually would become a slave state. Indeed, they had good reason to believe the California assembly was "friendly to their interests."[11] Enforcement was a non-issue. California's anti-slavery law was even more vague than the law enacted by Oregon's provisional government. There was nothing in the law before 1852 that told slaveholders whether they had to free their slaves upon arrival, or how long they might safely keep them. The legislature and judiciary "constructed a web of statutes and legal rulings that undercut enslaved peoples claims to freedom."[12] Among these was the California Fugitive Slave Act of 1852, which protected slave ownership in some circumstances.

Slaveholders typically encouraged slaves to work by allowing them to keep a portion of the gold they found. This was an obvious incentive for slaves, who might see it as an opportunity to buy their freedom, and possibly also freedom for their families.[13] In some instances, slaves were promised freedom in exchange for their labor. This seems to be the arrangement Ford made with Holmes. It was also not uncommon for a slave owner to hold a slave's family hostage at home as insurance against a slave escaping.

·⁓·

One of the best-known cases of a slave purchasing his freedom with gold earnings involved Alvin Coffey, a slave of a Dr. Bassett, who brought Coffey with him to California from Missouri in 1849. Coffey, then twenty-seven, was intent on purchasing his freedom. He mined $5,000 in gold for Bassett over two years; he earned $700 for himself by washing clothes for other miners. When Bassett decided to return to Missouri, however, Coffey had no choice but to return with him because his wife and two daughters were still there. Bassett sold Coffey to another Missouri owner after taking Coffey's $700. Fortunately for Coffey, the new owner was sympathetic and allowed Coffey to return to California to mine gold for his freedom. Coffey succeeded in earning $1,500 to buy his freedom, and similar amounts to free his wife and daughters from Bassett. Most of Coffey's earnings came from placer mining around Redding and Red Bluff.[14]

At least one Oregon resident may have sold slaves in California. A Congregationalist minister named Timothy Dwight Hunt said in a letter printed in the *Newark Daily Advertiser* that a man from Oregon—otherwise unidentified—sold a slave woman and her child in San Francisco for $1,900 to a purchaser from Rhode Island.[15]

·⁓·

Holmes said Ford promised that on his return from California, Ford "would comply with his agreement . . . as made in the State of Missouri, and discharge and liberate" Holmes and his family. He said he remained in California until 1850, and, upon his return to Oregon, the elder Ford "permitted" him, his wife, and an infant child, Lon, "to leave the service" of Ford. Holmes also said that while in California young Ford had informed him that he, Holmes, had mined $900 worth of gold dust and nuggets for Nathaniel Ford.[16] Holmes did not say how much, if any, of the gold he received, although Nathaniel Ford indicated in court testimony it had been Holmes' gold to keep.

Neither Ford nor Holmes addressed in their court testimony a tragedy on the return trip from California that claimed the lives of Marcus Ford and Scott. The incident is described in detail in several family accounts. According to Pauline Burch, Holmes and the others remained in California for about a year. During this time, she said Marcus' wife, the former Amanda Thorp—they married in 1847—died in San Francisco, where Marcus had taken her for treatment of an illness. Burch indicated the mining party set out on the return trip to Oregon in November 1849 with a large quantity of gold—Marcus had $14,000 of his own in gold and carried $2,000 of his father's gold. She said

Scott and Robin also had gold of their own—she put Robin's share at $900.[17] They decided to return to Oregon by ship, a fateful decision. The ship they boarded at San Francisco was "a leaky old lumber schooner" called the *Forest*. According to Burch:

The boat was old and storms drove it off its course. They were 50 days on the ocean. Food became scarce and an epidemic spread among the passengers; one had died and others were seriously ill. A storm and fog at the mouth of the Columbia prevented the captain from knowing their location. Mark A. Ford and three others volunteered to go in an open boat to shore to seek help. They misjudged the distance from shore, and their boat capsized. All four men lost their lives. One of the party reached shore at or near Shoal Water (sic) Bay, and was killed by the Indians. From testimony obtained later from a young Indian woman, and older Indians, it was thought that Mark reached shore. Scott died on board the boat the same night Mark lost his life. These two had been good friends from their days in Missouri.[18]

Another account said the *Forest* had been driven several hundred miles off-course by a storm. The passengers were low on provisions—one died of scurvy. When the ship finally arrived near the entrance to the Columbia River, no pilot came to escort them over the dangerous bar. It was at that point that Marcus, a man named Abner Stevens, and two other unidentified men attempted to reach shore in an open boat. A gale pushed them north to Shoalwater Bay. Three bodies, including Stevens, were found drowned, but there was no sign of Marcus.[19]

An account in the *Oregon Spectator* on January 24, 1850, offered yet another version of the tragedy, this one possibly reflecting the views of the ship's captain, identified as Williams. Under the headline, "Four Men Drowned," the article said:

The Brig Forrest [sic] was lying off the Mouth of the Columbia, and in consequence of not having made suitable provision for the voyage the passengers were put on short allowance. They, as was natural, became dissatisfied with their situation, and anxious to escape from such cheerless accommodations. Capt. Williams, at length and with great reluctance allowed a party of men to take a small boat and attempt a landing. The party consisted of Mark Ford, esq. of Polk county, two young men by the name of Stephens, whose friends reside at Portland, and John Plummer of Oregon City. They had with them a large amount of specie and gold dust.

Their attempt to go ashore proved disastrous. They were overwhelmed
in the breakers and perished. Three of the bodies were washed shore and
found.[20]

The newspaper lamented the death of young Ford, calling him "a gentlemen of much promise to the country" who "bid fair to stand high among the active and influential men of the Territory." The newspaper made no mention of Scott. The only reference to his death was in Burch's account. Holmes is not mentioned at all. He survived the voyage, but how much gold he came away with is unknown. If Marcus Ford was carrying all of the family's gold, it may have been lost.

The *Forest* would meet its end years later while carrying a load of coal to Hong Kong. It struck a rock off Taiwan and sank, a total loss.[21]

⁓

Marcus Ford was twenty-eight when he died. He was survived by a now-orphaned son, John Thorp Ford. The age of Scott, never mentioned in the Ford family accounts with a surname, isn't known. He left behind a widow, who may have been pregnant or had recently given birth to their child. The only reference to Scott's marriage is this sentence in Pauline Burch's account: "Scott had married a young negro woman from an adjoining county some time before he left for the mines, and our records do not indicate that she ever received the gold Scott started with from California."[22]

The 1850 U.S. Census listed a Maria Scott, age twenty-seven, living with the Holmes family in Polk County. Also listed was a one-year-old boy, George Scott. They possibly were the widow and son of Scott—and had moved in with the Holmeses after Scott's death. Maria's birthplace was given as Missouri; she probably was one of two slaves brought to Oregon in 1846 by Richard Linville, who was among the first emigrants to attempt the Applegate Trail. His slaves were identified in family records as Maria, age fifteen in 1846, and Johnson, age eleven.

Another 1850 census record listed Mary Scott, a twenty-six-year-old African American, living in nearby Salem with a one-year-old son named George. Mary's birthplace was also listed as Missouri. In the same household was a John Scott, age twenty-two, listed as a mulatto. If this was the family of the slave Scott, they may have been double-counted, with Maria, misidentified as Mary, counted first at her home in Salem, and later at the Holmeses. If John Scott was the slave Scott, it might indicate his wife hadn't yet learned of his death.

Marcus' son, John Ford, told journalist Fred Lockley in a 1922 interview that after learning of Marcus' death, Nathaniel Ford and other relatives went to Shoalwater Bay to investigate. He said they seized the chief of the Shoalwater tribe and took him and several other tribal members into custody as witnesses. Their intention, he said, was to take them to Oregon City for trial. But he said the chief drowned during the trip. As described by young Ford in a newspaper article, the circumstances of his death would today have prompted an investigation into whether the unnamed chief was murdered in an act of vengeance. According to John Ford:

They were going to have the chief tried for murder. They fastened a heavy ball and chain to his ankle and put manacles on his wrists. As they were coming up the river the chief jumped out of the boat and sank. They rowed around quite a while, but the water was deep and the Indian failed to come to the surface; so that stopped any chance of trying him for murder. They took the other Indians to Oregon City where they were tried. These Indians testified that the Indian chief had killed the white man and they had had nothing to do with it; so the Indians were turned loose to make their way back home.[23]

While John Ford said the surviving tribal members were released, Caroline Burch offered a conflicting outcome. She believed Marcus was stabbed in the back, allegedly by two Native Americans, the one who later jumped into the water and drowned, and a second, who was taken to Oregon City.[24] She said they were identified because they had in their possession "Spanish doubloons." Marcus, she said, had exchanged his gold for the Spanish coins before leaving California. Burch said the second man was not released. Rather, she said, he was "hanged at Oregon City." She didn't indicate whether there was a trial, but she said Ford had tried to talk with the suspect before the execution.

Grandfather went to talk with him while he was in jail, and tried to get him to tell where the body was buried. He said no white man should ever know the place. . . . A long time afterward an old squaw (sic) told someone they put him in a canoe and buried him on top of the mountain. Years afterward some men found near there a skeleton in an old cedar canoe, on the shore back away under the willows. The man's teeth were filled with gold. Uncle Mark's teeth had fillings of gold in them, and some felt it might be he [Ford].[25]

Whatever the circumstances of the tragedy, the Ford gold was lost. But Pauline Burch said Holmes, who safely reached shore, managed to keep a

A caption typed on this photograph identifies it as a home in Ellendale belonging to Nathaniel and Lucinda Ford, "with slave quarters" in the background. However, it more likely was a boarding house owned by James Nesmith where the newly freed slaves, Robin and Polly Holmes, worked for a time. They may have lived in the small cabin. (Oregon Historical Society).

share of the gold. Burch said that Holmes' gold, plus savings from sales of vegetables, enabled the Holmeses to leave the Ford farm and move to nearby Nesmith Mills where he found work at the gristmill for which the town was once named. We can only guess at the satisfaction and pride Holmes must have felt in the fortieth year of his life, finally earning a wage as a free man.

The gristmill and a boarding house belonged to James Nesmith, the one-time law partner of Marcus Ford and a future U.S. senator. Nesmith Mills would later be renamed Ellendale by Reuben P. Boise in memory of his first wife. Boise, who moved to Nesmith Mills in 1852, was to play a prominent role in Holmes' future.

One account said Holmes and his wife "conducted" the boarding house in Nesmith Mills until James Nesmith sold it in 1854.[26] The Holmeses would soon move again, this time to Salem, where they operated a plant nursery. But while Holmes and his wife—with their infant child, Lon, or Leonidas—could now live in freedom, they suffered the heartache of being denied their three children still in Ford's custody. Ford had refused Holmes' demands to give them up. Surely not forgotten by the Holmeses was that Ford had already separated them from their three children left behind in Missouri.

⌣⌣

While the two Ford family histories seemed to treat the issue of slavery with indifference, they maintained that the overall relationship between the Ford and Holmes families was a good one. Wrote Pauline Burch:

There are so many incidents witnessed and recorded by the pioneers in their personal association with the negroes that emphasize the unusually kind and protective feeling Nathaniel Ford had for them. This feeling he instilled in his own children and grandchildren.[27]

Burch said Ford and his son-in-law, James Boyle, would later build a new four-room house for the Holmes family in Salem, with Ford and Boyle each sharing one-half of the cost. She also said that when Nathaniel and Lucinda Ford built a new house for themselves in Rickreall in 1862, "Mrs. Ford had Robin bring a lilac bush and two locust trees from his little nursery in Salem."

A member of the Ford family witnessed a poignant scene involving the Holmeses in 1851. One of the children, Harriett, had died during a visit to her parents' home in Salem. Burch said Robin Holmes brought Harriett's body back to Rickreall for burial on a high bank on Ford property near Rickreall Creek. Another child, Celi Ann, had previously died and was buried there, and Holmes dug Harriett's grave alongside Celi Ann's. The Ford family was touched by the care Holmes gave to the gravesite. Wrote Burch:

A short time later Robin returned with three small oak trees, and when he stopped by the Ford home, Sarah accompanied him to the graves, where Robin planted the trees—one at the head of each little grave and one at the foot of the graves, forming a triangle. . . . Those three oak trees are still standing at the time of this writing in 1953. Sarah would never permit them to be cut down, and her descendants, the Burch family, who later became and are at this time owners of the land, revere her sentiment.[28]

The sympathy of the moment, however, didn't extend to giving the Holmeses what they most wanted, custody of their children.

"My Children Held as Slaves"

Harriett's death in 1851 seems to have galvanized Robin Holmes into taking action against Ford. Two of his children were dead, and he and his wife had little hope of ever being reunited with their three children in Missouri. On April 16, 1852, Holmes filed for a writ of *habeas corpus* in Second District Court in Polk County to require Ford to appear in court, with Holmes' three children to explain why he was holding them.[1] Holmes' subsequent testimony would strongly suggest he blamed Ford for Harriet's death and wanted to rescue the other children before something happened to them.

How Holmes came to file his suit is a matter of conjecture. Was he encouraged by a friend, a neighbor, perhaps someone who had witnessed his despair? At the time of Holmes' suit, there were no laws in Oregon prohibiting African Americans from filing a lawsuit or testifying in court, against whites.[2]

We know Holmes was someone who stood up for himself and his family. But think of the odds. He had lived his life as a slave, raised in a slave culture, bought and sold at the whim of others, unable to read or write. He was up against a powerful man with powerful connections, recently elected to the territorial legislature. Yet, despite all, Holmes was a risk taker. This would be evident again years later when he and wife would be among a handful of African Americans, all former slaves, who integrated a white church in Salem.

Prior to bringing his suit, Holmes had had several angry exchanges with Ford over custody of Holmes' children. Most likely these occurred at Ford's home. We don't know what was said, but we might guess how they started. Did Holmes arrive on foot, or by wagon, to confront Ford, who, after a shouting match, ordered Holmes to leave? Was it during one of these arguments that Ford threatened to seize the entire Holmes family under the new Fugitive Slave Act, and return them to slavery in Missouri? Did Holmes go in anger and frustration directly from Ford's home to the Polk County courthouse, a new two-story wood building in Dallas, and enter unannounced into the prosecuting attorney's office to seek help?[3] If so, he may well have been greeted with curiosity, even suspicion. Here was a black man, possibly ill-dressed in work clothes, covered with dust from the gristmill, unable to write his own name, and probably knowing little or nothing about legal procedures. One can imagine a clerk trying to shoo him away, ignoring the man's simple plea to help him get his children back.

Reuben Boise, the prosecuting attorney who handled former slave Robin Holmes' case against Nathaniel Ford. Boise later became a prominent member of Oregon's Supreme Court. (Oregon Historical Society)

Someone then, or earlier, or later, did take him in hand. That someone apparently was Reuben P. Boise, the prosecuting attorney for the Oregon Territory. A native of Massachusetts and a graduate of Williams College, Boise arrived in Oregon in 1851. He had traveled mostly by ship, with a land crossing at the Isthmus of Panama. After briefly practicing law in Portland, he settled on a donation land claim of six hundred and forty acres at Nesmith Mills in 1852. Along with his law practice and judicial career, he was a farmer.

It would be easy to romanticize a possible scene in Boise's office. While sitting at his desk on a warm afternoon in early spring, he hears Holmes pleading for help and resisting the clerk's attempts to get him to leave. At thirty-one years of age, Boise is new in his position, appointed prosecuting attorney only weeks earlier by the territorial legislature. He is from Massachusetts, a hotbed of abolitionist sentiment. This could be his first case, an important one—no slavery case has yet come before Oregon's territorial courts. He lives within ten miles of Ford's farm and no doubt knows who Ford is. Perhaps he doesn't care for Ford because he is a slave owner. Whatever it is that motivates him, he asks Holmes to come in and sit down.

All that could be true, some of it true, or maybe none of it true. Boise could have met Holmes at James Nesmith's gristmill, where Holmes worked as a laborer. Perhaps Nesmith, out of sympathy for Holmes' plight, mentioned him to Boise. But what is certainly true is that something, or someone, did bring Boise and Holmes together, and Boise took charge of his case.

Boise would go on to a prominent political and judicial career in Oregon, playing an important role as a delegate to the 1857 Constitutional Convention and serving several terms on the Oregon Supreme Court from 1859 to 1880. But during all these years, Boise and Holmes would maintain a friendly association—they attended the same Salem church; Holmes would name Boise as executor of his will. A photograph of Boise in the Polk County Courthouse reveals a man in his mid- to late fifties, fit in appearance, slightly aquiline in his features, graying, with a cropped beard and mustache, and a receding hairline. His eyes are dark, penetrating—you might not hold his gaze for long. Of Holmes, sadly, we have no photograph. But as a laborer in his forties we might imagine him as tall and muscular, possibly obsequious in his behavior toward whites—not unusual for African Americans who wanted to get along—but determined to stand his ground and see justice done.

⌣ ⌣

The case centered on Holmes' three children still in Ford's custody: Mary Jane, then eleven years old; James, seven; and Roxanna, five. Although Ford in 1850 had finally freed Holmes, his wife, and an infant child, Ford contended Holmes had agreed to leave the other four children, including Harriett—who had since died—in his care.

The forty pages of court records are hand-written, faded, and difficult to read. Holmes would have given his testimony orally to an attorney or clerk, who no doubt wrote as he talked. Some of the transcripts have multiple cross-outs and inserts, suggesting they were read back to Holmes for corrections or changes. Several attorneys lent their assistance, probably without being compensated; their names appear in the court record. But it was Holmes' case to make, and he made it with enough care to overcome the handicap of his illiteracy.

The records include lengthy testimony by Holmes, which opens a rare window into the relationship between a slave and his owner, from a slave's point of view. Holmes would deny at the outset that there was any agreement for Ford to have custody of his children. He said Ford had refused for two years to allow Holmes and his wife, Polly, to even see the children. Moreover, he said he had good reason to believe Ford "ill treats" the children and "does not furnish them with sufficient meat, drink or apparel. . . ." He feared "the treatment that they now receive will materially injure their health, and eventually cause their death, or be the cause of their enduring great suffering."[4]

Holmes vs. Ford, Day-by-Day

APRIL 16, 1852 (THE FIRST DAY)
Robin Holmes initiates his fifteen-month case against Nathaniel Ford by filing a writ of *habeas corpus* in Second District Court in Polk County, seeking the return of his "unlawfully detained" children. The intent of the writ is to require Ford to bring the children to court and explain under what authority he is holding them. If Ford fails to satisfy the court, he likely will be compelled to return the children to Holmes, or so Holmes hopes. According to the initial brief court record, Ford "admits that he detained" the children.

While there's no record of who is physically present in the courtroom, Ford and Holmes apparently are both there. How odd it must seem to both men to be, at least at this moment, equals before the law, the one accustomed to giving orders, the other to taking orders. Is there eye contact? Angry stares from Ford? Or do they ignore one another's presence?

Hearing the case is Judge O. C. Pratt, an associate justice of the Territorial Supreme Court. He orders Ford to bring the children to court at the next term as a first step toward adjudicating the dispute. Holmes and his wife live several miles from Ford at Nesmith Mills, where Holmes is employed.

APRIL 17, 1852
The sheriff of Polk County, Washington Smith Gilliam, serves the writ on Ford. However, the case will languish, and won't resume in earnest until the following April. Sheriff Gilliam is the son of Cornelius Gilliam, who led the wagon train that traveled alongside Ford's train in 1844. The young Gilliam no doubt became well acquainted with Ford on the journey west. He may remember Holmes as the slave accompanying Ford.

Subsequent records and testimony will be far more detailed than the initial record: Holmes will argue; Ford will respond; Ford will argue; Holmes will respond, and so on. Of the three Holmes children, most of the focus is on the eldest, Mary Jane—called "Jenny" by the Ford family.

APRIL 5, 1853

Ford waits nearly a year before responding to Holmes' writ. In a detailed affidavit, Ford claims his intentions are not to keep the children as slaves, but as "wards." He acknowledges he had considered, but rejected, the possibility of returning the entire Holmes family to Missouri to be sold back into slavery. He claims that after Holmes returned from California, they reached an agreement in early March of 1850 whereby "the said Robin and his wife were to be and remain henceforth free" with their youngest child, while Ford was "to keep all the rest of said children together with one who has since died"—a reference to Harriett—"and to hold them until they respectively became of age," which was twenty years for males and eighteen for females. He leaves no doubt he intends to put them to work.

That this respondent [Ford] has kept the said children at a heavy expense when they were young and their services of very little or no value—and now since they have arrived at an age when their services will be of some consequence the respondent insists that he has a right to retain the said children during their minority as part compensation and remuneration for the expenditure made in their behalf.

Ford attacks the Holmeses as unfit parents. Robin, in particular, Ford says, "is poor and ignorant and unfit to have the care, custody and bringing up of said children." Ford might be trying to make a case for guardianship. Oregon's territorial law provides that a court may appoint a guardian for a minor "if the father of a minor be insane, or be incapable, from want of understanding, to take care and provide for such minor," but only after an inquest to determine the father's mental health.[1] However, there is no record of Ford applying for an inquest or to have himself declared a guardian. Perhaps he hopes the judge will steer the case in that direction.

Chief Justice Thomas Nelson of Oregon's Territorial Supreme Court is now hearing the case. Nelson is the same justice who convicted Jacob Vanderpool in 1851 for violating Oregon's exclusion law and ordered him out of the territory. While national politics have little to do with the case before him, politics have influenced the selection of judges. Nelson is the outgoing chief justice. President Franklin Pierce, who was inaugurated in March 1853, had nominated Judge Pratt to succeed Nelson as chief justice, but the nomination was blocked by Senator Douglas.[2]

APRIL 6, 1853

Holmes responds to Ford's claims in a twelve hundred-word affidavit. He briefly reviews his slave background in Missouri, including his and his wife's previous owner, a "Major Whitman," and the unusual circumstances that led to his being claimed by Ford: A successful bidder backed out following a public auction "sometime in 1841"—a year that may be incorrect. The error is not difficult to explain, as Holmes would not have written the document himself. The attorney, or clerk, who took down his remarks, may well have confused the year—or Holmes confused the year—and the error went undetected.

In his affidavit, Holmes says after working as Ford's slaves in Howard County, Missouri, Ford's finances suffered a major setback in the spring of 1844 and he, Ford, "became very much embarrassed in his pecuniary circumstances, and he determined to emigrate to Oregon." Holmes continues:

That respondent solicited your petitioner [Holmes] and his wife Polly to go with him to Oregon, and represented to your petitioner that Oregon was a free country, that slavery did not exist there, and he did not think it ever would. That respondent would take your petitioner and his wife Polly to Oregon if your petitioner and his said wife would on respondent's arrival in Oregon assist said respondent to open a farm, and that when your petitioner and his wife had assisted said respondent . . . your petitioner and his wife Polly and family should be liberated and discharged absolutely from the service or control of said respondent.

Holmes says he and his family remained with Ford for five years until the spring of 1849, when Holmes approached Ford seeking his freedom. It was then that Ford asked Holmes to go to California to mine gold. When he returned, Ford "would comply with his agreement" made in Missouri "to discharge and liberate" Holmes and his family. He said Ford also promised him a share of the gold.

However, upon his return in the spring of 1850, Ford "refused to liberate the said Jenny or Mary Jane, Roxanna and James . . . but permitted your petitioner and his wife and one infant child . . . to leave the service of said respondent." Holmes denies there was any agreement for Ford to keep the children "for any period of time." He also says Ford frequently threatened to return the family to Missouri as a way of pressuring Holmes to back off his demand that his children be returned. He categorically dismisses Ford's accusation that he is an unfit parent.

*[Y]our petitioner is as well able in a pecuniary point of view to take care
of said children and raise said children as respondent, and denies that he is
unfit by reason of his poverty and ignorance to have the care and custody
of his own children, but on the contrary avers that his character for
honesty, society and industry is good, and this he prays may be inquired of
by the court.*

While the affidavit refers to Holmes' previous owner as a Major Whitman,
a later court filing will give the name as Major Whitmore. However, there was
no Major Whitman or Whitmore listed among Army paymasters in Missouri
at the time. Holmes may have been referring to Major Alphonso Wetmore, a
paymaster based in Franklin, twelve miles south of Fayette.[3] Wetmore and Ford
must have known one another as they served together in 1836 on a committee
studying the possibility of a railroad from St. Louis to Fayette.[4]

Major Wetmore was well known as an author and a chronicler of the Santa
Fe Trail. He was listed in the 1830 U.S. Slave Census with nine slaves. But by
1840, he had just two, both male, one age ten, and the other between ages ten
and twenty-three.[5] The decline in his number of slaves may reflect his economic
woes. But it also suggests that if the Holmeses were his slaves, he gave them up
before 1840. Wetmore was plunged into debt when the government sought to
recover $3,388 in salary that he allegedly overpaid himself from 1816 to 1831.
Wetmore had claimed pay at the higher rate of a staff major, rather than at
the lower rate of an infantry major, which the government maintained was his
correct pay grade. Wetmore lost at a jury trial in 1832 and appealed to the U.S.
Supreme Court, which, in 1836, upheld the lower court ruling that Wetmore
had, indeed, overpaid himself.[6] Wetmore died in 1849.

APRIL 6, 1853

Responding to a court order, Ford posts $3,000 bond as a guarantee that he
will not remove the children from the court's reach. While the judge doesn't
explicitly say so, he may have imposed the bond to discourage Ford from
returning the children to Missouri. The bottom line for Holmes, however, is
that his children are still with Ford.

APRIL 16, 1853

Ford requests to depose a prominent supporting witness, Joseph Lane. Known
for pro-slavery sentiments, Lane had been appointed by President Polk as
Oregon's first territorial governor in 1848, and, at the time of the Holmes suit,

was the territorial delegate to Congress. Ford says Lane can substantiate his claim of an agreement with Holmes for the children. But it also means delaying resolution of the case until Lane is available. Ford says "he expects to prove by said Lane that the said Robin made the agreement . . . that the said Robin and his wife and youngest child were to go free and that this respondent was to keep the other children of said Robin until they become of age . . . that he expects said Lane will be in this Territory so that his testimony can be taken by the next term of said court—and that this application is made, not for the purpose of delay merely but that justice may be done."[7]

JUNE 9, 1853

Holmes grows increasingly frustrated that after a year still nothing has been done to resolve his case. There has been delay after delay. One scheduled hearing was never held. He also suggests there has been complicity between Judge Nelson and Ford's attorneys.

In a new affidavit, Holmes says the children's lives may be in danger because of mistreatment by Ford.

> *Deponent [Holmes] further says he has been informed, and believes, that said Ford ill treats deponent's children, that he does not furnish them with sufficient meat, drink or apparel, and that deponent is fearful that unless said children are placed in a situation that they may be provided for by their parents, and that the treatment they now receive will materially injure their health, and eventually cause their death, or be the cause of their enduring great suffering.*

The case is now before Judge Cyrus Olney, another justice of the Territorial Supreme Court. The April hearing was Judge Nelson's last involvement in the case, as he has stepped down as chief justice.

In the affidavit, Holmes asks why Judge Nelson never ruled, as promised. Holmes is clearly worried that the court will take no action at all, leaving the children with Ford.

> *[D]eponent [Holmes]. . . says from causes unknown to him the term of said court last mentioned was never held, and that no return was made by said Ford to said writ till April term A.D. 1853 of said court, at which time the cause was heard before the Hon. Thos. Nelson, judge of said court. And deponent further says that the said Thos. Nelson, after having said cause (sic) fully tried refused to give an opinion or make an order in the case, but said that at some future day, not to exceed five weeks, he*

would make an order in the case, which the parties agreed to abide. And deponent further says that said order has never been made and that said Nelson has refused to make the same.

Moreover, Holmes says that he has heard "and believes" Judge Nelson informed Ford's attorney "he would make no order in the case but would turn it over to his successor to do." The delays are playing into Ford's hands.

Holmes also questions why Ford failed to bring Holmes' children to court as ordered by Judge Pratt fourteen months earlier. He says neither he nor his wife are allowed to visit or communicate with their children and "that although residing within five miles of said Ford, the mother of said children has not exchanged a word with, nor even seen them for the last two years." Holmes says he "has good reasons" to believe Ford is now seriously planning to take the children out of "this territory . . . and sell them into perpetual slavery." To keep this from happening, he asks Judge Olney to put the children in charge of the Polk County sheriff, or another appropriate party, until the case is decided.

JUNE 9, 1853

In a second action on June 9, Holmes sends a sworn statement to Judge Olney, alleging for the first time that his children are being held as slaves. This appears to be a shrewd new strategy by Holmes and his attorneys, since it moves the argument away from the question of whether Holmes and Ford have some sort of informal agreement for Ford to keep the children. If the case is to turn on whom to believe, the judge might well side with Ford, rather than a former slave. But Holmes is now arguing the case as a slavery case, where Oregon's territorial law prohibiting slavery seems iron clad, even though never before enforced.

Holmes alleges that Ford himself may now be planning to return to Missouri and take the children with him. He appeals to Judge Olney to order Ford to bring the children to his court to show cause "why he has imprisoned and restrained [them] of their liberties."[8]

[Y]our petitioner [Holmes] believes said minors are imprisoned and restrained of their liberties under the pretence that slavery is tolerated by the laws of this Territory, and that they the said Mary Jane, James and Roxanna are the slaves of the said Nathaniel Ford. That the said Nathaniel Ford has for a long series of years held said minors under a most galling and degrading servitude, has, and still claims them as his chattels, and that your petitioner has been informed and verily believes that the

said Nathaniel Ford intends ere long to depart this Territory, and your petitioner has reason to believe it is the intention of the said Nathaniel Ford to take along with him the said minors for the purpose of selling them into perpetual slavery in counties beyond the jurisdiction of the courts of his territory.

Holmes once again appeals to the court to issue a writ of *habeas corpus* to compel Ford to produce the children and "to show cause, if any he may have, why he has imprisoned and restrained of their liberties the said Mary Jane, James and Roxanna Holmes."

JUNE 13, 1853

Finally, some movement in Holmes' case.

Judge Olney places the Holmes children in the technical custody of Polk County Sheriff B. F. Nichols to await a further court order, although it doesn't appear Nichols actually takes the children. Olney also gives permission for Oregon's territorial delegate, Joseph Lane, to be deposed. Nichols, who succeeded Gilliam as sheriff, traveled to Oregon with the Burnett wagon train in 1843. Olney orders Ford to appear with the children at a hearing before the Territorial Supreme Court in Portland the following Monday and suggests final custody will be decided at that time.

Judge Olney to Nathaniel Ford:
You are hereby commanded to have the bodies of Mary Jane, James and Roxanna, negro children by you detained as it is said, together with the time and cause of their caption (sic) and detention . . . before the Supreme Court of the territory of Oregon, to be commanded and proven at Portland on the third Monday of June [June 24] instant, to do and receive what shall then and there [be done] by the said court, or by one of the justices thereof, upon a hearing at chambers be considered concerning them.

JUNE 14, 1853

Holmes notifies Ford that he will be in the office of Polk County Clerk John Lyle on June 16 for depositions in advance of the June 24 hearing before the Supreme Court in Portland.

JUNE 23, 1853

It is Ford's turn to express frustration that the case hasn't been decided—in his favor. He says in a deposition, given before a justice of the peace in Washington County, probably in Hillsboro, that he had expected testimony so far taken in the case would have settled the issue without subjecting him to the additional expense of another proceeding. He says he was advised—he didn't say by whom—that he could, if he chose, take the entire Holmes family back to Missouri as slaves, but he decided not to. And he offers excuses, both for failing to bring Mary Jane, James, and Roxanna to the Polk County District Court, as ordered by Judge Pratt on April 16, 1852, and for failing to respond sooner to Holmes' writ of *habeas corpus*.

Ford also raises anew his accusation that the Holmeses are "poor and ignorant," harsh to their children, and unfit as parents. He repeats his earlier assertion that he has a legal right to the children. And, for whatever reason, he lists some of the attorneys for both sides, A. G. P. Wood and M. P. Deady for Holmes; and James Malabin and Cyrus Olney for himself. Deady is known for pro-slavery views, so his mention on the side of Holmes seems curious and mistaken—Deady represents a different district on the Territorial Supreme Court and is not otherwise mentioned in the court record. Coincidentally, the county clerk who witnesses the depositions and handles the court records is John Lyle, the former school teacher who lived in the Ford home, and possibly still does.

The first half of Ford's deposition repeats virtually word-for-word the content of his April 16 deposition. It is at the midpoint of the deposition that he argues he has a right to the children and will be the better custodian.

Nathaniel Ford before Justice of the Peace Anthany (sic) S. Davis
    . . . this respondent was advised after it became settled that the people would not be permitted to hold slaves in this territory, to take the said Robin and his wife and said children back to Missouri, and there sell them—that he might have done so, but chose not to—and that from this fact, together with the fact that said children have always lived with him . . . the respondent had reasons to believe and did believe that the said relation, Robin, would have abided by his said agreement, and left said children with this respondent until they should have become of age . . . .

    And the respondent insists that he has, not only a legal and equitable right to retain the said children in his possession but also that it would be far better for said children to be so retained by him.

Ford denies Holmes' accusation that he mistreats the children and puts their lives in danger. He insists they "have always been well and kindly treated and used by the respondent and his family." On the contrary, he says it is Holmes and his wife who fail to provide adequate care. Holmes "is somewhat harsh and his wife is very cruel to their children."

As for failing to respond to the Holmes writ from fourteen months earlier, Ford explains the documents became mixed up with other papers in his coat pocket, and "in changing coats he forgot to take out the said papers and they were thus unintentionally all left at the respondents residence in Polk County."

Neither has Ford produced the children in court, as ordered, because "it is some sixty miles from here to the respondents place of residence, that the distance was so great and the expense which would follow the bringing of said children to their place so heavy that the same would have been a great hardship upon the respondent, and the same is the only reason why they were not brought here."

And in a lie that will be later be exposed, Ford "denies that he now has or ever had any intention of taking said children or either of them out of this territory, or even out of said Polk County."

JUNE 24, 1853

A setback for Holmes. Still no decision. Judge Olney in Portland continues the case to the next term of the Territorial Supreme Court in Salem, scheduled for December 1853. Olney says a new chief justice has been appointed for the territory, and a decision will await his arrival. Olney does issue a temporary ruling that must be especially disappointing to Holmes. He says Mary Jane shall be free to go where she wants. He inexplicably divides temporary custody of the other two children, awarding Roxanna to Ford, and James to Holmes. Singling out Holmes in his order, Olney forbids him from trying to influence Mary Jane's decision on where to stay. He also directs Ford and Holmes to each post $1,000 bond within ten days before they can gain custody of the children. It surely is an impossible sum for Holmes to raise, and there is nothing to indicate he manages to raise it, or even attempts to raise it.

Reflecting the prevailing disrespectful attitude toward blacks, Olney uses Ford's last name in his rulings and Holmes' first name. He also refers to Mary Jane, as "Jenny," the name Ford uses. The weight of the ruling, albeit temporary, seems to tilt favorably toward Ford.

JUNE 25, 1853

Holmes' attorney, A. G. P. Wood, files a formal statement with the court agreeing that Joseph Lane, the territorial delegate, may be deposed in Salem on one day's notice by Holmes, as well as by Ford, who has requested the deposition.

JULY 5, 1853

Lane, the territorial delegate and former governor, is deposed before Justice of the Peace Leonard Williams on whether he knows of any agreement for the custody of the children. Lane tries to be helpful to Ford, without being specific. Lane also discloses he offered Holmes a job in a mill, and Polly a job as a cook.

The attorneys at the deposition are George K. Sheil for Ford and Joseph C. Wilson for Holmes—Wilson will be appointed a justice of the Oregon Supreme Court in 1862 and will incur the wrath of *Statesman* editor Asahel Bush for attending the wedding of a black couple in 1863. Sheil, regarded as pro-slavery, will be elected to Congress in 1860.[10]

Sheil to Lane: Have you ever any conversation with the said Holmes touching the conditions under which his children viz. Jenny, James and Roxanna were held by the said Ford or under his control?

Lane: Recollect being at Col. Fords March 1850, heard a conversation between Ford and Holmes which left the impression on my mind that Holmes was to go where he pleased, but that the children were to be left with Ford. This however is only an impression as I do not recollect the words which passed between them.

Sheil: Please state the time, place and substance of that conversation.

Lane: Had a conversation with Holmes about keeping house for me in Oregon City, that is I proposed to employ him and his wife to work, her to cook and him to work about the mills. My proposition to Holmes brought about the conversation between the parties.

Wilson to Lane: Please state what led to such conversation; state also what was Robin's purpose in such conversation in your opinion.

Lane: My proposition to employ Robin and his wife, do not recollect the words, impression as above stated.

Wilson: If such conversation happened [,] state as to which and how many of the children specified, any admission was made, and what if anything was said concerning each.

Lane: Do not recollect any one of the children being named, nor do I recollect distinctly any word or words spoken, further than that the conversation between the parties left the impression on my mind that the children were to remain with Ford.

By this time, however, the focus of the case has turned to whether Ford's real intention is to keep the children as slaves.

JULY 13, 1853

Holmes files a long affidavit with the Polk County court restating his positions. He and his attorneys are evidently aware a new chief justice is about to take over the case, and they fully detail Holmes' previous arguments so the new justice will have all their evidence before him. Holmes also responds to Ford's new charge that Holmes is harsh in his behavior, and that his wife is cruel to the children. Holmes invites the court to investigate Ford's charge and predicts it would find the Holmeses are kind and good parents. Moreover, he says he is as financially capable of raising his children as Ford.

Holmes reviews the circumstances under which he became Ford's slave and the agreement they had to come to Oregon—freedom for Holmes in exchange for helping Ford make the journey and establish his farm. Holmes also hints at what must have been angry and highly disturbing arguments with Ford over the children.

Holmes also suggests he may not have come away with any gold from the mining venture in California, as he says Marcus Ford informed him he had dug $900 in gold dust "for" Nathaniel Ford. Holmes also says that in addition to mining gold he served as cook for the mining crew. He says after he returned from California, and after Ford freed him, his wife and infant son—but not his other children—Holmes "has ever since sought to obtain the custody and control of said children."

Your petitioner [Holmes] further answers and says, that said respondent [Ford], has no legal or equitable right to the service or control of said minor children. That your petitioner does not know whether said respondent has ever been advised to take your petitioner and his family back to Missouri and sell them into slavery or not, but he does know and states the fact to be that respondent has often threatened to do so, for the purpose of deterring your petitioner from seeking to obtain the custody and control of said children, as your petitioner believes.

That your petitioner is as well able in a pecuniary point of view to take care of and raise said children as respondent, and denies that he is unfit by reason of his poverty and ignorance to have the care and custody of his own children and further denies that he is harsh, or that his wife Polly is cruel to their children, but on the contrary avers that his and his wife's reputation for kindness and parental care for their children is such that he can safely ask the court to enquire thereof, and that his character for honesty sobriety and industry is good as petitioner believes, and this he prays may be inquired of by the court.

As on previous documents, Holmes signs the affidavit with an X.

⸱⸱ ⸱⸱

Holmes and Ford by this time have laid out in great detail their respective cases. There appears nothing more for either man to say. But a ruling will await the arrival of a new judge.

Ford's Secret Strategy

Nathaniel Ford told the court he delayed responding to Robin Holmes' suit because he misplaced the court papers and also couldn't afford the expense of transporting the children to court. The delay lasted more than a year, frustrating Holmes. But these were fraudulent excuses. In truth, Ford was using the time to try to circumvent Holmes' suit by devising a plan to return the entire Holmes family to Missouri to sell them back into slavery.

Holmes told the court in his affidavit that he didn't know whether Ford was serious about sending them back, or whether the threat was merely a ruse to discourage him from trying to regain his children. For his part, Ford told the court someone else suggested he return them, but he decided against it. However, a letter that turned up later in Missouri revealed that Ford had a very specific plan in mind to send the Holmeses to Missouri. He hoped to claim them as runaway slaves under the new, more rigid, Fugitive Slave Act, which Congress enacted in 1850.

While no one in the Holmes family, by any stretch of the imagination, could be considered a runaway, the Fugitive Slave Act required no more evidence than a claimant's sworn testimony that the person was a runaway and belonged to him. Law enforcement officers, even in non-slave states and territories, were required to enforce the law, or face a fine of $1,000. Anyone helping the suspect was also subject to a fine and six months in jail. Nor could the suspect testify on his or her own behalf. With such flimsy evidence free blacks might be fraudulently conscripted into slavery, although there is no recorded instance of this happening in Oregon.

Ford, however, may also have been exploring whether a new fugitive slave law in California could be replicated in Oregon. Although California had a constitutional prohibition against slavery, hundreds of slaves were brought from slave states to help mine gold. Not wanting to give up their slaves, slaveholders won approval from the legislature for the highly controversial California Fugitive Slave Act of 1852, which provided that owners had a legal right to return slaves to their slave states, if they brought them to California prior to statehood.[1]

The California Supreme Court upheld the law in "one of the most deeply proslavery decisions ever rendered in a free state," said Stacey L. Smith, an assistant professor of history at Oregon State University. The court ruled that the constitution's anti-slavery clause did not free anyone because it lacked an enforcement provision.[2] Thus, the new fugitive slave law potentially authorized the enslavement or re-enslavement of nearly all of California's two thousand enslaved and free black residents. As it happened, some African Americans who thought they were free were returned to their former owners, although there is no way of knowing how many.

Ford evidently felt no remorse about devising a strategy to reclaim Robin and Polly Holmes as slaves two years after he gave them their freedom. The letter outlining his plan was addressed to James A. Shirley in Howard County, Missouri, on June 22, 1852, two months after Holmes initiated his suit and ten months before Ford responded to Holmes. Ford revealed to Shirley he had sold a slave in Oregon—he didn't identify him or her. It was also in this letter that Ford complained about having no Missouri friends. The following excerpts, with misspellings and grammatical mistakes included, detail Ford's strategy:

> *Dear Sir: I have for the first time since I left Howard County come to the conclusion to write to you and I assure you it has not been out of any disrespect to you that I have never wrote to you. I have wrote several letters to Dr. Lowery and also several to my brothers and my brother in laws and have never received a line from them. I have long since come to the conclusion that I had no friends in that country even amongst my relatives. . . .*
>
> *I am very poore except a fine tract of 640 acres of land one-half being my wifes in her own right by the act of Congress. We have no patent for it nor shant for some time. You know I brought some negroes with me*

to this country which has proved a curse to me and my fambly. Scott died. Robin and his wife done verry well untill the spring of '50 when the abolitionists interfered—and the country is full of them—the interference was so great that I had to let them go. They have stoped (sic) in some six miles of me with a man who owns a mill and the abolitionists are so much about them that the negroes are continuly harrissing my fambly by attempts to slander them.

Now my dear friend I wish you if you care to befriend me—though I am in a distant land, you know Crigler the sheriff had leveyed an execution on the negroes and they were brought off to this country. I am of the opinion that the execution may be so renewed as to send it here and take the negroes back to Missouri under the fugive slave law. If so if you will have it attended to and appoint an agent here, I will pay all the expenses here and git all the evidence which is in my neighborhood. Samuel Gass bought [one] of the negroes and Cary S. Embree knows all about the matter. I can get a lawyer here to attend to the business if you can appoint an agent here and leave his name blank, for me to fill in, I will arrange the whole matter. Robin and his wife Polly are very likely—they have five likely children if you can make the arrangement you may make some 1500 to 2000s out of them and do me a great favor.

If the negroes can be taken under the fugive slave law I will make the arrangements to send them to you in short order (don't send a judgment here to hariss me for I am not able to pay any old debts) if the case of the negroes can be attended to it will releave me and my fambly of much trouble and you may be benefitted by it. Whether there can be anything done or not please write to me amediently. I should like if there can anything be done to have the writ here by the first of October next—that is the time of the setting of our district court.[4]

The letter gives a much different insight into Ford's thinking than the family histories. The timing of the letter suggests Ford was delaying his response in order to remove the Holmeses from the jurisdiction of Oregon courts, and return them to Missouri where he might sell them to pay off past debts, or make a profit, or both. Ford's reference to Crigler is to Howard County Sheriff Lewis Crigler, who took possession of one of Ford's Missouri slaves in 1843 to pay off some of Ford's other debts. An introduction to the letter in the *Missouri Historical Review* said that the slaves Ford took to Oregon had been mortgaged by Ford—he probably never fully paid for them. The writ of execution would have been Sheriff Crigler's threatened seizure of Ford's slaves.

Several other points in the letter stand out. Ford says pressure from abolitionists forced him to free the Holmeses, not his promise to Holmes. And the enactment of the new Fugitive Slave Act encouraged him to try to reclaim all of the family as slaves. Also, Ford's meaning isn't clear when he wrote that a Samuel Gass "bought" one of the slaves. There is no way of knowing which of his slaves were so sold. Was it Mary Jane Holmes? It might explain why Ford was so reluctant to give her up. But she was in the household of Ford's son-in-law, James Boyle. There also is no record of a Samuel Gass in Polk County. However, the Ford family was close to a man called Goff, a relative of Ford's by marriage, who crossed the plains in the Ford wagon train and settled at Rickreall. Ford may simply have misspelled his name.

·, ~ ,·

In his letter, Ford also wrote of the family's ill-fated gold mining expedition to California, and the death of his son, Marcus—two events which seemed to cripple his outlook on his life in Oregon.

From the time I arrive on farm I now live on up to the fall of 1848 I was in fine spirits and so was my family as we ever was enjoying fine helth. In the fall of 1848 I went to California on the search of gold and for the first ten days was very successful when I was taken sick in the mountains some 15 or 20 miles from any settlement and lay sick some 90 days when my friends, Morons [Mormons?] took me to a little village in the fall of 48. After I left Origon—my sons wife fell into the consumption and the doctor advised him to take her a trip on sea—he took her to the bay of Santfranciso (sic) where she died in two days after his [son's] arrival which was some time in December. He had heard of my being sick and reached me about the 10th of January 1849, and took me to the city of Sacramento and weighted on me until I was able to leave for home—there we parted never to see each other in life. He went into the mines and was very successful and some time in Nov. '49 left for Origon with $2000 of my money and some 14 or 15000$ of his own and was either drowned or killed by the Indians or the white men—most proble killed—the Indians and whites certainly got his money—I have never received one dollars of the money.

. . .

My sickness in California and the troubles about the loss of my only son has brought me down in helth and spirits. I have a very helpless famley to support. I have got 4 of my daughters with me and 2 of them are grown.

I have by heavy exertions given my daughters a good English education—
we have the finest country for a pore man to make a living in I have ever
seen if the man is only able to labour. But now with bad helth and of the
age that I am [I] have hard times to keep up.[7]

It isn't known whether Shirley replied to Ford. The scheme may have seemed
too bizarre for Shirley to take seriously, and he chose to ignore the letter. But
for whatever reason, it doesn't appear Ford made any concrete attempt to
reclaim Robin and Polly Holmes.

Enter Judge Williams

Judge Cyrus Olney told Robin Holmes on June 24, 1853, that the court would
await the arrival of a new Supreme Court justice before deciding whether
Holmes would get his children back—or whether Nathaniel Ford could keep
them. The new judge arrived within a few days, and within a few more days,
on July 13, issued a landmark ruling in favor of Holmes. For a new judge, it
was an extraordinarily quick resolution of a controversial and important case.

The judge was George H. Williams, newly confirmed by the U.S. Senate as
chief justice of Oregon's Territorial Supreme Court, following his nomination
by President Franklin Pierce. Williams had never been to Oregon and had only
the briefest possible time to familiarize himself with the Holmes case. The
thirty-year-old Williams was described by a biographer as "tall, heavy framed,
rather awkward." Born and raised in New York, Williams lived at the time
of his nomination in Fort Madison, Iowa, where he owned a newspaper and
served as an elected district judge. His nomination as Oregon's chief justice
was seen as a political reward—he had been a presidential elector for Pierce,
whose first choice, O. C. Pratt, had been rejected by the Senate.[1] Williams
would play an important role in organizing Oregon for statehood. He would
later serve as a U.S. senator from Oregon, and U.S. attorney general under
President Ulysses Grant. Grant would also nominate Williams for chief justice
of the U.S. Supreme Court, although the post would be denied him. He would
end his political career as mayor of Portland.[2]

When Williams arrived in Oregon, the Holmeses had been subjected to
delay after delay, and the case was still unresolved after fifteen months. Had

George H. Williams, the chief judge of Oregon's Territorial Supreme Court, who ruled in Robin Holmes' favor in his suit to free his children from Nathaniel Ford. Williams later became a U.S. senator and the U.S. attorney general. (Oregon Historical Society)

he chose, Williams would have had ample reason to also go slowly—he had arrived in Portland only days earlier with his wife, Kate Van Antwerp; they were moving into a new home; he barely knew his fellow justices; and he could legitimately say he needed more time to consider the legal issues. Williams also didn't give himself much time to learn the major players in the new Oregon Territory—those who called the shots, so to speak—or familiarize himself with local attitudes toward slavery and blacks. In today's judicial system, any one of these might be a reason—spoken or unspoken—for a judge to take his time. However, Williams not only did not proceed slowly, he moved the decision forward by several months, well ahead of the hearing Judge Olney had scheduled for the following December in Salem.

⸱⸱⸱

On July 13, 1853, Judge Williams issued the following ruling on Ford v. Holmes:

> [S]aid Judge having heard the allegations and evidence of the petitioner and respondent, orders and decrees that the said children Jenny or Mary Jane, James and Roxanna be and they hereby are awarded to the care and custody of their parents, Robin Holmes and his wife, to be and remain with them as their children as fully and in all respects as though they, the said children, had not been in the custody of the said Ford.[3]

The *Oregon Statesman* published the verdict in a brief article on July 19, 1853, saying, "The court decreed that the lawful custody of said children belonged to the parents and ordered said Ford to deliver them up." It listed Reuben Boise and Wood as the attorneys for Holmes.[4] The newspaper followed up its report on the verdict by running verbatim Judge William's opinion on July 25 under the headline "The Negro Case." In his opinion, Williams dismissed out of hand Ford's allegations that the Holmeses were unfit as parents.

> *Nothing appears in evidence to show that the charge of harshness against respondent is true and the evidence is abundantly sufficient to prove that petitioner and his wife are not only affectionate parents but that they are sober honest and industrious people entirely competent to have the charge of their own children. . . . Difference of color does not destroy parental power and authority in this Territory, and unless voluntarily and legally relinquished petitioner has the same right to his children as respondent has to his.*[5]

In his most assertive declaration that slavery was illegal in Oregon, Williams said that while Ford held the family as slaves in Missouri, "as soon as the laws of Oregon touched the parties, the relation of master and slave was dissolved." He found the evidence of an agreement between Holmes and Ford for the children flimsy and unconvincing. He said Joseph Lane's "impression" of an agreement didn't help.

> *Vague and unsatisfactory as this evidence is, no liberality of construction can make it prove a complete and binding contract. No issues or conditions are made known. What said children were to have or do during the time of service, when that time was to cease; what they were to have at its expiration, in no way appears. Mutuality of obligation is essential to a valid contract, but the contract as disclosed by this evidence does not bind respondent to do anything, therefore it does not bind petitioner.*

As for the suggestion that Ford had granted the Holmeses their freedom in exchange for keeping the children, Williams declared freedom wasn't Ford's to give. "To convey that to a person which at the time is absolutely his by law, plainly amounts to nothing."

It was a bad period for Ford. Not only did he lose the Holmes children, he also lost an election for a seat on the legislative council the year before. Ford had concluded a two-year term in the House in 1852 and sought election to the more prestigious Council, on which he'd previously served. However, the seat went to James Fulkerson, who received two hundred and forty-two votes to Ford's one hundred and eighty-three.[6]

Judge Williams would refer in later years to negative fallout from his ruling, saying it probably prevented him from being elected one of Oregon's first senators after statehood in 1859. In an address to the Oregon Legislative Assembly on the fortieth anniversary of statehood, Williams left no doubt of his own feelings about the significance of his ruling:

> *Whether or not slaveholders could carry their slaves into the territories and hold them there as property had become a burning question, and my predecessors in office, for reasons best known to themselves, had declined to hear the case. This was among the first cases I was called upon to decide. Mr. Ford contended that these colored people were his property in Missouri from which he emigrated, and he had as much right to bring that kind of property into Oregon and hold it here as much as he had to bring his cattle or other property here and hold it as such; but my opinion was, and I so held, that without some positive legislative enactment establishing slavery here, it did not and could not exist in Oregon, and I awarded the colored people their freedom. Judge Boise was the attorney for the petitioners.*
>
> *So far as I know this was the last effort made to hold slaves in Oregon by force of law. There were a great many virulent pro-slavery men in the territory, and this decision, of course, was very distasteful to them.[7]*

The *Statesman* offered no editorial comment on Williams' ruling. But another newspaper reference to the case portrayed the ruling as "radical." It appeared as an "Historic Footnote" on July 13, 1959, in a so-far unknown newspaper that was said to quote a news account at the time of Judge Williams' ruling:

> *Judge George H. Williams has decided this day for the plaintiff Holmes, and against the defendant, and has ordered the release of the children into the custody of Holmes. The judge based his opinion upon the theory that once Ford brought slaves into this territory where slavery is illegal, the relationship of slave and master was dissolved. This is considered a radical position and is much criticized by the several other slaveholders in the territory.[8]*

It may have been fortunate for Holmes that Williams ruled quickly. Had he waited, it might have given him pause to learn that a number of judicial colleagues and territorial leaders were sympathetic toward slavery. Maybe he knew this. Maybe he would have ruled as he did anyway, but Williams would later show a proclivity to bend principle in the face of a political wind. Nevertheless, Williams' scalpel-quick decision on a major slavery case in Oregon was in contrast to the debilitating imbroglio over slavery then under way in Washington, D.C., where lawmakers were tied in knots over whether slavery should be legal in the future new territories of Kansas and Nebraska.

⸱⸱⸱

We don't know how Robin and Polly Holmes reacted to the ruling. We can only imagine the elation and relief they must have felt at winning a fifteen-month legal battle to regain their children after two years of being denied contact. Moreover, they had regained custody from a slave owner who for years had held the entire family in bondage both in Missouri and Oregon, and had sold—or had forfeited because of unpaid debts—three of their children in Missouri. They had, in spite of their lack of education, triumphed over a prominent member of a community known to be sympathetic to slavery. The importance of Holmes' achievement, for his family, and for the course of the slavery issue in Oregon, cannot be overstated. Yes, Holmes clearly needed—and received—help from Boise and other sympathetic attorneys in making his case. But there would have been no ruling if Holmes hadn't persevered against what to him, and others, must have seemed like overwhelming odds.

It was probably also fortunate for Holmes that Judge Williams chose to preside over the Salem judicial district, one of three districts in Oregon's court system. The two other Oregon districts were supervised by Justices Deady and Olney.[9] Had Deady taken the Salem district, the outcome might have been different, as he was known for pro-slavery sympathies. In later years on the bench, Deady would acquire a reputation as a defender of human rights. But not then. John McBride, who served with Deady in the Oregon Constitutional Convention in 1857, said Deady was a Democrat "of the ultra-pro-slavery type, who advocated the adoption of slavery in the new state."[10]

Williams' photograph is today prominently displayed on a courtroom wall in the Polk County Courthouse in Dallas, Oregon. A caption reads in part: "[In] 1853 Judge Williams presided over Polk County's most notable case, Robin Holmes vs. Nathaniel Ford which held that slavery could not exist in Oregon."[11] Although Holmes vs. Ford received little publicity at the time, the case marked a major milestone in the evolution of the territory's attitudes toward slavery, when, in the words of Darrell Millner, "It was still an open question whether Oregon would have slavery or be free."[12] Millner, of Portland State University, told the author, "We need to appreciate what it took [for

Holmes] to challenge the racial conventions of his day: a black against white, a former slave against a former owner . . . All those factors make it quite remarkable."

·~·

Several years later, a slave case in California would deal with similar issues, but unlike Holmes vs. Ford, it attracted extensive public interest and a great deal of press coverage, both in California and nationally. The case involved a slave owner, Robert Mayes Smith, originally from Mississippi, who brought two women slaves, Biddy Smith and Hannah, and their children to California from Utah in 1851 to work on Smith's cattle ranch near San Bernardino. The two women had ten children, ranging in age from two to seventeen.

When Smith's once-successful ranch failed for complicated reasons—the Mormon Church ended up with his land—he prepared to move the twelve women and children to Texas, a slave state. But a writ of *habeas corpus* was filed on January 1, 1856, contending that the African Americans were no longer slaves in California, and Smith could not compel them to go to Texas against their will.[13]

Judge Benjamin Hayes of the U.S. District Court for Southern California in Los Angeles ruled on January 16 in favor of the blacks. Although Hayes was a former southerner who had himself once owned slaves, he determined that Smith had severed his slave relationship to the women and children by bringing them to California, and that they were henceforth "free forever" and fully able to make their own decisions about where they wanted to live.[14] There were a number of complications in the case. One was the apparent reluctance of the former slave Hannah to say in front of Smith that she didn't want to accompany him to Texas. Judge Hayes concluded Hannah was afraid to stand up to Smith. Moreover, he was certain Smith had every intention of returning her to slavery in Texas, and possibly selling her. He finally prevented Smith from taking Hannah by placing her in jail in protective custody. Smith eventually went to Texas without his former slaves.

·~·

One apparent outcome of Holmes vs. Ford was retaliation against Oregon's African American population to prevent any future such court cases. The 1853-1854 territorial legislature voted to deny to African Americans, as well as Native Americans, the right to testify against whites in Oregon courts. The record of the debate, if there was debate, is lost. But it is fair conjecture that the law resulted from Williams' ruling in Holmes vs. Ford. It was approved unanimously in the Council on January 5, 1854, and apparently without objection in the House two days later.[15] The law, as written into the Revised Statutes of the Territory of Oregon for 1855, provided, "The following persons shall not be competent to testify: Negroes, mulattoes and Indians, or persons having one-half or more of Indian blood, in an action or proceeding in which a white person is a party."[16] However, the law seems to have been ignored by some judges, as blacks would testify against whites in at least two court cases in later years.

Despite the ruling in Holmes vs. Ford, the legacy of slavery would remain very much alive for African Americans in Oregon in the mid-1850s. One whose ordeal wasn't over was Holmes' daughter, Mary Jane.

Reuben Shipley

The slave known as Reuben Shipley arrived in Oregon on September 1, 1853, just six weeks after Judge Williams' ruling in favor of Robin and Polly Holmes.[1] Oregon's 1849 exclusion law was repealed in 1854, and thus did not seriously threaten Shipley with removal. Shipley, who was born in Kentucky, traveled from Missouri to Oregon in a wagon train with his white owner, Robert N. Shipley. Census records for 1850 in Missouri listed Robert Shipley with three slaves. These were two women, ages thirty-one and fifty-five, and one male, age forty-four, who no doubt was Reuben Shipley.

Reuben served as overseer on the Shipley farm near Saline in Miller County in central Missouri. Overseer was a position of prestige for a slave, indicating he was well-thought-of and trusted by his owner. Robert N. Shipley owned five properties in Miller County over the years, totaling one hundred and eighty-six acres, although it's not clear he owned them all at the same time.

Several accounts, including the author's family genealogy, said Reuben Shipley—"Uncle Reuben Shipley" in the genealogy—was promised his freedom if he would help Robert Shipley move to Oregon with his first wife, Charlotte Mulkey, and their seven children.[2] Reuben was to drive a team of oxen, pulling a wagon. Should he refuse Shipley's offer, his other option was to remain in Missouri and be sold again as a slave. In a 1938 interview, Robert Shipley's daughter, Amy Shipley Lurwell, indicated that the choice for Reuben was a painful one, as going to Oregon meant leaving behind his wife and two sons, who belonged to another owner or owners. As Lurwell told the story, Robert Shipley's two female slaves were given the same option, but chose to stay in Missouri.

> *Before leaving Missouri my father was a slave holder in a small way.*
> *He had two women and one man slave. When he prepared to leave for*
> *Oregon he offered these slaves their choice. Either they could go with him*
> *and help on the journey and then be free in Oregon, or they could stay*
> *behind where their relatives lived and have another master. The women*
> *chose to stay in Missouri with their husbands and families (belonging to*
> *other masters), but the man, though married, chose to go to Oregon. He*
> *worked faithfully all the way across the plains and then took his liberty.*
> *After reaching Oregon this man whose name was Reuben went to work to*
> *earn money to purchase his wife back in Missouri.*[3]

The Robert Shipley family settled in Benton County, establishing a claim for one hundred and sixty acres south of present-day Philomath, near the foothills of the Coast Range. Shipley's wife, Charlotte, died soon after they arrived, and in 1856 he married Elizabeth Jane Goodman. In addition to farming, Robert Shipley also identified himself as a wheelwright. Unlike Nathaniel Ford, Shipley did not enter politics. The 1860 U.S. Census listed the combined value of his real and personal property as $3,600.[4] He died in 1883 and is buried in the Monroe Cemetery in Benton County.

More is known about Shipley's son, John L. Shipley, who no doubt would have worked alongside Reuben. John Shipley married Rachel Ann Henkle and became postmaster and collector of toll charges on the Yaquina Bay Wagon Road in Lincoln County. He later moved to Philomath where he purchased a store from The Reverend Thomas J. Conner in 1872.[5]

Keeping his word, Robert Shipley gave Reuben his freedom in Oregon, after which Reuben went to work for a nearby landowner, Eldridge Hartless, who had a mile-square claim along Marys River, a mile east of Robert Shipley's farm.[6] Reuben established a reputation in the community as a hard and intelligent worker. Over the next few years, he saved his money, intending both to buy a farm of his own and to buy back his wife and two children, still in Missouri. Jeremiah E. Henkle, who was familiar with the family history, said in a 1936 interview that Reuben saved $1,500 while working for Hartless.[7]

Benton County records show that on November 21, 1857, Reuben Shipley paid $700 to Charles and Eleanor Bales for one hundred and one acres of farmland, a mile and a half east of today's downtown Philomath.[8] Shipley likely was the largest African American landowner in the Willamette Valley at the time. He purchased an additional five acres for $50 from George Howell on November 10, 1865. Shipley's farm extended in a rectangle across the high southeastern slope of what is today known as Neabeack Hill. The location offered, and offers still, an expansive view of the lush valley farmland south and east of Philomath.

Shipley built a cabin on the property where he hoped to make a new home for his family, bringing them from Missouri. However, when he tried to purchase their freedom, he learned his wife had since died, and the owner of his two young sons refused to sell.[9]

It was around this time that Reuben Shipley met Mary Jane Holmes, living thirty miles away in adjoining Polk County. She was still in a situation that would further complicate her life and Reuben's as well.

They Weren't Alone

African American slaves were scattered throughout Oregon. Few records survive of who they were, where they were, or what happened to them. But repeated efforts in the territorial legislature to protect slave property suggested slaveholding was more widespread than previously thought.

Representative William Allen of Yamhill County submitted a petition to the territorial legislature on January 7, 1858, on behalf of M. R. Crisp and forty-seven other county residents urging enactment of a law "for the protection of property in slaves in this territory."[1] Crisp, the lead petitioner, was a prominent Yamhill County farmer. If each of the signers owned a single slave, the total would amount to forty-seven slaves. However, while it's likely some slave owners were on the list, most who signed were probably farmers and others who either wanted slaves, supported the rights of others to own slaves, or signed as an expression of solidarity with the South.[2] In support of his petition, Allen declared in a speech on the House floor:

> *It has been proven upon this floor that slavery does exist in the Territory in several counties. There are some in Benton, Lane, Polk, Yamhill and I know not how many other counties.*[3]

Another legislator, James W. Mack, also argued for protection of slave property, declaring that "my neighbor in Lane County owns slaves and is now in California endeavoring to test the validity of the Fugitive Slave Law."[4]

Allen submitted his petitions in support of a bill he introduced weeks earlier, on January 9, 1858, seeking protection for slave property. He argued that the U.S. Supreme Court's decision in the Dred Scott case in March 1857 had overturned the territory's anti-slavery laws—making slavery legal—and therefore slaveholders were entitled to protection.[5] By protection, he meant a law to corral runaway slaves and return them to their owners.

Allen said that in the event Congress rejected Oregon for statehood, "we shall remain as we are, under our territorial government, and by passing laws protecting property in slaves, we shall encourage immigration." His measure failed on a procedural vote, fifteen to seven.[6] However, that wasn't the end of it. There would be other petitions in other legislative sessions.

ᴗᴗ

In any discussion of the slaves brought to Oregon, it is important to keep in mind that slaves had an opportunity to gain their freedom, an opportunity denied them—except in rare cases—in Missouri and other slave states.[7] It was an opportunity that was realized for Reuben Shipley, and, after a painful decade, for the Holmes family. Once slaves were freed in Oregon, they and their descendants could afterward live free from the threat of bondage.[8]

Some slaves were freed unconditionally by their owners; a few—the Holmes children—were freed by the courts, and some bought their freedom. Although Oregon's anti-slavery law made no mention of a purchase requirement, some slaves did pay if an owner insisted. Given Oregon's ambivalent attitudes toward slavery, and hostility toward African Americans in general, it is understandable that some who paid probably didn't want to take any chances that their freedom might someday be snatched away.

There is no recorded instance of anyone in Oregon ever being charged with violating the anti-slavery law, even though slaveholders could hardly have kept slaves secret from their neighbors. Blacks working in a farmer's fields would have been conspicuous by their very presence. Thus the anomaly of the time: despite laws forbidding both slavery and free blacks, there were both slaves and free blacks in the territory.

Uncertainty over whether Oregon might become a slave state is reflected in a poignant document written in 1851 on behalf of the former slave, Maria Scott, who had paid $200 to her Polk County owner, Richard Linville, to buy her freedom. Maria Scott was very likely the wife of Scott, the slave of Nathaniel Ford, who died during the journey home from the Ford family's gold-mining expedition to California. Assuming she was Scott's wife, she had purchased her freedom before their marriage. Linville later returned the $200 to Maria Scott because slavery was illegal. However, she pledged to re-purchase her freedom in the event Oregon became a slave state.

The hand-written document is a receipt dated August 2, 1851, addressed to "Polk County, Oregon Territory."

> *Received of Richard Linville the sum of two hundred dollars in full for the money and property which I paid him for my freedom as we then thought I was not free having been a slave of his in the United States and brought to Oregon by him and whereas it is now thought that it will be a free state the aforesaid Richard Linville has paid me back the aforesaid two hundred dollars which two hundred dollars I promise to pay back to the said Richard Linville if in case it should be a slave state.*[9]

The letter is signed with an X scrawled across the words: "Mariah Scott a colored woman now the wife of Jackson Scott." Maria Scott lived with the Holmes' family in Polk County in 1850 after her husband, Scott, died on returning from California. The mention of Jackson Scott is puzzling. If he is the same person as the slave Scott, he had been dead for over a year.

A witness to Maria's signature, and possibly the person who wrote the document, was M. Vanderpool. In the same file is a codicil to Richard Linville's will, dated February 25, 1847, in which Linville bequeathed to his son, Harrison Linville, "all rights I may have in my two slaves called Maria and Johnson now in Oregon." Maria had evidently purchased her freedom after the will was written.

The second Linville slave, Johnson, is not further identified, but he possibly was William Johnson, one of three former slaves admitted years later into the First Congregational Church in Salem. The M. Vanderpool in the document was undoubtedly Medders Vanderpool, who traveled to Oregon in 1846 along the Applegate Trail. Harrison Linville and his wife were in the same wagon train.

ᵕ ᵕ

What little is known about most slaves in the Oregon Country is largely anecdotal—a mention in a family history, an incident on the Oregon Trail, a name in a census record or on a gravestone, an unexplained document randomly found. And there were undoubtedly slaves for which there is no record at all. Three blacks—two women and a child—were listed as "slave" in the 1860 U.S. Census.[10] The census was taken three years after voters added a clause to Oregon's constitution prohibiting slavery, suggesting slave owners had little fear of enforcement.

A court document in the files of the Benton County Historical Museum reveals more information about one slave than is available for most. It involved a case brought by a Luteshia Carson, a slave—or a former slave—against the estate of the late David Carson, who was born in Ireland and emigrated from Missouri in 1845. Luteshia filed suit on February 27, 1854, in Benton County Probate Court against the executor of the estate, Gransbury Smith, seeking compensation for work done for Carson prior to his death in 1852.

Luteshia Carson—her first name appeared in census records as Letitia—claimed David Carson promised during the journey from Missouri that if she would live and work for him during the remainder of his life, "he would make me his sole heir or that he would give me his entire property" upon his death. However, Carson failed to put the agreement in writing, and Luteshia evidently was denied a share of his estate. She went to court seeking $7,450—$5,000 for seven years of work, plus the value of livestock and other property to which she claimed she was entitled.[11]

Luteshia was twenty-nine in 1845, when Carson brought her to Oregon. Carson evidently fathered her children. A child, Martha, described as a mulatto, was born in the Rocky Mountains during the trip West. A second child, Adam, also described as a mulatto, was born in Oregon. Luteshia, Martha, and Adam were listed with the last name Carson in the 1850 U.S. Census.[12]

The *Oregon Statesman* of October 7, 1854, said a jury rejected Luteshia Carson's claim. It suggested the lack of a written agreement probably doomed her case. The newspaper, however, appeared to take the former slave's side.

> *This was an action by a black woman to recover the value of her services rendered in this territory to defendant from the year 1845 to 1852. Luteshia was a slave in Missouri, but came to Oregon and served her master faithfully until his death.*[13]

There was no mention of the daughter, Martha, although another account said Martha later married and raised a family on the Umatilla Indian Reservation. Luteshia may have subsequently moved to Douglas County where she was said to have operated a boarding house.[14]

The Carson case brought together leading figures from the Holmes vs. Ford suit. Judge Williams presided at the trial, and Reuben Boise was the prosecuting attorney. Oddly, and for no apparent reason other than probable carelessness, the *Oregon Statesman* misnamed both Luteshia and David Carson, giving their surnames as "Censor" and listing the title of the case as "Luteshia Censor v Green B. Smith."[15]

In December 1854, Judge Williams would preside at another case involving minority rights, ruling in favor of Native American widows who sought to keep land their white or "half-breed" husbands had lawfully claimed under the Donation Land Act "He [Williams] decides in favor of the right of such persons and argues the question ably in support of the decision," the *Oregon Statesman* said. It added that unnamed persons had already "jumped" some of the claims in Marion County, wrongfully anticipating Williams would rule against the Native American widows.[16]

·–~·

Much of the available information on slaves in Oregon has been randomly accumulated by historians, authors, and journalists. That the accounts often differ, sometimes significantly, underscores the difficulty of ascertaining verifiable facts.

Unlike the unique court depositions and testimony of Robin Holmes, most slaves left few records. And how could they? Without the ability to read and write, they would send no letters to family and friends for descendants to read. Neither could they keep journals or diaries for future generations to ponder. Except in rare cases, they would leave behind no photographs or portraits to help identify them. Oral accounts of their lives were spotty and often remembered differently by whoever was doing the telling. The many colorful accounts left by white families telling of their ordeals and adventures on the Oregon Trail have no counterpart among African Americans. Their experiences on the journey West are lost to history.

Below are the mostly fragmentary accounts of the lives of some of the slaves and former slaves, brought to Oregon by early settlers.

LOUIS SOUTHWORTH

Louis Southworth was born July 4, 1830, in Tennessee to Louis and Pauline Hunter, slaves of James Southworth.[17] He was brought to Oregon from Franklin County, Missouri, in the 1850s by his owner, who also brought Louis' mother. The slave Southworth mined gold in the Jacksonville area to buy his freedom. After the death of his mother, Southworth moved to Yreka, California, where he made a living by playing the fiddle at dancing schools. He earned the last $400 toward the $1,000 needed to pay for his freedom.[18]

Louis Southworth with his fiddle. He was brought to Oregon as a slave in the 1850s and worked as a gold miner and played his fiddle at dancing schools to raise money to buy his freedom. Southworth Creek in Lincoln County is named for him. (Oregon Historical Society)

Different dates are given for Southworth's freedom, 1855 and 1858. Once free, Southworth worked as a blacksmith in Buena Vista in Polk County where he operated a livery stable and learned to read and write. He married a woman named Mary—one account gave her name as Mariah Collins—and they moved with a stepson to Tidewater, near Waldport, where he established a homestead and later donated land for a school. He lived and worked along the Alsea River, operating a ferry for passengers and freight.[19] Southworth's wife died six years after the move, and he married a second time to Josephine Jackson of Portland.

Two early pioneers interviewed in 1938 described Southworth as a good blacksmith who dressed well and "drove a fine team of black horses." He "was respected by all and treated almost as an equal even by the southerners."[20] His wife, Mary, was said to have "an education above the average of the community."[21] Southworth died June 28, 1917, at nearly age eighty-eight, and is buried in the Crystal Lake Cemetery near Corvallis. A road and creek through Southworth's old homestead in Lincoln County were disparagingly named Darkey Road and Darkey Creek. The Oregon Geographic Names Board honored Southworth by changing the name of the creek to Southworth Creek in 1999.[22]

AMANDA GARDINER-JOHNSON

Amanda Johnson was born at Liberty, Clay County, Missouri, on August 30, 1833, and arrived in Oregon in 1853 with the Anderson Deckard family. In an interview from her home in Albany in 1921, Johnson told journalist Fred Lockley that although a slave, she was proud she had never been bought or sold. Wrote Lockley:

When I asked her if she had ever been sold as a slave, she said, "No sir, I was never sold nor bartered for. I was given as a wedding present to my owner's daughter. I belonged to Mrs. Nancy Wilhite. Mrs. Wilhite later married Mr. Corum. When her daughter, Miss Lydia, was married, she gave me to her as a wedding present. I have known seven generations of the family. I had five brothers and six sisters; none of us were sold like common negroes. We were all given away as the different young folks got married.

"In 1853 my owners came to Oregon. A man offered my master $1,200 for me. I was 19 years old then. My owners said, 'Amanda isn't for sale. She is going across the plains to the Willamette Valley with us. She is like one of the family. I don't care to sell her.'

"It took us six months to come from Liberty, Missouri, to Oregon City. We reached our destination on September 13, 1853. Lou Southworth, also a slave, crossed the plains the same year I did. So did Benjamin Johnson, another slave, who later became my husband."[23]

Amanda Johnson said Deckard offered to free her if she wanted to stay in Missouri, but, as she explained to Lockley, she was afraid:

The word of a Negro, even if a free Negro, was of no value in court. Any bad white man could claim I had been stolen from him and could swear me into jail. Then in place of keeping me in jail, he could buy my services for the time I was sentenced for . . . and do whatever he wanted to me, for Negroes were the same as cows and horses and were not supposed to have morals or souls. I was afraid to accept my liberty, so I came to Oregon with my owners.[24]

The 1860 U.S. Census listed Amanda, then twenty-eight, as a servant in the Deckard home.[25] She died in 1927 at age ninety-four.

AMERICA WALDO BOGLE

Tracing America Waldo's direct connection to the Waldo family is challenging. What is known is that America, then eighteen, married a Jamaica-born free black, Richard A. Bogle, in Salem in 1863. Both the Waldo and Bogle families have been prominent in Oregon and the Northwest.

Was America the daughter of Daniel Waldo? There is disagreement among descendants in the two families. Was she the daughter of Daniel's brother, Joseph? Possibly. Or was she a former slave belonging to another Waldo brother, John? That's possible, too. Renita Bogle-Byrd of Decatur, Georgia, a Bogle descendant, told the author in an email that the family's position remains that Daniel was America's father. "We had always been told through family tradition that Daniel was the father of America . . . and so we as a family will keep this tradition until we find out otherwise."[26]

However, America's birth year on her headstone was given as June 1844. If this is accurate, she could not have been Daniel Waldo's daughter, since he emigrated to Oregon in the spring of 1843. Brian Waldo Johnson, a descendant of Daniel Waldo's, said this leaves Waldo's brother, Joseph, who emigrated in 1846, as the next best candidate to be America's father. Joseph, a bachelor and a former deputy sheriff in Gasconade County, Missouri, apparently did bring slaves, Johnson said, but Daniel Waldo did not—although he had owned slaves in Missouri.[27] Johnson said that Daniel Waldo raised America in Oregon and "acted as a father figure," giving rise to the later confusion about her father's identity. However, Bogle-Byrd said the date on the headstone could well be a mistake. She said that her grandmother, Kathryn Bogle, purchased the headstone "and some information that she had in regards to the Bogles has been found to be an error."

Johnson said it is not out of the question that a third brother, John Waldo, was America's father. John Waldo died in California in 1849, and family records say he directed his widow, Avarilla, to free his slaves in Missouri. This was before Avarilla emigrated to Oregon, where she later remarried. Said Johnson: "America could have come to Oregon with Avarilla . . . technically a free black."

Was America a slave in Oregon? That's unclear, too, although the preponderance of evidence suggests a slave background. America's surname of Waldo was the surname of the white Waldos. Moreover, several of the eight Waldo brothers did report owning slaves, including Daniel, Joseph, and John. Johnson said he wouldn't "disagree" that America was born a slave in Missouri, but added she was apparently treated as free in Oregon.[28] A newspaper article at the time of her wedding in 1863 refers to America as "a servant and a great favorite" of a Salem family, which was not named.[29]

Bogle-Byrd said the family did not believe that America was a slave, although Kathryn Bogle, a prominent Portland journalist and community activist, said in a 1974 interview that both America and her mother were slaves.[30] America lived with the Daniel Waldo family in what are now known as the Waldo Hills east of Salem, but her name does not appear in the 1850 or 1860 census. Neither does the name of her mother, whose history is unknown. America's name first appears in census records in 1870 when she was America Bogle, living with her family in Walla Walla in the Washington Territory. The Bogles had eight children.

There is no obvious explanation for why America wasn't counted in the early censuses. However, it can't be ruled out that the family was secretive about her presence, as well as that of the other blacks known to be at the Waldo farm. The 1850 census failed to identify any of twelve people listed in the Daniel Waldo household by race, which was unusual. Neither did it record family relationships, although some can be guessed, including Joseph, Daniel's brother, who lived with Daniel in 1850. Daniel was then fifty-four; Joseph was forty-five.

TOM DAVIS

Under the headline "Tom Davis, slave," the *Salem Statesman* of December 26, 1930, reported the death of Thomas Davis at age ninety-two in Vancouver, Washington.[31] Davis said he was a slave brought to Oregon at age fifteen by Avarilla Waldo, the widow of John Waldo, one of the eight Waldo brothers. John, known as John B., died in 1849 in California, quite possibly while following the gold rush. He owned slaves in Missouri and had at least one slave, known as "Uncle Knee," with him in California.[32] According to an account in a Waldo family genealogy, Avarilla followed her late husband's instructions to return to Missouri and free his slaves.[33] But according to Thomas Davis' version in the newspaper, Avarilla didn't free all the slaves. Rather, she left for Oregon in 1853 with Davis, his sister, Susan, and their grandmother—the grandmother died en route. Avarilla and the Davis children resided first with the Daniel Waldo family at Waldo Hills near Salem. Avarilla later moved to Douglas County, taking Thomas Davis with her. Still later, she returned to Salem where she married The Reverend J. C. Moreland about 1864.

In the meantime, Davis learned that under Oregon law he couldn't legally be held as a slave, and left the family in 1863 to strike out on his own. He held various jobs, including a cook on a railroad dining car. He first appears in census records in 1880 at age thirty-three, listed as a servant in an East Salem household. Davis said his sister, Susan, died in Salem—she is not found in census records. Never married, Davis lived the final years of his life in a two-room house he built in Vancouver in 1907.

AME

Gravesite in Corvallis of a slave known only as Ame, brought to Oregon in 1847 from Missouri. (Photo by author)

A small gravestone at the Odd Fellow's Pioneer Cemetery in Corvallis bears the simple name "Ame." The only other words on the marker identify her as "A Slave of Mary and John Porter." No birth or death date is given. But quite a bit is known about Ame, who was also variously referred to as Aim and Annie, the latter in the 1850 census, where her age was given as thirty-four. She came to Oregon in 1847 as the slave of Johnson and Susan Mulkey, who emigrated from Johnson County, Missouri, with their large family.

Ame was born about 1816 in Kentucky. Her owner, Johnson Mulkey, was also from Kentucky where he owned slaves, and she may have been with the family from birth. According to Mulkey descendants, Johnson Mulkey freed his slaves before leaving Missouri, apparently including Ame. However, a Mulkey granddaughter, Maude Cauthorn Keady, said Ame suddenly appeared after four days on the Oregon Trail, and, "There was nothing to do at this late hour, but take her along."[34] She was said to have left behind her own children.

The Mulkeys settled in Benton County near Corvallis where Ame served the family for the remainder of her life. Keady said Ame avoided being seen. "If there was knock at the door, unless it was a close friend, Ame had disappeared from the room before the guest had entered."[35]

Ame is believed to have died about the year 1874. Her polished granite gravestone is alongside the graves of five members of the Porter family.

HANNAH GORMAN AND ELIZA J. GORMAN

The mother, Hannah, and daughter, Eliza, were brought to Oregon by Major John Thorpe—or Thorp, or Tharp—in 1844. Thorpe, who settled at Rickreall, was captain of a small wagon train of immigrants that preceded the Ford train. His daughter, Amanda, married Marcus Ford. It is thought that Hannah and Eliza were Thorpe's household slaves. The 1850 census identified both with the last name of Thorpe, at a time when they were living in the Thorpe household. By 1860, they had moved to Corvallis, and had the last name of Gorman.[36]

At some point, Hannah and Eliza apparently received their freedom, after which they began to accumulate real estate in downtown Corvallis. Eliza Gorman purchased two adjacent lots in Corvallis in 1857. The next year, Hannah purchased a single lot on the same block, and Eliza added a fourth lot.

The 1860 census listed them as living together in a home which was still standing in 2012. Their real estate was valued in 1860 at $1,200. Hannah was then fifty-two; Eliza was twenty-four. Hannah, or Hanna, was listed in the census records as a "wash woman" born in Tennessee, who could neither read nor write.

Hannah died in 1888. Eliza, listed as a seamstress, preceded her mother in death; she died in 1869.[37] An obituary for Eliza said that mother and daughter "seemed to live only for each other, and to make others happy." Of Eliza, it said, "Her intelligence, modesty, kind and sympathetic disposition, consistent Christian life, and uniform courteous behavior, has won the respect and confidence of the entire community." It said that the "large number of citizens" who attended her funeral "was the strongest proof of the high estimation in which she was held."[38]

ALICE AND GEORGE WASHINGTON

The 1860 U.S. Census listed a sixteen-year-old named Alice as a "slave" in the household of James Cochran in Harrisburg in Linn County.[39] Cochran, then seventy-three, evidently had no misgivings about giving the girl's true status. They were the only two people listed in the household. Beyond the census document, there is no further record of Alice.

Another James Cochran, or Cochrane, traveled to Oregon in 1850 with George Washington, a black he freed from slavery before making the trip. Cochran settled on a land claim near Centralia in present-day Washington. He later sold the land, or a major portion of it, to George Washington for $3,400.[40] George Washington should not be confused with George Washington Bush, who settled near Puget Sound. The land acquired by Washington was at the juncture of the Skookumchuck and Chehalis Rivers in Lewis County. He became prominent in his community and founded the city of Centralia in 1875.[41] He died in 1905 at age eighty-eight.

George Washington and his dog. Washington was a former slave, who came to the Oregon Territory with his former owner in 1850, established a farm and later founded Centralia, Washington. (Oregon Historical Society)

CORA COX

The 1860 census listed thirty-two year-old Cora Cox as a "slave" of Jefferson Huff, a Linn County rancher. Her daughter, Adeline, five months old, also was listed as a slave. Cora Cox, who was born in Virginia, was purchased in New Orleans in 1837 by Emeline Carey-Johnson. She was brought to Oregon in 1850 by Emeline and her then-husband Samuel Johnson. Emeline, who later married Jefferson Huff, deeded thirty-six acres of the family farm near Brownsville to Cora Cox in 1864 for "the consideration of faithful services rendered." Cora Cox married an African American named John Cox, also believed to have been a slave, with whom she had her daughter, Adeline.[42] John Cox was listed as a "farm laborer" in the Huff household.[43]

RACHEL BELDEN: "THE LAST SLAVE GIRL IN OREGON"

Rachel Belden, the slave brought to Oregon by Daniel Delaney in 1843, was listed in the 1860 census with two sons, described as mulattoes, and both with the surname Delaney. Rachel was just fourteen when she was purchased by Delaney in 1842 in Missouri for $1,000—or $550—versions differ.

Belden apparently received her freedom in 1864, a year before Delaney was murdered. She married a seventy-year-old widower, Nathan Brooks, in 1863. Brooks was an Illinois-born laborer living in Douglas County and had five children from a previous marriage. Rachel and Brooks had two additional children. Brooks died in 1874. The 1880 census listed Rachel as a housekeeper in Polk County, living with her three sons. She later bought a home on Miller Street in Salem. Belden died on October 12, 1910, and was buried next to her son, Noah, in Salem's City View Cemetery. The *Daily Capital Journal* wrote her obituary under the headline, "The Last Slave Girl in Oregon."[44]

⌣ ⌣

An unknown number of blacks brought to the Pacific Northwest between 1840 and 1860 were probably slaves in fact, if not so identified.[45] The 1850 census data reveals instances where an African American was the only black in the household in a situation where he or she may have been a slave. At least a few blacks and slaves in Oregon were not counted at all—or, in some instances counted, but not identified by race. The omissions may be the fault of slave owners, who did not want their slaves identified, or an attempt by white employers to protect African Americans from Oregon's exclusion laws.[46] But, whatever the reasons, such omissions suggest an undercount of African Americans, although there is no way of knowing how significant.

The historian Quintard Taylor has written that a slave's true status was frequently disguised with the pseudonym "servant." Among those African Americans listed as servants in census documents:[47]

Yamhill County: Miranda, age eighteen, born in Virginia, lived in the home of James P. Graves.

Marion County: Edward Ross, age eleven, born in Missouri, lived in the home of James Campbell and his five children.

Washington County, including a major portion of present-day Multnomah County: Eliza, age nine, born in Missouri, lived in a boarding house run by A. L. Davis.

Washington County: Jane Snowden, age thirty-five, lived with Andrew Skidmore, a merchant. Snowden, who was born in Virginia, later married Morris Thomas and returned to Missouri in 1852 to buy freedom for a son, William, a slave. She paid $500 and brought him to Portland, where he died at age fourteen in 1857.[47] Morris Thomas was one of the free blacks accused of violating Oregon's exclusion laws, but was allowed to remain.

Washington County: Henry, age thirty, born in Virginia, listed as a "steward" in the home of William W. Chapman, a lawyer from Virginia, and his wife and seven children. [48]

These were but a few. Several other blacks in Washington County were also identified as stewards.

·– ·–

Caroline Burch made mention in her family history of four blacks living with white families in Polk County. She didn't say they were slaves, but the context of her remarks suggested they were.

> *There was a negro girl, Tilly, with Mrs. Frances McDaniel. She lived on the south side of the Rickreall about two miles below here. Mr. Linville, who settled near Parker, had one negro woman. John Tharp, who settled near Independence, brought two Negro women.*[49]

Tharp is John Thorpe, and the "two Negro women" were Hannah and Eliza Gorman. The "negro woman" with Linville was probably Maria Scott.

There is also an advertised reference to one or more slaves belonging to a Corvallis barber, Samuel Harris. In an advertisement in a Corvallis newspaper on March 5, 1859, Harris announced that "owing to the intermeddling (sic) of northern abolitionists he has disposed of his entire interest in his *negro property*." The italics are in the ad. The "negro property" is not otherwise identified. It's notable that Harris blamed abolitionists for forcing him to give up his negro property rather than Oregon's new constitution, which banned slavery.[50]

·– ·–

There are apparently no recorded instances of beatings or other physical abuse of African American slaves by their owners. It doesn't mean there weren't beatings—it would have been unusual if there weren't. But Pauline Burch sought to portray Nathaniel Ford and other slaveholders as largely benevolent toward their slaves.

> *Many of the newcomers to the Oregon Territory had not grown up with the colored folk and their children and could not believe or understand the kindly feeling a good owner would have for his negroes.*[51]

But benevolence toward a slave was in the eye of the beholder. To say slaves were treated with "kindly feeling" overlooks entirely the psychological impact the denial of freedom has on another human being. Burch either didn't comprehend, or chose to ignore, the impact of forced servitude on an individual when he or she is denied an education, freedom of movement, choice of labor, and, all too often, spouses and children. There was the added insult of not even having a surname of one's own.

Burch also blamed abolitionists for the problems that beset her family over the slavery issue: "The abolitionists and others who had prejudice against the negro race began in 1850 and earlier to agitate against and harass the several pioneer families who had brought negroes."

An Army Slave

At least one Army officer—and probably others—brought a slave to the Oregon Territory. The following documents refer to a slave named Monimia Travers, freed by an officer at Fort Vancouver in 1851:

> *Mommia (sic) Travers, a black woman, aged about forty-five, bought by me from Isaac Burbayge (sic), in April 1849, I have this day given her freedom unconditionally, and she is in all respects free to go and do as may seem most to her advantage, without let or hindrance from me, my agents, heirs or assigns. Witness my hand and seal, at Vancouver, May 5th, 1851. Llewellyn Jones, Captain, U.S.A.*

Also:

> *The above named woman, Mommia, is an honest and perfectly conscientious woman and deserves kind and good treatment at the hands of every one. Llewellyn Jones, Captain, U.S.A., Recorded, July 29th, 1857.*[1]

It was not uncommon for an Army officer to hold a slave as a servant or personal assistant. Dred Scott, the subject of the Supreme Court's 1857 decision, had been a slave of John Emerson, a U.S. Army surgeon.

The 1850 U.S. Census for Clark County, then part of the Oregon Territory, listed Travers' first name as Monimia and gave her birthplace as Virginia. She lived with Captain Jones, his wife, and two daughters at the Columbia Barracks, adjacent to Fort Vancouver.[2] Jones was a recent West Point graduate from New York, assigned to the U.S. Army's Regiment of Mounted Riflemen.

He purchased Travers in St. Louis in April 1849 from Isaac Burbbayage, a well-known dealer in slaves.[3] This was just a month before Jones' unit of mounted riflemen departed on May 10, 1849, on a five-month, two thousand-mile march from Fort Leavenworth to Fort Vancouver. The cross-country march is chronicled in a book, *The March of the Mounted Riflemen.* Jones was one of four officers who brought families.

The mounted riflemen's march gained fame because it was the first military unit to travel the entire length of the Oregon Trail. As first envisioned, a unit of ten companies of sixty-four privates each was authorized by Congress in May 1846 to establish and secure military posts along the Oregon Trail to protect emigrant wagon trains.[4] However, once organized, the regiment was instead diverted to Mexico to fight in the Mexican-American War, during which it lost four officers and forty-five men in combat.[5]

At war's end, the regiment returned to its original mission of safeguarding the trail to Oregon. However, while Captain Jones and the other officers stayed with the original regiment, their veteran troops were released from service. According to Major Osborne Cross, the chief quartermaster, the replacement troops were undisciplined and poorly trained, "many of them foreigners who scarcely knew enough of the English language to understand an order given to them."[6] The unit was plagued by desertions of men lured to California by the discovery of gold. Seventy men either died or deserted during the trip.[7]

The expedition set out from Fort Leavenworth with about six hundred and forty mounted riflemen, plus thirty-one officers. Counting teamsters and other non-military personnel, there were as many as one thousand personnel. They took with them seven hundred horses, twelve hundred mules, five hundred cattle, and one hundred and seventy-one wagons. They staffed military posts at Fort Kearney, Fort Laramie, Fort The Dalles, and, temporarily, a post near the Hudson's Bay Company's Fort Hall known as Cantonment Loring. Jones was in charge of Company D, one of several companies that made the entire trip. A camp along the way was named Camp Frederica after his ten-year-old daughter.[8]

There was a second African American at the Columbia Barracks, nineteen-year-old Zacara Richardson, listed in the 1850 Census as a servant born in Pennsylvania. Richardson resided in quarters with eight military personnel, including Lieutenant Colonel Andrew Porter, the second in command. There is little in the historical record about Travers or Richardson. While the story of the riflemen's march has been extensively chronicled, with a mile-by-mile account of the trek and the many participating soldiers, they are not mentioned.[9]

The men in the unit were not always well received by local residents. Some were temporarily housed in Oregon City, where they occasionally behaved like an unruly mob. The book about their journey suggests considerable relief among the townspeople when the unit moved across the Columbia River in April 1850. "The people of Oregon City, to whom the Mounted Riflemen had been most obnoxious because of drunkenness and disorderly conduct, celebrated their departure by burning down the buildings they had occupied."[10]

Coincidentally, one of those traveling with the regiment was Matthew Deady, the future Oregon judge who would play an important role in Oregon's slavery debates. Deady was skilled as a blacksmith, and traded his skills for passage with the regiment.[11] During the march, Deady was credited with helping disclose a plot to kill a paymaster. The conspirators had evidently tried to recruit Deady to the plot, but he exposed them instead.[12] Possibly it was the same incident that resulted in a further promotion for Lieutenant Colonel Porter. According to Major Cross' account:

Companies G and B (sic) under Major Simonson . . . arrived at Fort Hall about two weeks ahead of the regiment, therefore their animals were rested. Major Simonson was relieved of the command of this post, arrested for some military dereliction, and Brevet-lieutenant-colonel Porter placed in command.[13]

The regiment was stationed at Fort Vancouver for two years. It was ordered in May 1851 to prepare for a new deployment in the American Southwest to confront the Comanche tribes then fighting white incursions into traditional tribal lands. The riflemen and their horses and equipment were transferred to the 1st Dragoons, a mounted U.S. Army unit, in California, while the officers returned to the Jefferson Barracks in Missouri for reassignment. Two companies of the 1st Dragoons would later fight in the Rogue River War against tribes in southern Oregon, losing as many as twenty-five men at the Battle of Hungry Hill in 1855.[14] The 1st Dragoons were re-designated as the 1st Cavalry Regiment, and, subsequently, became part of the 1st Cavalry Division based at Fort Hood.

⌐ ⌐

Captain Jones' decision to give Monimia Travers her freedom may have been less than the altruistic act it might at first seem. Quite possibly, with the return to Missouri and the pending reassignment, Jones decided he didn't any longer need his slave, who he evidently had bought expressly for Fort Vancouver.

In giving Travers her freedom, Jones may have wanted to be relieved of an obligation to look after her well-being, which he would have been legally compelled to do in Missouri. Slave laws in that state, dating to 1804, prohibited a slave owner from freeing slaves over the age of forty "to prevent the free negro becoming a burden to society."[15] The owner was held responsible for aging slaves and could not simply set them free to fend for themselves with nowhere to go, and no way to earn a living. Oregon had no such law, so there was nothing to prevent Jones from freeing Travers. It doesn't appear from the wording of Jones' documents that he had made any provision to care for Travers, and nothing has been found to indicate what happened to her.

For Travers, it was probably the first time she had been free to make her own decisions. But without resources and most likely illiterate, did she approach her future with dread and uncertainty? Or, did she quickly find employment in another household that provided her with income and security?

·~ ~·

The experience of some other former slaves in Oregon suggests the difficulty Travers might have faced in making a new life for herself in an atmosphere of hostility and disregard toward African Americans.

A former Mississippi-born slave, who called himself Julius Caesar, was found dead "on a pile of lumber" under a Portland dock in July 1906. He was identified as Caesar Taylor in the 1870 census when he was then nineteen-years-old and listed as a "servant" in the family of Benjamin Taylor, a Corvallis butcher. A sarcastic account of his life, written following his death, said, "Instead of aspiring to become the world's greatest monarch, the local Julius Caesar contented himself with a desire to drink up all the gin in Chinatown."[16]

Travis Johnson, a former Missouri slave, also ended up homeless. After thirty years of slavery, he was freed by his owner, Philip Glover, in exchange for driving a family wagon to Oregon in 1849. The Glover family took out a mile-square claim east of Salem. Glover and Johnson apparently had an understanding that Glover would support Johnson's return to Missouri to purchase his wife and children from a different owner. However, Johnson decided to remain in Oregon. He worked for a time as an ox driver and owned a horse. In later life, he became a "wanderer," traveling with a pack of dogs, and considered by some as "a disreputable tramp" and occasional drunk. Yet others welcomed him as a source of gossip.[17]

According to a family history by Glover's granddaughter, Mabel Glover Root, "Travis did not like freedom in the new country and he was ever returning to his old master, asking to split fence rails, 'grub' in the oak wood lot, and could scarcely be prevented from doing those things." As a result, some thought Johnson remained a slave. However, wrote Root, "such was not the case and only showed that Travis' devotion to grandfather was not understood." She also wrote of strong pro-slavery sympathies in the local Baptist church. Johnson's date of death is unknown.[18]

The Free State Letter

If all that was known of Judge Williams was the road he paved, leading away from slavery in Oregon, he might be seen as a heroic figure. And to some in his day, he was such a figure. However, the arguments he used would today earn him more condemnation than praise.

During the summer and autumn of 1857, "slavery overshadowed every other issue" in Oregon.[1] Pro-slavery forces believed their views were ascendant. One argument they used was that slavery would provide cheap labor for the farms and other needs of the developing region. Wrote historian Charles Carey:

> *Some pro-slavery democrats, confident of the approval and patronage of the Washington administration, would not be silenced . . . and they were far more numerous than those democrats of free-state proclivities who dared speak out. And, of the latter, some would say, 'I shall vote against slavery, but if it carries, I shall get me a nigger.' Add to these the fact of the great donations of land by the general government . . . and the scarcity and high price of labor, and we may not wonder at their [opponents of slavery] anxiety.[2]*

⸱⸍ ⸌⸱

Judge Matthew P. Deady was considered "the point man for slavery" in Oregon.[3] Deady, who sat with Williams on the Territorial Supreme Court, was originally from Maryland. He was remembered as an imposing figure, tall for his day at six-foot-two, and, in middle age, "inclined to portliness, which was fashionable among substantial people, with large protuberant eyes."[4] During the height of the slavery debate, Deady wrote to a friend, "If a citizen of Virginia can lawfully own a Negro (of which there is no doubt) then I a citizen of Oregon can lawfully obtain the same right of property in this Negro by either purchase or inheritance."[5]

Another prominent supporter of the right to own slaves was Joseph Lane, Oregon's first governor and later its territorial delegate to Congress. Lane was not an imposing figure physically—five-foot eight-inches tall, with dark hair, a high forehead, and a "long leathery face"—but he "was endowed with an ego sufficient for two men."[6] After Lincoln was elected president in 1860, Lane supported the right of southern slave states to secede from the Union rather than bow to the growing anti-slavery dominance of northern states. In later years, Lane would be described by the future president Andrew Johnson as "more Southern than the South itself."[7]

Williams, Lane, and Deady were all prominent members of the Democratic Party, which dominated Oregon politics until the outbreak of the Civil War. While the party took no official position on slavery, many of the most recognizable names in the party voiced pro-slavery views. Among them was the soon-to-be first statehood governor, John Whiteaker, who "championed the introduction of slavery on the ground that to do otherwise would be to invite race equality."[8] The smaller political parties, the Whigs and the emerging new Republican Party, were firmly opposed to slavery.

Judge Williams stepped into the middle of the debate in a letter that came to be known as the "Free State Letter" in which he argued forcefully that slavery would be wrong for Oregon. A remarkable document at the time, it appeared in the July 28, 1857, *Oregon Statesman*, three weeks before the convening of Oregon's Constitutional Convention. Rather than challenge slavery on moral or ethical grounds, however, Williams attacked it as wrong for Oregon's young economy—a dollars and cents argument. He had nothing good to say about blacks, nor did he condemn their treatment as slaves. He seemed even to defend slavery in the South as an economic necessity for Southern states.

As with his ruling in the Holmes vs. Ford case, Williams' Free State Letter hasn't received the attention it has deserved in Oregon history. Partly this is because Williams' approach to the issue makes people uncomfortable. His arguments are repugnant, insulting, and highly racist to most modern-day readers. However, it would be hard to overstate the letter's importance in helping to frame the intense debate over slavery on the eve of the Constitutional Convention. At nearly eight thousand words, the letter took up the entire front page of the *Statesman*. Williams first addressed the divisions arising from the slavery issue.

Much has been said for slavery. Candidates for office have become its champions on the stump—documents have been circulated—a paper has been set up for its advocacy. These things invite, in fact, force discussion. Men are rapidly perhaps inconsiderately, taking sides, and determining as to their votes upon this question. Differing reluctantly from many friends for whose opinions I have respect, I am constrained to think that Oregon had better become a non-slave-holding state.[9]

Williams said he did not object to slavery as such, and, "I do not reproach the slaveholders of the South for holding slaves." They were as "high-minded, honorable, and humane a class of men as can be found in the world." The best argument for slavery in Oregon, he said, was to help relieve a shortage of labor, especially on farms. But that argument was shortsighted because slaves would actually be a burden to their owners. Williams said the reason "outweighing all others" to reject slavery is that so many Oregonians were opposed. "I say that slavery can no more stand as a useful institution with one half of public opinion arrayed against it than a house can stand with one corner stone."

Immigration from other countries would be discouraged. "Slavery has a terror in its very name to foreign immigration. . . . Establish slavery here, and the effect will be as it has elsewhere. You will turn aside that tide of free white labor which has poured itself like a fertilizing flood across the great States of Ohio, Indiana and Illinois, and is now murmuring up the eastern slope of the Rocky Mountains."

Continuing with the argument that slavery would result in a far less productive labor force, Williams said slaves "are an ignorant and degraded class of beings" and if white workers were brought into regular contact with them, "the white men will go down and the negroes go up, till they come to resemble each other in the habits, tastes and actions of their lives." After directing insult after insult toward blacks in the course of his anti-slavery arguments, Williams closed his letter with an appeal to the white community.

I know what siren song self-love sings for slavery; how pleasant it seems in prospect to have a slave to till our ground, to wait upon us while we wake, and fan us when we sleep. But are these the ideas to possess men whose business it is to lay the foundation of a State? History, philosophy, and posterity plead with us not to be wholly absorbed in the present but to learn from the past and look to the future, and if we hear and obey this appeal, the lapse of twenty-five or fifty years which is as nothing in the life of a State, will find Oregon teeming with a people, intelligent, prosperous and happy, and every man a free man.

Years later, in an address to the Oregon Legislative Assembly on the fiftieth anniversary of statehood in February 1909, Williams would say he intended in his letter to emphasize "with all the arguments at my command, the inexpediency of establishing slavery in Oregon." He said he spoke out because few other Democrats would.

Whether Oregon should be a free or slave state had now become the paramount issue in our local politics. . . . Many of the most influential Democrats, with General Lane their head, were active for slavery and there was little or nothing said or done among the Democrats on the other side of the question.[10]

On the same day that Williams' letter appeared in the *Statesman,* Judge Deady wrote a four-page letter to a friend, Benjamin Simpson, in which he made an impassioned defense of the right to hold slaves in Oregon and elsewhere. "There is no middle ground between the position represented by the so-called abolitionists and pro-slavery men," he wrote. He didn't mention Williams' letter, but it would not be surprising if he was writing in response, as he took issue with the claim that slavery wouldn't work in Oregon.

I believe and can show that Negro labor will pay better in Oregon than in any state in the Union simply because labor of any kind is more valuable here than in any of the states. Yet if it would not pay . . . it would not affect the question of the individual right pro or con because the question of profit and loss is for each man to determine for himself.[11]

Williams believed he paid a price for his letter. He said his outspoken opposition to slavery derailed his hopes of becoming one of Oregon's first senators after statehood: "With this address that chance vanished like the picture of a morning dream. I was 'unsound' on the slavery question."[12]

·-· ·-·

It was significant that Williams directed his letter to the *Statesman,* because its editor, Asahel Bush, was one of the most powerful voices in the Democratic Party and the acknowledged leader of the so-called "Salem Clique," which for years dictated party policy and picked its candidates. Other key members of the clique included James Nesmith, Reuben Boise, B. F. Harding, and LaFayette Grover. The Massachusetts-born Bush has been described as "a cold, calculating, relentless" editor and political opportunist, who used the *Statesman*'s news columns to help dominate Oregon politics.[13] But Bush was also credited with helping give Oregon "efficient and responsible government."[14] His newspaper served as the official organ of Oregon's Democratic Party.

Bush was twenty-six when he was recruited to Oregon from a small newspaper in Westfield, Massachusetts, by Samuel Thurston, Oregon's first territorial delegate to Congress. Thurston, who also imported the newspaper's presses, wanted to establish a newspaper to support both the new Democratic Party in Oregon and his own political ambitions.[15] But he never saw his newspaper. While returning home from the nation's capital, anticipating a hero's welcome for helping engineer enactment of the Donation Land Act, he fell ill with fever and died aboard a ship off the coast of Mexico in April 1851.[16] He was just thirty-six. Lane succeeded him as territorial delegate.

Thurston's death freed Bush to pursue his own interests. And he did. Bush cultivated alliances with men who could be useful to him, including Lane, although that relationship would later badly sour. Within a short period of time, Bush became "the foremost political kingmaker in the Territory."[17]

Bush remained largely silent on the subject of slavery, in part because he didn't appear to have strong feelings on the subject, but also to avoid taking sides between the pro- and anti-slavery factions within the party. The *Oregonian* in Portland, under its Whig editor, Thomas Dryer, was strongly opposed to slavery. But several other newspapers were sympathetic, including a new publication in Corvallis called the *Occidental Messenger*, established for the sole purpose of pushing a pro-slavery agenda. Timothy Davenport, an abolitionist who helped organize the Republican Party, said opponents of slavery found Bush's position on slavery suspect. "The *Statesman* was intensely feared and hated by them."[18] But whatever Bush's personal views, he did give Williams important access to the *Statesman*'s front page.[19]

⁓

Williams' negative comments about blacks seemed directed at the slave culture—slaves and freed slaves—rather than at African Americans per se. He did appear to understand the impact of slavery on the human psyche when he said, "Negro slaves it must be admitted, are an ignorant and degraded class of beings." To the extent slaves were ignorant, it was because they were denied an education, and to the extent they were degraded, it was because they were denied freedom and family, and forced to work under the lash.

But even considering that Williams' comments were aimed at the institution of slavery, it still is puzzling that he seemed to overlook his experience four years earlier with the former slave, Robin Holmes, who had demonstrated success in his new freedom as a mill worker and nurseryman. Despite Holmes' lack of education, he had prevailed in a complicated court case in which

Williams recognized in his opinion that Holmes had shown himself to be neither ignorant nor degraded.

Reuben Shipley, the newly freed slave in Benton County, was another example of someone who, freed from bondage, would achieve success as a farmer and make a major contribution to his community. Louis Southworth was yet another. Perhaps Williams chose to ignore black success stories because he wanted to keep his focus on the one issue that would be persuasive: the adverse economic impact slavery would have in Oregon.

Walter Carleton Woodward, writing in 1910, quoted Williams as telling him that while he had always opposed slavery for reasons of morality, "to have hinted that side of the question would have roused opposition to me as a 'd------d abolitionist' and Black Republican, and my letter would have gone for naught."[20] That said, however, it still fails to justify or adequately explain the ugliness of his criticisms of African Americans.

⁓

Anti-slavery Whigs and Republicans gave Williams' letter the name by which it became known, the "Free State Letter," while pro-slavery Democrats labeled it Williams' "Infamous Letter." Whatever else might be said about the letter, its publication proved to be a pivotal moment for the slavery debate in Oregon. According to Woodward, "As pro-slavery sentiment had up to this time been steadily rising, from the publication of the Free State Letter on to the election in November, it seemed steadily to recede."[21]

Not lost in Williams' long letter was his flat declaration that the general public opposed slavery in Oregon, even if leaders of the Democratic Party couldn't make up their own collective mind. The controversy would roil the party for the rest of the decade and, as the Civil War loomed, tear it apart.

Let Voters Decide

Oregon voters were ambivalent about statehood. On four occasions in the 1850s, they rejected proposals to write a state constitution. Likewise, Joseph Lane, as Oregon's territorial delegate to Congress, had been unsuccessful in an effort in 1856 to gain congressional approval for statehood.

The Democratic Party and the *Oregon Statesman* supported statehood, but they faced strong opposition from *Oregonian* editor Thomas Dryer, who argued statehood not only would not benefit the territory, but would harm it economically. He said whereas the federal government paid governmental expenses for the territory, the people of Oregon would pay these under statehood, imposing a heavy tax burden they could ill afford.[1] Congress, meanwhile, declined to act on Lane's statehood bill, in part because of doubts over which side Oregon would take in the intensifying national debate over slavery. Whig Party members of Congress were apprehensive that because Oregon "had persistently sent a Democrat as a delegate to Congress, [it] should array itself on the side of slavery in both House and Senate."[2]

Wilson Blain, a Presbyterian missionary who served in the first territorial legislature with Nathaniel Ford in 1849, estimated that as much as one-third of Oregon's population supported slavery. In a letter to the *Oregon Argus*, Blain warned of political maneuvering intended to make Oregon a slave state: "Circumstances might arise through which the dominant party of the Territory by a 'fusion' with the friends of slavery might secure them a complete victory."[3]

In 1856, Whigs and the *Oregonian* had a change of heart about statehood, in large part because of uncertainty over the intentions of the incoming president, James Buchanan. They feared Buchanan, president from 1857 to 1861, might somehow force slavery on the territories in the wake of the Kansas-Nebraska Act of 1854. The act, maneuvered through Congress by Senator Douglas, created the new territories of Nebraska and Kansas, with each to determine its own policy toward slavery—an application of popular sovereignty. In a major blow to the anti-slavery North—and a later blow to Douglas' presidential aspirations—the act repealed the Missouri Compromise of 1820, which for more than thirty years had fixed the boundaries for the spread of slavery to new territories. Douglas justified the decision to shelve the Missouri Compromise by arguing, disingenuously, that the Compromise of 1850, which Douglas also helped write, had superseded the Missouri Compromise. The 1850 accord had established the Utah and New Mexico territories, parts of which were north of the boundary in the Missouri Compromise, and allowed them to decide on slavery for themselves.

Douglas' initial strategy behind the Kansas-Nebraska bill was to facilitate development of a transcontinental railroad. But the railroad was overshadowed by the slavery issue, and failed to win approval. After enactment of the Kansas-Nebraska bill, Nebraska became a free territory. Kansas, on the other hand, was torn by violence between pro- and anti-slavery factions. There were other consequences of the bill, none of them favorable to the nation's unity. Douglas lost much of his earlier northern support, while the concept of popular sovereignty, which he championed, would henceforth be tarred by a "fatal proslavery taint."[4] The once cohesive Democratic Party, already divided between anti- and pro-slavery factions, would be further fragmented by rivalry between Douglas and President Buchanan. And the controversy over the bill gave rise to a new Republican Party, succeeding the Whigs, who were in decline.

·⁔·

While much of the nation focused on the implications of the Kansas-Nebraska Act for the spread of slavery, many in Oregon were drawn to what they hoped would be more self-government. Settlers had bemoaned the loss of self-government in the years since Oregon gained territorial status in 1848. Until then, they were accustomed to, and comfortable with, making their own decisions. As emigrants, they had made the rules by which they lived and worked; they established a provisional government suitable to their own needs and picked their own leaders. With territorial status, however, appointments and decisions were made in far-off Washington, D.C., by officials unfamiliar with Oregon's needs. The popular sovereignty in the Kansas-Nebraska Act was limited in scope, applying solely to decisions on slavery, but many in Oregon saw it as a potential breakthrough toward restoring self-government.[5]

But there were also those in Oregon who welcomed what they viewed as an opening to slavery. One of these was Delazon Smith—detractors called him "Delusion" Smith—a slavery-leaning member of the Oregon Territorial Legislature. He argued during the 1854-1855 legislative session that the Kansas-Nebraska Act nullified the anti-slavery provisions in Oregon's organic act. At Smith's urging, the House passed a joint resolution welcoming the provisions in the act that prohibited "the interference of Congress in the domestic affairs of the States, and which established its inability to legislate slavery into or out of the organized Territories of the nation." The resolution also declared the legislature "has no sympathy for, or confidence in, the many-headed fanaticism [to abolish slavery] of the north and east."[6]

Asa Lovejoy would later argue during debate over the exclusion bill in the 1856-1857 legislature that although he didn't think slavery would benefit Oregon, the Kansas-Nebraska Act had "destroyed" the anti-slavery clause in Oregon's voter-approved organic act. He declared on the floor of the House that "I believe that masters have a right to bring their negroes into Oregon and hold them as slaves, today."[7]

The next blow to African Americans and the anti-slavery movement came in the Supreme Court's 1857 Dred Scott decision, which denied citizenship to African Americans, both slave and free, and held that Congress lacked the authority to ban slavery in the territories.[8] Dred Scott was a slave taken from Missouri into Illinois by John Emerson, a U.S. army surgeon, in 1834, and later to the free Wisconsin Territory. After being returned to Missouri as a slave, with a new owner, he filed suit claiming he had gained his freedom by residing in jurisdictions where slavery was prohibited. The majority opinion, written by Chief Justice Roger Taney, held that Scott remained a slave and, moreover, even if he were free, could not be a citizen. He said a person had to be born a citizen, or naturalized, neither of which could occur for a slave or free black. Taney said African Americans:

> *are not included, and were not intended to be included, under the word "citizens" in the Constitution, and can therefore claim none of the rights and privileges which that instrument provides for and secures to citizens of the United States. On the contrary, they were at that time considered as a subordinate and inferior class of beings who had been subjugated by the dominant race, and, whether emancipated or not, yet remained subject to their authority, and had no rights or privileges but such as those who held the power and the Government might choose to grant them.*[9]

Taney also ruled that the Missouri Compromise was unconstitutional as a violation of due process because a slave owner had the same right to safely take slaves into a territory as he would any other property.[10] Wrote Taney: "The Constitution of the United States recognizes slaves as property, and pledges the Federal Government to protect it. And Congress cannot exercise any more authority over property of that description than it may constitutionally exercise over property of any other kind." In short, slavery was protected in the territories from congressional interference.

The court's six to three ruling—five of the six justices were from the South— proved "a disaster for the American people," in the words of the late historian David M. Potter.[11] Southern slave interests were encouraged by a ruling in their favor, while northern abolitionists were outraged. A national compromise on slavery was even further out of reach.[12]

The ruling marked another setback for Douglas' already badly bruised concept of popular sovereignty. If Congress lacked authority to restrict slavery in the territories, how could it authorize the territories to act on their own? The Buchanan administration's interpretation of popular sovereignty was that the territories could decide on slavery only when applying for admission as a state. Douglas, however, refused to concede that the court's decision was everything it seemed. He fashioned a new argument to the effect that even though a slave owner might theoretically bring his slaves into a territory, slavery could nonetheless not survive unless the territories took action to sustain and regulate it. "Slavery cannot exist a day in the midst of an unfriendly people with unfriendly laws," Douglas said.[13]

Douglas and President Buchanan parted ways politically over the fallout from the Kansas-Nebraska Act. The Pennsylvania-born Buchanan was not considered pro-slavery, although he drew most of his support from the South, and was intent on keeping that support. In a strategy to end the conflict in Kansas, he backed a flawed pro-slavery constitution—called the Lecompton Constitution—and urged Congress to admit Kansas as a slave state. "Kansas," he said, "was as much a slave state as Georgia or South Carolina."[14] But Douglas argued the Lecompton Constitution was invalid and violated the concept of popular sovereignty. He led the congressional campaign to derail it, much to the chagrin of Buchanan. Although Douglas had been seen as something of a hero in the South because of his leadership on the Kansas-Nebraska Act, he now became an adversary. Buchanan and party leaders tried to engineer his defeat in his 1858 campaign for reelection to the Senate from Illinois.[15] However, Douglas narrowly won reelection over Abraham Lincoln.

Popular sovereignty had gone through a metamorphosis in the space of a few years. Viewed by anti-slavery advocates in 1854 as a strategy to encourage slavery in the territories, it was seen by pro-slavery advocates in 1858 as a strategy to defeat slavery in the territories.[16]

⸱⸱⸱

One influential Oregonian who took a more jaundiced view of the Kansas-Nebraska Act—and popular sovereignty—was Thomas Dryer, editor of the *Oregonian*. Dryer warned in an editorial on November 1, 1856, that Kansas might soon be admitted as a slave state—although that didn't happen—and Oregon could be next. He said the national Democratic Party "has been, is now, and still continues to be the handmaid for the extension of slavery over free territory." He concluded, "If we are to have the institution of slavery fastened upon us here, we desire the people resident in Oregon to do it, and not the will and power of a few politicians in Washington city (sic)."[17]

Dryer wasn't alone in his fears. The constitutional historian, Charles Carey, wrote of "a peculiar combination of circumstances . . . which made it seem not only possible, but even highly probable, that slavery would be imposed upon the territory."[18] When statehood appeared on the Oregon ballot at the next election in June 1857, it was overwhelmingly approved by a vote of 7,617 to 1,679. A convention to write a constitution was scheduled in Salem for August 17, 1857, with the constitution to be submitted to voters the following November. According to Carey, the weeks and months between June and November 1857 "were filled with political agitation in which slavery overshadowed every other issue."[19]

Sixty delegates to the Constitutional Convention were chosen at the June election. All were white males, the only people entitled to vote. Forty-two were Democrats. One, John McBride, was a Republican. The others were unaffiliated with a major party.[20] Democrats Deady, Williams, Olney, and Boise were among the delegates. So were Jesse Applegate, an independent, and Dryer, a Whig.

·–· –·

Nathaniel Ford might well have been among the delegates, had he not angered Asahel Bush and other party leaders. While serving in the territorial legislature in January 1857, Ford joined with eleven other dissident party members, known as anti-Democrats, to organize opposition to the iron-fisted rule of the Salem Clique, which nevertheless continued to dominate the party. Oregon Democrats saw themselves as part of the national Democratic Party, but were differentiated by Oregon's focus on landholding and agriculture rather than commerce. One historian wrote: "Oregon Democrats were extremely wary, if not downright suspicious, of the liberal, market-oriented, economic individualism identified with Jacksonian Democracy elsewhere."[21]

The clique-led Oregon Democrats decided on April 13, 1857, that they should neither debate slavery at the upcoming Constitutional Convention, nor consider pro- or anti-slavery clauses. Instead, they favored submitting the slavery issue to voters in November, along with the constitution itself. With Democrats controlling the convention, their view was expected to prevail.

The hands-off approach to slavery was in keeping with the concept of popular sovereignty—let the people decide. However, it also enabled party leaders to avoid a split in the party's already fractious ranks over the issue of slavery. According to the early twentieth century historian Walter Carleton Woodward, "The one consuming desire of the regular or machine Democrats was to maintain the organization intact."[22] The attempt to promote unity was temporarily successful. Dryer wrote that the dissident Democrats "who had opposed the machine organization in the late election, now did penance and joined the clique forces in caucus."[23]

The Constitutional Convention convened in the Marion County Courthouse in Salem on August 17, 1857.[24] The courthouse was a wood-frame building, sixty-eight by forty feet, built in 1854 in the center of a block facing High Street between State and Court streets. Its sole distinctive feature was four Doric columns at the High Street entrance. Next door, on the southeast corner was the county jail.[25]

The delegates elected Judge Deady convention president, a choice alarming to anti-slavery members. Dryer reported that "no delegate opposed to the Salem Clique had been placed at the head of a committee and (he) declared that every committee had a pro-slavery majority."[26]

Judge Williams was named chairman of the judicial committee, where he anticipated the slavery issue would be assigned. It wasn't.

The Great Slavery Non-Debate

Jesse Applegate, the independent anti-slavery delegate from what was then Umpqua County, introduced a resolution on August 18, 1857, to prohibit any discussion of slavery during the Constitutional Convention. He introduced it on the second day, while the convention was still getting organized. His resolution declared:

> [T]he discussion of the subject of slavery by this body is out of place
> and uncalled for, and only calculated to engender bitter feelings among
> the members of the body, destroy its harmony, retard its business and
> unnecessarily prolong its session.[1]

Applegate's motive was to prevent a pro-slavery clause from slipping through the convention. He "feared a trick would be played, as in Kansas, and slavery be forced upon the people of Oregon without their consent," wrote Timothy Davenport. Also troubling to Applegate, and others as well, was the sight of Deady, "the most influential pro-slavery man in the Territory," at the head of the convention, with Democratic partisans in the majority.[2]

Applegate had abhorred the slave culture in Missouri, and once declared "whoever is against the extension of slavery is of my party; whoever is for it is against me. My platform has but one single plank."[3] Anti-slavery delegates didn't want a clause prohibiting slavery to emerge from the convention either. They were concerned that such a clause "would have turned every pro-slavery voter into an opponent of the Constitution as a whole [and] insured (sic) its defeat at the polls and kept a free state out of the union."[4]

⌐ ⌐

Applegate's resolution was at once debated, giving a strong flavor of the delegates' attitudes toward slavery itself. So the subject Applegate didn't want discussed, was, in fact, discussed, albeit obliquely. The excerpts below are taken from a convention transcript:[5]

James K. Kelly, Clackamas County, in opposition to the resolution:
. . . it may, if adopted, prohibit us from discussing the mode in which the
question shall be submitted to the people . . .

Applegate: . . . nothing is mentioned as to the mode of submitting the
question . . .

Delazon Smith, Linn County, in opposition: . . . I would as soon sever
my right hand as to vote for a constitution that would either inhibit or
adopt slavery here . . . But I do not want to put a padlock upon my lips
or upon the lips of any other gentleman. . . . The slavery question is
the question in Oregon now. We may resolve and re-resolve upon this
question, and yet every man in the country will form his opinion.

Thomas J. Dryer, Multnomah and Washington Counties, in opposition:
. . . the people sent us up here to discuss the question and to submit it
to them for final decision . . . the question of slavery is the all-important
question now agitating the public mind. . . .

Judge George H. Williams, Marion County, in qualified support: .
. . would favor the principle of the resolutions if not the resolutions
themselves . . .

David Logan, Multnomah County, in opposition: . . . some counties
have elected delegates here with the express understanding they shall go
for a free state constitution at all events. The county of Washington sent
their whole delegation here upon that understanding, and Yamhill also,
and other counties, perhaps. Would it not be unfair to the counties of
Washington and Yamhill to say by our action that their delegates shall
remain silent upon this floor . . . ?

Erasmus D. Shattuck, Washington County, in opposition: . . . it should
be known to our children whether they live under a free or slave state
constitution. . . . But if the question must be debated, then I go for a free
state, and I wish that to be understood. . . .

Stephen F. Chadwick, Douglas County, in support: . . . it was the wish of the people that they be left to discuss this question at the polls. . . . As to the manner of its submission, this convention can decide that. But as to the merits of the question, the convention has no right to discuss it. . . .

At this point, the convention transcript leaves off with a notation by the convention reporter that he lacked the time to "write out all the speeches," but might return to them later "as we find the time."

However, both the *Oregonian* and the *Oregon Statesman* carried additional comments, some of which were heated.[6] One quote, attributed by the *Statesman* to Delazon Smith, linked the question of excluding blacks to the slavery question.

Smith: Hundreds in the country were for a free state if free negroes were kept out of the state; but if we were to have negroes at all, let them be slaves.

Dryer: . . . He wanted every man to show his hand. General Lane, the great bellwether of the democratic party, had dodged. He did not dare to say to the South that he was opposed to slavery, and he did not dare say to the North that he was in favor of it, and here, when interrogated, he had refused to tell the people where he did stand. . .

Cyrus Olney, Clatsop County, in opposition: . . . The adoption of the resolution would make it out of order to offer any provision looking to a settlement of the slavery question directly in the constitution . . .

Applegate: . . . thought Mr. Olney's positions were contradictory. He had thought the discussion of the slavery question here productive of harm, and had sought to cut it off by this resolution . . .

A. L. Lovejoy, Clackamas County, in opposition: . . . You can't keep this negro question out; it will come up in some shape, and the convention has got to meet it. . . .

Williams, now in support: . . . Open this question, and he believed the session would be swallowed up by it. . . . He said opposition to this resolution was based upon some other motives than the professed ones; it was founded upon party considerations.

William H. Watkins, Josephine County: . . . called Mr. Williams to order [regarding his] . . . questioning the motives of the members. The president [Deady] overruled the motion on the ground that no individual was named.

Williams: . . . said that he had not named the gentleman [Mr. Watkins], but if the coat he had prepared fitted him, he was at liberty to put it on, as he had done . . .

Applegate's resolution was eventually tabled. However, slavery from that point on shadowed nearly every issue to come before the convention, although the question itself was never directly debated.

During a discussion the following day, on August 19, about a resolution to limit speeches to forty minutes, Charles Meigs of Wasco County was opposed, still citing a hoped-for debate over the slavery issue.

> *Meigs: . . . [The public] may reasonably expect that a debate shall be had upon the slavery question . . . the proposition to introduce slavery into this country would require someone like himself more than forty minutes to address . . .* [7]
>
> *Dryer, opposed to limiting debate: The effects and the results of the deliberations of this convention will tell upon the future generations who inhabit this goodly land of ours . . . if there is an element, a single element, that will tell on its weal or woe, it is the very question which we debated here yesterday afternoon—this question [of] slavery. . . . It is the destroying element, the evil principle, the besetting sin of the body politic of the United States, and when a proposition is made to introduce it into our midst, shall we pass it lightly by? God forbid. . . .*
>
> *Williams: I will oppose in this body the discussion of the slavery question upon its abstract merits. . . . I am not afraid to answer for that position to the people of Oregon.* [8]

The forty-minute rule was imposed.

·~·

Controversy arose over whether to assign to Williams' judicial committee, or to a special committee, the questions of when and how to submit the constitution and accompanying slavery and black exclusion clauses to the voters. These questions were ambiguously referred to as "the schedule." Party line Democrats, the pro-slavery delegates among them, distrusted Williams because of his Free State Letter.

Logan, regarded as an anti-slavery delegate, made a motion to assign the schedule to Williams' judicial committee.

> *Smith, favoring the judicial committee: This schedule is a matter of the first importance; so far as absolute accuracy is concerned more important than any other portion of the constitution . . . because the chairman of that committee [Williams] has frankly stated the facts in relation to the matter, I conceive no reason why the house should not avail itself of the service of that committee.* [9]

Logan's motion was defeated. Olney moved to amend Logan's original motion by excluding "the subjects of slavery and the apportionment of representatives in the first state legislature" from the issues assigned to Williams' judicial committee.

> *Kelly, favoring special committee: . . . if the gentlemen from Marion (Mr. Grover) wishes to have them referred to a special committee of nine, I will vote for it . . .*

At this point, Williams gives up, but not without a parting shot at the pro-slavery delegates.

> *Williams: . . . suspicions have been excited as though somebody had come here to steal something . . . to avoid any feeling of jealousy or suspicion, I think it would be advisable to refer all this matter to a select committee.*[10]
>
> *P. B. Marple, Coos County, favoring judicial committee: . . . we expect to refer two current propositions in one form or the other to the people. I mean the subject of slavery. And that schedule must remain as part and parcel of the constitution. For this reason, I conceive it highly improper that it should be referred to special committees. . . .*
>
> *Olney, favoring special committee: . . . if the resolution of the gentlemen from Multnomah (Mr. Logan), as amended, should prevail, it would leave the subject of slavery and the subject of the apportionment yet to be referred or otherwise disposed of . . .*
>
> *President Deady, Douglas County, calling the vote: The question will be upon striking out all of the original motion and substituting a select committee of nine.*

A special nine-member committee was named to write the slavery and exclusion measures to be put before the voters. Members included LaFayette Grover as chairman, Delazon Smith, and Reuben Boise. All nine were Democrats and most were said to be pro-slavery.[11] Williams was not included.

⋅⌒⋅

Race surfaced in the discussion of nearly every issue, no matter how mundane. The debate was frequently absurd, and might be considered comical—were the subject not so serious.

On August 25, a provision on voting was introduced to the convention declaring "all elections shall be free and equal," but limiting voting to "every white male citizen" twenty-one years or older. A follow-up discussion dealt

Matthew Deady, chairman of Oregon's 1857 Constitutional Convention, described by an historian as "the point man for slavery in the territory." After the Civil war broke out, he supported the Union and was a distinguished U.S. District Court judge in Portland for many years. (Oregon Historical Society)

with limiting military service to "free" whites. Dryer suggested striking the word "free," saying all white men in Oregon should be free. This ignited protracted debate.

John Kelsay, Benton County, supporting "free" white: It is well known to a large majority of this convention that there will be a constitution submitted to the people having a clause establishing slavery and one making Oregon a free state.[12]

Dryer, interrupting: It is not decided yet.

Kelsay: It is not decided but is expected to be. There is a general move among a good many farmers on the side of slavery. And in the event that slavery should be admitted here, upon that contingency happening, this word is necessary. Every one who is from a slave state knows that there are slaves there as white as any man in this house. . . . They will be introduced in Oregon as sure as slavery be brought here. . . .

Dryer: The gentleman . . . [seems to be saying] he would consider himself disgraced by being put upon an equality with a slave in the battlefield. That reason will not apply here . . . it is not necessary to specify that they shall be free able-bodied white citizens in Oregon, for there are no able-bodied white citizens in Oregon but what are free men, and I have no fear there ever will be . . .

Kelsay: That is the idea, I am in favor of closing the door against the slaves [in the military]; I care not if they are as white as the driven snow. There are but few white slaves that I have seen; but I have seen a few in Kentucky and Missouri. I do not intend to be led into the discussion of the question of slavery, but I intend to stand by what I conceive to be right and proper in the military. . . .

Olney: The principle ought to be settled by this convention that none but free white persons can be citizens, and we ought not to adopt a word that would implicitly admit that other than white persons may be citizens.

The amendment to strike the word "free" passed.

ᵕᴗᴗ

On August 29, Applegate introduced a new resolution, stipulating the question of slavery should be decided by "a direct vote of the people" and should not be debated at the convention. At Williams' urging, the resolution was tabled. Applegate was soon to walk out of the convention in disgust over the proceedings and would not return; he objected to his measures being tabled because it allowed the delegates to avoid "explicitly saying they wouldn't debate slavery."[13]

On September 3, Luther Elkins of Linn County offered the following resolution: "Resolved, that a clause be inserted in the Constitution to prevent free negroes and mulattos from coming into or settling in this state." Williams favored the resolution, "but thought it was unnecessary to consider the matter now." He said it was "understood" it would be included in the measure sent to voters. Elkins said his object in introducing the resolution was to bring the subject before the convention, but the matter was tabled once again.[14]

On September 10, in a discussion of voting rights, Judge Deady questioned the meaning of the word "free" as used in proposed wording that "All elections shall be free and equal."

Delazon Smith replied, "It did not mean Chinese or niggers. He thought the term sufficiently explicit."[15] Section 6 of a proposed bill of rights included a provision that: "No negro or mulatto shall have the right of suffrage." Grover moved to also deny the vote to Chinese, and this was approved.[16]

A series of racially motivated actions were taken in a discussion of the bill of rights. If the debate was ridiculous before, it became even more so. Quoting from the newspaper accounts:

Deady: . . . moved to . . . insert "No person, other than those of the white race, shall have the right of suffrage."
Logan: moved "free white . . ."
Dryer: opposed "free . . ."
William H. Farrar, Multnomah County: . . . it was uncertain who were free . . . Irishmen were not free at home. They lived under the worst slavery in the world.

Logan: . . . this would admit quarter-blood negroes—they had a predominance of white blood, and would be entitled to vote under Mr. Deady's amendment.

Deady: . . . the word white was well understood. But he would move to make it "pure white."

Dryer: . . . it was hard to determine who was pure white. There was his friend Kelsay; he was not as white as his friend Burch, and Mr. Waymire's nose was not as sharp as his.

Kelsay: . . . he was for free white; he would risk it.

William W. Bristow, Lane County: . . . moved to insert "Simon" before pure (Laughter).

Watkins: . . . opposed to "pure white"—it would exclude two men of doubtful white color in his county, who had voted for his opponent.

On September 11, John McBride of Yamhill County, the only Republican delegate and an opponent of slavery, sought to bring the slavery issue to the convention floor by proposing a new section for the bill of rights to say:

There shall be neither slavery nor involuntary servitude within the state, otherwise than for the punishment of crimes, whereof the party shall have been duly convicted.[17]

Although the wording was nearly identical to the anti-slavery provision in the Organic Laws of Oregon, endorsed by Congress, and approved by voters, it received scant convention support. Farrar of Multnomah County immediately called for a vote, cutting off debate. McBride's amendment was defeated by a vote of forty to ten. Dryer was one of the few voting with McBride. Among the no votes were judges Williams and Deady. By this time, Applegate had walked out of the convention.

During a discussion of schools, Logan moved to insert "white" before "children" who should attend public schools. The official record quoted him as saying: "He could wring in [bring in?] a nigger or an Indian under the provisos as it stood." His motion was adopted.

Bristow moved to substitute wording to the effect that the legislature should provide for a system of common schools. It was adopted by the narrowest of votes, twenty-one to twenty.

John W. Watts of Columbia County then moved to insert "white" before "children" in another section, setting off a new debate:

Smith: . . . he had no objection to the amendment, but did not think it necessary—thought negroes and Indians could be excluded without it.

Dryer: . . . opposed to the white (sic). He saw it sticking out that we were to have slavery here, and he wanted that gentlemen should have an opportunity to educate their own children.

Deady: . . . in Ohio, under a provision similar to that of this report, they had admitted negroes into their schools. He favored the amendment.

John S. White, Washington County: . . . he was opposed to the amendment. There were many half-breed children in his county.

C. Peebles, Marion County: . . . there were many voters in his county whose children had Indian blood—half blood or less. They paid taxes, and their children ought to enjoy the benefits of common schools.

Farrar: . . . thought some provision ought to be made for that class. The report of the schedule committee had made no provision concerning the negroes now here.

The Holmes and Reuben Shipley families, of course, were among those "now here." By this time, Shipley's children attended school near Philomath, while the Holmes children received home schooling in Salem.

Possibly because of the question Farrar raised about blacks already living in Oregon, Smith "thought the section had better be adopted as it stood." The Watts motion failed, making it a rare instance where the convention backed away from wording that would have explicitly excluded blacks from something, in this instance, schools.

·~·

The next racially charged debate concerned how, and when, to submit the constitution to Oregon voters.[18]

The select committee on the "schedule" recommended on September 11 that separate measures be submitted to voters on whether Oregon should be a slave state, and whether free negroes should be excluded. It proposed that the constitution and other measures be submitted to voters on November 9, 1857, just two months away. The recommendations came up for discussion on September 15. The convention record had little to say about the debate, but the *Statesman* offered some details.

Paine Page Prim, Jackson County: . . . said a November election would not give voters enough time to properly consider the Constitution. He proposed moving the election back to February, six months away.

Farrar: . . . thought April, eight months away, was even better. Give the people time . . . the longer time they had to consider it, the better would be their judgment. What need was there of haste? He would even move it to May or June.

Dryer: The people of Oregon would understand this Constitution as well in two months as in two years. A majority of the people were prepared to vote today. Dryer saw slavery as a hidden motive in proposals to delay the election. The only argument he heard urged for extending the time was that it did not give the pro-slavery Democrats a chance—they wanted to stump the territory in behalf of slavery. For himself, he was a free-state man, and did not feel under obligation to put off this submission to please them. . . .

As the debate ensued, some of those who had previously indicated pro-slavery or strident anti-black sentiments, lined up in support of delay. They included Deady, Kelsay, and Logan. Deady acknowledged he did, indeed, want more time for voters to consider slavery.

Deady: It had been said by Mr. Dryer that this delay was asked for to give pro-slavery men a chance to discuss the slavery question. Why not give them a chance to discuss that question? You propose to submit it to the people—and it was an important question. For one, he wanted an opportunity to discuss that question with the people . . .

Frederick Waymire, Polk County: November is better. Both the constitution and slavery had a better chance of passing sooner rather than later. He said if he favored slavery—which he didn't—"the sooner you submit it, the more votes it will get."

Deady: . . . If this constitution was adopted in November, we should still be a territory. . . We were not a state until we were admitted.

Dryer: . . . not convinced of the sincerity of those who wanted more time . . . he was satisfied that he hit the nail on the head when he said it was the slavery question which influenced them.

Williams: . . . heard no sufficient reason for changing the time of submission, and was opposed to so doing. . . . we ought to know whether or not we are to become a state by the next session of congress.

The motions to delay were rejected. November 9 stood. Voting was to be *viva voce*, with voters casting their votes orally in front of electors. The 1854-1855 legislature had narrowly approved public voting to substitute for the secret ballot in territorial elections. It was a strategy partly designed to expose members of the secretive Know Nothing party, which at the time was an emerging threat to the Democratic Party.[19] But public voting was also a way to enforce party discipline. The requirement to vote publicly on the constitution and the slavery and exclusion clauses, rather than by secret ballot, was opposed by Dryer and some others, but it stood.

"Consecrate!!!" Oregon for Whites

To this point in the debate, little had been said about the moral implications of slavery; whether slavery would be good for Oregon; or why blacks should be excluded from the new state. The silence on these issues reflected the earlier agreement among Democrats to avoid meaningful debate, and simply submit the issues to voters.

But in a session late on September 15, the convention's attention turned to Chinese immigrants, and the lid came off the restrained debate like an exploding teapot. It elicited the seemingly most improbable—and ugly—statement from Judge Williams, whose judicial decisions and Free State Letter had so far helped steer Oregon away from slavery. Williams said he would "consecrate Oregon to the use of the white man," excluding all other races.[1]

William Watkins of Josephine County ignited the debate on Chinese immigrants when he proposed asking voters to exclude Chinese from Oregon. By 1857, there had been a significant movement of Chinese immigrants from California into Oregon to mine gold and later to help build the new railroads. Chinese gold miners in southern Oregon were the initial target. Again, it was the Salem newspaper, not the official record that provided details of the debate:

> *Watkins: Chinamen in his county were practically slaves. They were bought and sold to one another, and to white men, as much as negroes were in the South. If Chinese continued to come into that county, he predicted that in five years no white man would inhabit it. White men could not compete with them—they would work for $1.50 or $2.00 per day.*
>
> *Peebles: . . . thought it was quite possible that the people of the territory might vote to exclude Chinamen, but he thought it had better not be coupled with free negroes, but submitted separately.*

Grover: . . . the people did not want this question separately submitted; two-thirds of them know nothing about it.

Reuben P. Boise, Polk County: . . . the people of the whole territory were not prepared to pass upon this question now, and he thought the most we should do was to give the legislature power over it . . . If their [Chinese] increase became an evil in the future, the legislature could prohibit such immigration.

Waymire: . . . could not vote to exclude Chinamen; so far as his constituents were concerned, he believed they would like to have a lot of them come among them. They made good washers, good cooks, and good servants.

Prim: . . . Chinamen were an evil in the mines, and were growing to be a greater one.

Deady: . . . should vote to couple Chinamen with negroes and should vote for submitting the question of excluding both, though he believed it would be impotent—that it would not amount to anything. But he saw no reason for making a difference between Chinamen and negroes. The negro was superior to the Chinaman, and would be more useful.

Marple: . . . in favor of the exclusion of Chinamen, though he agreed with Mr. Deady that such legislation would be impotent.

Watkins: . . . thought that the negroes far surpassed, morally and physically, the Chinamen; if there were any class of thieves who understood their profession so thoroughly it was the Chinamen.

Williams: He was in favor of excluding both Chinamen and negroes. And he did not agree with Mr. Deady that such attempted exclusion would prove inoperative and impotent. . . .

It was at this point in the debate that Williams said he would "consecrate Oregon to the use of the white man." Blacks, Chinese, and "every race of that character" would be excluded, he said.

Dryer: . . . should vote for the amendment, but would separate the clause from the negro one. In this portion of the country Chinamen had not become an evil, and people might desire to vote to exclude negroes and not Chinamen. He would vote to exclude negroes, Chinamen, Kanakas [Hawaiians] and even Indians. The association of these races with the white was the demoralization of the latter.

William H. Packwood, Curry County: Chinamen . . . were an evil in this country. They spent very little in the country.

Chadwick: . . . the people of the Willamette [Valley] had not found the Chinamen to be an evil, and might vote against excluding them . . .

Watkins: . . . withdrew his amendment—said he would offer it another time.

We don't know why Watkins withdrew his motion after arguing so forcefully in favor, and receiving support from other delegates. Possibly it was because including the Chinese, who were a significant presence only in southern Oregon, might doom the measure to exclude African Americans.

·~ ~·

To suggest that Oregon be reserved for whites—apparently even excluding the Native Americans who were indigenous to the region—would today be seen as bizarre in the extreme. Perhaps Williams was playing to sentiments of the Democratic Party, angling for support for a nomination to the U.S. Senate, trying to recover ground lost because of his Free State Letter. Whether that was his motive, or whether his statements reflected his true feelings, make little difference. The words were said, although Williams would later attempt to explain them away.

Voters Do Decide

Convention delegates approved the proposed constitution on September 28, 1857, by a vote of thirty-five to ten, sending it on to voters for their decision on November 9. Fifteen delegates failed to vote, either absent or abstaining. A day earlier the convention had approved wording for the proposed slavery and exclusion measures, also to be submitted to voters. The vote on those measures was thirty-six to thirteen.

Among the "No" votes on the constitution was Thomas Dryer, who, in an angry speech, denounced the Democratic majority for shutting down all debate on the slavery and exclusion issues.

Did any man here avow his principles upon that slavery question? Was there not a studied effort to crush discussion upon the question? Yes, sir.

Was there not a predetermined, foreordained ordeal by the party in power to crush that question in its infancy, and not permit it to come before the convention? . . . Sir, we have been choked off. We have been not allowed to discuss that question.[1]

Years later, John McBride, who abstained from the final vote, recalled how he was shut down when he tried to insert an anti-slavery provision in the bill of rights. He thought he had some support. But when he introduced it, one of the expected supporters "immediately rose and called for the previous question," cutting off debate. When he asked later why his support had evaporated, he was told his proposal was "too radical."[2]

But it was William Watkins, another "No," who addressed the moral issue. It was the only time during the entire six weeks of the convention that the question of fair, equal, and humane treatment of blacks was raised. In explaining his vote, Watkins said "the black man in my estimation has as much right to live, eat, drink, read, think, and in the various avenues of life, to seek a livelihood and means of enjoyment and happiness as has the proudest Caucasian." He went on:

But what is proposed in this constitution, sir? That no negro shall maintain any suit. Under this barbarous provision (for I can use no milder term) the negro is cast upon the world with no defense; his life, liberty, his property, his all, are dependent on the caprice, the passion and the inveterate prejudices of not only the community at large but of every felon who may happen to cover an inhuman head with a white face. . . .

Sir, no power, no conceivable contingency of circumstances, no motives of interest, however great, can induce me to vote either directly or otherwise to sustain a proposition so radically wrong, or even give it my implied assent by submitting it to the people for their approval . . . the free negro has claims upon us which we can neither ignore nor destroy; he was born upon our soil, he speaks our language, he has been taught our religion, and his destiny and ours are eternally linked.[3]

Not one of the delegates who endorsed the constitution addressed the morality of enslaving blacks—or at least there is no record of their doing so.

In a long speech defending the convention's work, Delazon Smith said it was up to the people "to say at the ballot box whether they will endorse the proposition [of slavery] or refuse and reject it." He seemed to suggest that approving slavery in Oregon would be no big deal, since, he said, an individual would probably want only a few slaves at most.

If a majority of the people of Oregon . . . say they will have slavery; if they say that they desire to introduce slave labor into this country, that they desire to have constitutional authority for so doing, I shall acquiesce in that decision. As a sequence (sic) of that decision, I shall anticipate nothing more than a nominal existence of slavery within the boundaries of this state for a time to come, not extending practically beyond a few body or household servants.[4]

Smith held out slavery as the solution to the shortage of labor in Oregon—addressing the complaints of hard-pressed farmers that they couldn't find laborers to work on the mile-square farms they had claimed under the Donation Land Act. Smith, who would later be elected one of Oregon's first U.S. senators, slyly suggested farmers would face an uphill struggle to bring help from elsewhere if slavery were defeated.

Vote on slavery in Oregon's 1857 Constitution by county*		
	For slavery	Against slavery
Marion	214	1055
Linn	198	1092
Benton	283	368
Lane	356	602
Yamhill	107	522
Clackamas	98	655
Multnomah	96	653
Columbia	11	84
Clatsop	25	71
Douglas	248	377
Coos	19	72
Polk	231	484
Washington	68	428
Jackson	405	426
Tillamook	6	22
Umpqua	32	201
Curry	35	95
Wasco	58	85
Josephine	155	435
Totals	2645	7727

Source: *Oregon Statesman*, Dec. 22, 1857
* There were nineteen counties at the time.

If the majority of the people decide otherwise, it will then in my judgment, become the policy of the people of the future state of Oregon to put in requisition those influences and causes which shall divert labor from the over-populated and over-burdened cities of the Atlantic coast to this country, to divert some portion of the tide of immigration from the European states to this continent to the Pacific coast to supply the wants and necessities of the country. . . . The people of this country have been discussing this question [slavery] for the last year, and even for years, for it is the question of the nation and of the age.

⌐~

The constitution was submitted to voters for a decision on November 9, 1857. As agreed, voting was done orally, before judges, with only white males eligible to participate. They were asked "yes or no" on three issues:

1. *Do you vote for the Constitution?*
2. *Do you vote for slavery in Oregon?*
3. *Do you vote for free negroes in Oregon?*

When the votes were counted, Oregon voters had approved the constitution decisively, 7,195 to 3,215. They defeated the slavery clause by an even larger margin: 7,727 to 2,645. But the vote to prohibit free negroes was more lopsided yet, with 8,640 favoring an exclusion clause, and 1,081 opposed. The clause did not apply to existing black residents.[5]

Timothy Davenport wrote in 1903 that while the vote against slavery was gratifying, "Is it not a most astounding fact that they would seriously consider such a question?"[6]

The election resulted in the following clauses being added to the constitution's Bill of Rights, as sections 34 and 35:

Section 34: There shall be neither slavery nor involuntary servitude in the state, otherwise than as a punishment for crime whereof the party shall have been duly convicted.

Section 35: No free negro or mulatto not residing in this state at the time of the adoption of this constitution, shall come, reside or be within this state or hold any real estate, or make any contracts, or maintain any suit therein; and the legislative assembly shall provide by penal laws for the removal by public officers of all such negroes and mulattoes, and for their effectual exclusion from the state, and for the punishment of persons who shall bring them into the state, or employ or harbor them.

Had slavery won, the constitution would have read:

Persons lawfully held as slaves in any state, territory or district of the United States under the laws thereof, may be brought into this state; and such slaves and their descendants may be held as slaves within this state, and shall not be emancipated without the consent of their owners.

The constitution thus approved has been described as "thoroughly a white man's document" designed "to put blacks and mulatto residents in a state of complete subordination and even rightlessness."[7] They were not eligible to vote, hold public office, serve on juries or in the militia, or sue in the courts. Land ownership was in doubt as well.[8]

·~·

When Congress approved Oregon as the thirty-third state on February 14, 1859, Oregon became the only free state admitted with an exclusion clause against blacks in its constitution. While the clause was never enforced, it remained part of the constitution for nearly seventy years, until finally removed by voters on November 2, 1926.

In addition to the exclusion clause, the constitution approved in 1857 contained these additional race-related restrictions:

> *Bill of Rights, Article 31: White foreigners only, who become residents, will have the same rights as native-born citizens.*
>
> *Article II, Section No. 2: Voting restricted to every white male citizen.*
>
> *Article II, Section No. 6: No Negro, Chinaman, or Mulatto shall have the right of suffrage.*
>
> *Article VII, Section No. 10: Growth in the white population only will determine expansion of the state courts.*
>
> *Article XV, Section No. 8: No Chinaman, not a resident of the State at the adoption of this Constitution, shall ever hold any real estate, or mining claim, or work any mining claim therein.*

Jesse Applegate would, years later, underscore his disgust at the way the convention dealt with the issues of slavery and African Americans. In a letter to Judge Deady, he singled out for criticism the exclusion measure put before voters:

> *It is hard to realize that men having hearts and consciences, some of them today in the front ranks of the defenders of human rights, could be led so far by party prejudice as to put such an article in the frame of government intended to be free and just.*[9]

·~·

Judge Williams, who had argued for exclusion in his Free State Letter, and again in the convention, appeared in later years to soften his views. Quite possibly speaking of himself, he would say in 1909, that "Many of those who voted for the exclusion of free negroes were at heart opposed to the policy, but it was considered necessary to throw the 'tub' (sic) to the whole of the pro-slavery [Democratic] party to secure the success of the free state clause of the constitution."[10]

·~·

Disagreements over slavery, and control over the party, finally led to an irrevocable split in 1858. The faction dominated by Asahel Bush and the Salem Clique was known as the state Democratic Party. The breakaway group, which included Nathaniel Ford and eleven other legislators, was called the national Democratic Party—national because they supported the 1856 national party platform. The two factions held separate conventions and nominated competing sets of candidates. The dissidents' efforts to create a new party apparatus led Bush to denounce them in a vitriolic editorial as, among other things, "nigger-loving apostates for the Democratic Party."[11] And when the dissidents prepared to meet in Eugene on April 8, 1858, Bush called them "the Eugene negro equality movement."[12]

Bush seemed to take special delight in mocking Ford's apparent effort to seek the national Democrats' nomination to higher office. The *Statesman's* account of a national party caucus in Dallas in late March said Ford was nominated to run for a new state Senate seat, but was forced to withdraw. The reason, the newspaper said, was that Ford had attended a recent legislative caucus of the state Democrats, who had previously expelled him.[13] Ford's national supporters didn't take kindly to his crossing the aisle. "Their complaint is that two years ago, Ford . . . denounced Bush and the Salem Clique and the Democratic organization and pledged himself to their overthrow," the *Statesman* wrote. They "claimed he was elected by them [to the Legislature] and ought to have represented them."

Ford next sought a nomination for governor. But that didn't happen either. In an account oozing with sarcasm, the *Statesman* wrote that Ford "modestly retired from the building, but listened outside until he heard the result of the vote through the weather-boarding of the old courthouse, and, returning, inquired what had been done, demurely resumed his seat and commenced counting over the first crude sentences of a badly spelled 'National' inaugural [speech], which he will never have an opportunity to deliver."[14] Ford was left with a nomination to a seat in the final session of the territorial legislature.

The split in the party was all about power. Both factions included pro-slavery advocates. The views of the dissidents were reflected in the pro-slavery *Occidental Messenger*, "which held even a state did not have the right to keep slavery out of its borders."[15]

Ford himself contended in a convoluted letter to the *Jacksonville [Oregon] Sentinel* on May 29, 1858, that there was little difference between the two party factions in their attitudes toward race. The letter was in a defensive response to a complaint by Lucien Heath, a state party candidate for secretary of state, who had accused Ford of "a base slander" against him.

Heath, in a letter in the *Statesman* on May 18, 1858, did not offer details of Ford's alleged slander, while demanding "a public denial."[16] Moreover, without being specific, Heath complained that "Col. Ford also threatened that the report (which is said to have originated with Mr. Embree, of his family), should be sent south [southern Oregon]." Carey Embree was Ford's brother-in-law, who crossed the plains in the Ford wagon train.

The alleged slander had occurred in a conversation between Ford and a Jacksonville attorney, Benjamin Franklin Dowell, concerning a rumored racial incident at the Heath home. The incident, if it was an incident, involved Ford's unnamed fourteen-year-old niece—Embree's daughter—and a sixteen-year-old African American girl working for the Heath family. While Heath didn't go into detail, Ford seemed to take delight in giving the specifics of what he claimed he was told about the incident, as he wasn't there. According to Ford, his niece was residing with the Heaths while attending school in Dallas and was told by Mrs. Heath she must either sleep in the same bed with the African American girl, or in a small bed with the Heath children. Ford said his niece "very naturally agreed to sleep with the children."

Embree, however, separately wrote the *Statesman* on April 12—his letter ran under Heath's—saying any suggestion that his daughter had been coerced to sleep in the same bed with an African American girl was "utterly and unqualifiedly fake." He added, "I neither reported such slander, nor did such a thing ever occur to my knowledge, and further I will do Mr. Heath the justice to say that I do not believe he would be guilty of *so great an indiscretion* [author's italics]."[17]

But even knowing his brother-in-law had denied the incident, Ford feigned outrage and seemed only too eager to spread the rumor. He said he had been told that the African American girl was allowed to dine with the Heath family. Ford said his comments to Dowell were prompted by an article in the *Statesman*.

The conversation between us grew out of some remarks of the Oregon Statesman about the Nationals being of the negro-equality party. I referred to Heath's case for the purpose of showing to Dowell, or any others it might concern, that the Bush ticket for state offices, or a part of them, might with as much propriety be called the negro equality ticket as any other party.[18]

Both the state Democrats, meeting in Salem March 16, 1858, and the national Democrats, meeting two weeks later in Eugene, endorsed the Kansas-Nebraska bill. Both also expressed support for Joseph Lane, Oregon's congressional delegate and soon to be a U.S. senator. The one real issue dividing them had been control of the nominating process for candidates in the upcoming June election.

The state Democrats swept the state offices. They elected John Whiteaker as governor, and LaFayette Grover to Congress, along with majorities in both houses of the new state legislature. Both Whiteaker and Grover were considered pro-slavery. Lucien Heath was elected secretary of state. It was a rout. Ford was elected to the largely toothless territorial legislature—Oregon was still a territory. With the state Democrats in control, the state legislature, meeting in July 1858, elected Lane and Delazon Smith as Oregon's first two U.S. senators, even though Oregon hadn't yet been confirmed as a state. Lane's vote was forty-five in favor, with none opposed, and four blank votes. Both Lane and Smith were pro-slavery, which led historian Charles Carey to marvel at an incongruous outcome.

> *Thus, the people of Oregon that (sic) had just adopted a free-state constitution and voted against slavery, elected violent advocates of slavery for the first state officers, and they now proceeded to select pro-slavery senators to represent them in the senate at Washington.*[19]

The influence of pro-southern Democratic leaders in both Oregon and California during this period is partly explained by the power of the political

Joseph Lane, a witness for Ford in the only slavery case brought in Oregon courts. Lane was Oregon's first territorial governor and a U.S. senator. He was pro-slavery and ran for vice president on a secessionist ticket with John Breckinridge of South Carolina in 1860. (Oregon Historical Society)

patronage that flowed to them from the Democratic administrations in Washington, D.C.[20] Smith served just seventeen days—he and Lane drew lots to determine who would serve the long and short terms. Lane served until 1861.

After nearly a decade, Bush was about to lose control of the Democratic Party. Although he had for years nominally supported Lane in his political ambitions, tensions were never far below the surface. The break between the two was instigated by Lane with support from Delazon Smith, after Oregon became a state in 1859. Using influence cultivated during his years in Washington, Lane succeeded in getting the Buchanan administration to remove Bush partisans from appointed positions, replacing them with Lane supporters.[21] Lane and Smith formally seized control at the state Democratic convention in April 20, 1859, when their supporters elected W. W. Chapman as convention chair. The defeated Bush loyalists walked out.

Bush-supported members of the central committee were purged and replaced with members supportive of Lane and Smith's interests, including Nathaniel Ford.[22] The dissident national Democrats were now in control. Tilting ever more toward slavery, they endorsed the Dred Scott decision and supported President Buchanan for reelection in 1860, although Buchanan would not be the nominee.

The Bush faction, now in opposition, took its first definitive stand in the ongoing debate over slavery, aligning itself with the Douglas Democrats and popular sovereignty. This position, and the party split, created an opportunity for Oregon's small Republican Party to join forces with the Bush Democrats and enhance its own status. Cooperation between the two was a "unique Western development," made possible because both were controlled in Oregon by advocates of popular sovereignty.[23] Elsewhere in the country, Republicans were adversaries of the Douglas Democrats.

Nationally, the Democratic Party was badly divided between the Douglas Democrats, who favored the popular sovereignty option for slavery, and the pro-South and pro-slavery faction, which supported President Buchanan. When delegates to the 1860 Democratic National Convention, meeting in Baltimore in June, were poised to nominate Douglas for President, a number of southern delegates walked out. They were joined by the delegations from Oregon and California. The head of Oregon's delegation "by proxy" was Isaac Stevens, the Washington Territory's congressional delegate, and a friend of Lane. Just one regular Oregon delegate and one alternate attended.[24]

The dissidents organized their own rump convention in Baltimore where they nominated John Breckinridge—Buchanan's vice president—for president and Lane for vice president. Stevens was named chairman of the party's executive committee and managed the Breckinridge/Lane campaign, supervising campaign literature and scheduling events.[25]

Senator Douglas received the nomination of the regular Democrats, while the Republican Party nominated Abraham Lincoln, setting up a four-way race. The fourth candidate was John Bell of the Constitutional Union party, who had some southern support.

While Lane had become a major player on the national stage, his role in Oregon was becoming much diminished. Although he had won control of the state's Democratic Party, his partisans lost their hold on the more important Oregon legislature. It was Bush's turn to do the maneuvering. Working together, the Bush Democrats and Republicans controlled a joint session of the 1860 Oregon Legislative Assembly, which met in October to elect Oregon's next two U.S. senators. After fourteen contentious ballots, the legislators elected James Nesmith, a Douglas Democrat and a longtime member of Bush's Salem Clique, and Edward Dickinson Baker, a popular Republican—and a friend of Lincoln's—who had been recruited from California to run for the U.S. Senate.[26] Lane's ally, Delazon Smith, was defeated in his attempt to recapture his old seat, which had been vacant.

Both Baker and Nesmith were supporters of popular sovereignty, giving northern interests two more votes in Congress. Covered extensively by the national press, Lane's repudiation was seen as a personal embarrassment, one that eroded his standing nationally.[27]

Lane's still significant popularity in Oregon wasn't enough to carry the state for the Breckinridge ticket. It split Oregon's Democratic vote with the Douglas Democrats, allowing Lincoln to squeak through to victory. Lincoln carried Oregon by 270 votes out of nearly 14,500. In a similar situation in California, Lincoln won by 700 votes. However, even without Oregon and California, Lincoln's margin of victory was such that he would have been elected.[28]

There were those in Oregon opposed to slavery and racism on moral grounds. One of the most notable—and most controversial—voices was that of the Reverend Obed Dickinson, pastor of the Salem's First Congregational Church from 1853 to 1867. The Salem church had only four members and held services in a log house when the Massachusetts-born Dickinson was assigned as minister by the American Home Missionary Society. Dickinson, thirty-four, and his wife, Charlotte, made the journey by ship, traveling with seven other missionary couples, some of whom disembarked in California.

Congregational ministers in Oregon were on record against slavery—in addition to Salem, there were also churches in Corvallis and Albany. At a meeting in 1857, the ministers expressed "disapproval of churches that did not permit free expression of such opposition to slavery from their pulpits." In 1859, they agreed not to "invite into their pulpits persons known to own slaves or persons sympathetic to slaveholding."[1] These statements were interpreted as disapproval of Methodists and other church bodies, which were less outspoken in their opposition to slavery.

Dickinson's vocal opposition to slavery embroiled him in controversy, even within his own church. In explaining why he had never attended Dickinson's church, acting Governor George Curry was quoted as saying, "I won't hear an abolitionist preach."[2] Equally controversial was Dickinson's stand in favor of racial equality. There were just twenty or so African Americans in Marion County in 1860, among them the Robin Holmes family. Dickinson welcomed blacks into his church, and argued for integration of local schools. After Salem's schools refused to integrate, Dickinson's wife home-schooled the black children.

Two incidents caused Dickinson particular difficulty with his congregation. The first was his insistence on admitting three former slaves into the church alongside whites on March 3, 1861. The former slaves included Robin and Polly Holmes. A parishioner recalled years later of seeing "Dear old Aunt Polly, as she swayed to and fro with her sincere singing."[3] The third may have been William Johnson, brought to Oregon by Richard Linville on the Applegate Trail in 1846.[4] The Holmeses and Johnson—if it was Johnson—were the first blacks to unite with the Congregational Church in Oregon and among the first accepted into any white church in Oregon.[5]

In a lengthy letter to the American Home Missionary Society on February 15, 1862, Dickinson defended his decision to admit the former slaves:

These came to me, and with the utmost modesty, asked if I would be willing to let them come into the church. I said yes, if you love Christ. I talked with them faithfully several times after that at their houses, and was satisfied that they were sincere disciples of Christ. I then told them that they might come before the brethren of the church and, if after examination, they voted to receive them, they could become members of the church. . . . Before the time of public examination came, however, there were six others (white persons), part ladies, and one the only daughter of a leading merchant (a most humble Christian) (she) who wished to unite with the church at the same time. As soon as this was known the wife of our brother (the deacon) came to me wishing to have a "separate" meeting on Saturday or some other day for the blacks to unite with the church. She thought this merchant and wife would not like to have their daughter join the church on the same day with these negroes. I told her Christ had given us no warrant for such distinctions. . . . The black people were accordingly examined—were voted to be admitted without a dissenting voice, on the part of the members, and on the Sabbath following stood forth with six white persons to take the vows of God upon them. Our little church was crowded to overflowing. . . . Even breathing seemed to be suppressed by the intensity of this feeling. God bless Old Black Robert. He has been a cause of trouble, but I believe he loves his God.[6]

The "Old Black Robert" in the letter must have referred to Robin Holmes, as Holmes by this time frequently used the name Robert, evidently his true name. Dickinson didn't explain what he meant by Robert being "a cause of trouble," although he may simply have referred to Holmes' application to join the church. On June 16, Dickinson delivered a sermon that contributed to the controversy surrounding him. Again, quoting from his letter:

In that sermon I said there is a wrong public opinion in this town. It has closed the doors of all our schools against the children of these black families dooming them to ignorance in life. I said it was wrong to take away the key of knowledge from any human being. Especially wrong when their property was taxed to support our schools not to let them have some privileges in the schools. . . . A brother came to me the next day and said "that sermon will take away five hundred dollars from our Church Building."

Dickinson had also denounced the apparent torture and near murder of a young African American boy wrongly accused of a series of burglaries, including a burglary at the home of a relative of the church deacon. His stand again put him at odds with important members of his congregation.

> *The husband of a cousin of our deacon (a southern man) lost money also.*
> *He laid it to a negro boy so ignorant that he hardly knew his right hand*
> *from his left, and to compel him to confess gathered a company and hung*
> *him till some supposed he was dead. For parts of three days an excited*
> *gang of men in our streets trod down all law and right (sic)—hanging*
> *choking and whipping that poor boy. . . . I spoke out against it, and yet*
> *many of our citizens being southern men, they were able to carry on their*
> *work so long. The boy was finally lodged in the jail and after two months*
> *[and] tried and acquitted as an innocent boy, and is now as harmless as he*
> *was before.*

As a consequence of Dickinson's actions, the church membership urged him to temper his preaching on "the general equality of race." Both Holmeses are listed in a church document as attending a meeting on January 20, 1863, at which members voiced concern that Dickinson's outspokenness on the issue "has greatly lessened his influence for good in the community."[7] One unhappy parishioner withheld vital financial support from the church. Dickinson said the parishioner accused him of being "stubborn," adding he accepted the criticism because it spoke to his values.

> *I am stubborn because I would not yield to their counsel in having a*
> *separate meeting for the blacks to join the church. I am stubborn because I*
> *maintain the rights of the blacks to an education for their children, against*
> *the popular opinion of the place. I am stubborn because I set myself firmly*
> *against hanging before they are proved to be guilty.*

Among critics was the *Statesman*'s Asahel Bush, who criticized Dickinson as among "ministers meddling in politics." Dickinson also courted controversy when he presided at the New Year's Day wedding in 1863 of America Waldo and Richard A. Bogle, a black couple. Bogle, originally from Jamaica, crossed the plains to Oregon in 1851 and had been a successful miner in northern Idaho.[8] He owned a barber shop in Walla Walla and became wealthy with ranching interests.[9]

The Waldo-Bogle wedding occurred on the day President Lincoln's Emancipation Proclamation became effective, freeing slaves in the Confederate states. The manufactured controversy over the wedding focused on the prominent whites who attended, including two justices of the Oregon Supreme Court, Joseph Wilson and Chief Justice Reuben Boise.

In a letter to Matthew Deady, Bush said that the wedding, held at the Dickinson's home, was "generally regarded as shameful" by the Salem community. He named Boise and Wilson among guests, along with at least six white women, including Boise's sister, "Lizzie," and the wife of O. C. Pratt, a former justice on the Supreme Court. "They had a feast, and Jo [Wilson] presided at the table. . . . It was a negro equality sentiment mixed up with a little snob-aristocracy"[10] The *Oregonian*'s Dryer, however, saw nothing extraordinary in the event. "We can see no impropriety in any white person who may have a favorite—even if she were as black as the ace of spades—in attending the wedding of such a person." He noted that America Waldo "had long been a servant and a great favorite in a family at Salem," an apparent reference to the Waldo family.[11] In its account, the *Oregonian* suggested Bush might have been among the guests, which Bush denied.

Deady, who reported Oregon news to the *San Francisco Bulletin*, sent the *Oregonian* article to the San Francisco newspaper, which reprinted the article with a commentary, possibly written by Deady himself. The commentary denounced the "scandal-mongers" and appeared to take the side of "the certain distinguished white ladies and gentlemen, who saw proper to witness the ceremony and participate in the festive proceedings."[12] The article included mention that Bush might also have attended. "What did you do that for?" Bush complained in his letter to Deady. "You know I did not" attend.[13]

Dickinson survived the controversies. He tried to resign in 1865 but was urged to stay on. However, financial support for the church diminished significantly. Dickinson left the church voluntarily in 1867 to devote his time to a successful seed and nursery business in Salem.[14]

There were other voices, many in the clergy, who defended the rights of blacks on moral grounds, but who, like Dickinson, found little support among business and political leaders.

Reuben and Mary Jane

Only a few details are known of the lives of Robin and Polly Holmes following the 1853 court decision that gave them back their children. But a great deal is known about their eldest daughter, Mary Jane, who was soon to meet another former slave, Reuben Shipley.

When Judge Williams returned to the Holmeses the custody of their children, only Roxanna and James went to live with them in Salem. Another child, Leonidas, or Lon, was already living with his parents. But Mary Jane continued to live apart. Several accounts say Mary Jane Holmes had been given by Ford as early as 1850 to his daughter, Josephine Boyle, probably as a house servant. The 1850 census lists Mary Jane as a member of the Boyle household. Ford's comment in a letter in 1852 that he sold one of his slaves possibly referred to Mary Jane.[1]

Boyle and her husband, James Boyle, a doctor, lived near the Fords on seven hundred and fifty acres north of Rickreall Creek, where they built a large colonial house with a portico above, and a porch in front, "a very fine house"—recalled Caroline Burch. According to Burch, James Boyle began his medical practice in Indiana and was the first physician in Polk County. He saw patients over a wide area.

Notwithstanding Judge Williams' decision, Mary Jane continued living with the Boyles, "not as a slave, but a member of the household."[2] It may well have been her decision to remain with the Boyles, as she legally was free to go. There is one known description of Mary Jane as a younger woman, and that is from Pauline Burch, who wrote approvingly that "Mary Jane through the years found time to answer calls for help when her neighbors were in need. Mary Jane as a girl and young woman was short and quite stout and very loveable. This sweetness of disposition would have made her many friends in the Philomath community."[3]

Burch insisted that Ford never sold nor gave Mary Jane to his daughter, Josephine Boyle, and that Mary Jane did not live with the Boyles. She said Mary Jane would sometimes visit the Boyles and stay with them temporarily. A census taker who recorded her living there in 1850 was mistaken, Burch insisted. "Mrs. Boyle had Mary Jane stay with her during the weeks just before the court decision. . . . Robin and Polly had a very small house at that time, and there was little room for the three additional children, nor provisions for them."

However, the evidence shows that years after Judge Williams' ruling, Ford was still trying to maintain his hold on Mary Jane. The 1857 Dred Scott decision may have encouraged him to think that Judge Williams' ruling against him was no longer valid.

·~·

We don't know how Reuben Shipley and Mary Jane Holmes met. They lived about thirty miles apart. Shipley was fifty-seven in 1857, twice the age of Mary Jane, then twenty-eight. The little known about Mary Jane's early life would seem to indicate she had scant leeway to venture very far from home. Shipley, then a free man and a successful Benton County farmer, evidently sought a new wife. He had learned his wife in Missouri was dead. He also had been unable to regain his sons, who remained in Missouri as slaves.

Someone brought Reuben and Mary Jane together. Could it have been Dr. Boyle, whose practice extended into Benton County? Had Boyle realized that he and his wife could not keep Mary Jane and looked for an opportunity to send her elsewhere? It is certainly conceivable that Reuben Shipley, or one of his white friends, was a patient of Boyle and that Boyle learned from one of them that Shipley was looking for a wife. Whether Boyle played a role or not, Shipley found out about the black woman living single in Polk County, met her, and proposed marriage. The couple wed on July 18, 1857, at the Holmeses'

Former slave Mary Jane Holmes Shipley Drake in a photo taken about the year 1924, a few years before her death. As Mary Jane Holmes, she was a central figure in a suit brought in Polk County by her father to free her from her slave owner. She had two marriages, to Reuben Shipley and Alfred Drake, both of whom preceded her in death. (Benton County Historical Society)

home in Salem. The probate judge who married them, J. D. Boon, listed an incorrect surname for Shipley in the Marion County marriage book, carelessly recording his name as Reuben "Shepsherd."[4] He did correctly list the name of Mary Jane Holmes. There were two witnesses, Charles Rowe and L. Rowe.

.⸱ ⸱.

The wedding was not without complications. Once again, it was Ford who made things difficult. He claimed to Shipley that Mary Jane remained his property—despite Williams' court ruling. In the only known interview during her life, in 1924, Mary Jane said that when the newlyweds prepared to leave for Shipley's Benton County farm, Ford informed Shipley that he, Ford, had purchased Mary Jane, and Shipley must pay him before he could take her away.[5] Jeremiah Henkle shared a slightly different version in the 1936 interview:

> *Ford allowed Reuben to marry this girl and take her to his farm. Then, having heard that Reuben had money, he came without the knowledge of Reuben's white friends, and made him believe that he must purchase his wife's freedom which he did for $700.*[6]

Mary Jane said two white friends of Shipley's—his former employer, Eldridge Hartless, and the Reverend Thomas J. Connor, pastor of the Beulah Chapel of the United Brethren Church, which the Shipleys attended—learned of Ford's demand and tried to convince Reuben he didn't need to pay. But, for whatever reason, Shipley apparently paid anyway.[7] Seven hundred dollars may have seemed a small price to have his marriage unencumbered by controversy.

There are other versions of how the money was paid. One was that Shipley was forced to pay as a condition of marrying Mary Jane. Another was that he paid in installments until Hartless, Connor, and others finally persuaded him the debt was bogus. But Henkle's interviewer was convinced Henkle had the story right. "Since Mr. Hinkle (sic) was for years a business partner of Mr. [John L.] Shipley, a son of Reuben's master, and his intimate friend, it seems reasonable certain that Mr. Hinkle is correct."[8]

John B. Horner, who conducted the 1924 interview with Mary Jane, wrote that she was born in Pike County, Missouri, and once worked on a farm owned by a Captain Taylor—"The captain was always interested in breeding speedy horses and fine cattle," she told him. Horner also quoted her as saying that, while she was a slave, Ford never struck her, but "she would not favorably compare slavery with freedom."[9] Horner said Mary Jane was "undoubtedly the last of those sold as property in Oregon where slavery was occasionally practiced, but not authorized by law."

The black Shipleys had six children, three sons and three daughters—Wallace, Ella, Thomas, Martha, Nellie—or Nettie—and Edward. At some point, they must have gone to San Francisco, or at least Mary Jane did—or there was an adoption—because Edward said he was born in San Francisco in 1871. According to recollections of neighbors, the family got along well in the community. They attended the United Brethren Church. Mary Jane was known for her cooking. They hosted white families for dinners, and were guests at dinners in white homes. However, their children apparently didn't have an easy time at the nearby Union School, facing occasional harassment.

Recalled a neighbor, George Bethers: "His [Shipley's] children got along with everybody except the Scott boys, who bullied them shamefully."[10] Even so, it must have been enormously satisfying to the Shipleys to see their children gain access to an education that, as slaves, they were denied. One can imagine Reuben and Mary Jane stressing to their children, at the end of a tough day at school, the opportunity they had been given, and urging them to persevere in spite of the harassment.

Grain and corn would have been the probable crops on the Shipley farm. Shipley owned livestock, and recorded the following brand, or mark, with Benton County on September 18, 1865: "Reuben Shipley's mark for his stock is a crop and under bit on the left ear and under slope in the right ear."[11] Shipley may also have been involved in at least one local political campaign even though, as a black man, he was denied the right to vote. A letter in the *Oregon Statesman*, written from Corvallis and dated June 2, 1857, referred to campaigning by "Hartless old nigger" during the contentious 1857 campaign that followed the split in the Democratic Party. Shipley didn't buy his farm until November 1857, so he may still have worked for Hartless at the time of the election. From the insulting and racist wording in the letter, it appeared Shipley—assuming it was Shipley—may have campaigned on behalf of candidates who defeated candidates supported by Asahel Bush and the Salem Clique. The letter, signed only "N. C.," referred vaguely to two other unidentified men. It said in part:

Jim and the man . . . voted, but the negro I believe did not, although he did good service in the opposition ranks. Doubtless the "old darkey," even if he had been allowed, would have been ashamed to have supported such a variegated shirt-tail ticket, yet he was willing to electioneer with "Jim" for the sake of the whiskey which both obtained at Avery's grocery.[12]

⌣⌣

As for Ford, it should be noted that his descendants dispute the notion that Shipley paid Ford for Mary Jane's hand, or that Ford had given her to his daughter. Wrote Pauline Burch:

Nathaniel Ford had no contact . . . with Mary Jane or her husband before or after they were married. In fact he had no desire to, and made no attempt to get control of any one of the negro children after they had gone from his home in June 1953 [1853].[13]

However, Reuben Boise, the prosecuting attorney who represented Robin Holmes in his suit against Ford, said in a letter to Timothy Davenport, dated June 4, 1906, that Ford had given Mary Jane to Josephine Boyle some time prior to 1853.[14] Reviewing the case, Boise said Ford had claimed the Holmeses' "children as slaves and continued to claim them until 1853." He went on to say, "One of these children—a girl [Mary Jane]—had prior to that time, been given by Ford to Mrs. (Dr.) Boyle, a daughter of Ford."

The letter to Davenport was one of his few public comments Boise made about the case. Boise said that Judge Williams ruled "these children being then (by the voluntary act of Ford) in Oregon, where slavery could not legally exist, were free from the bonds of slavery, and awarded their custody to their father."

Who Was Reuben Ficklin?

The name Reuben Shipley is not found on any headstone in the Mt. Union Cemetery, although Mary Jane is buried there with four of their children. The cemetery is on land once belonging to the former slaves. Reuben and Mary Jane Holmes Shipley donated three acres from their hillside farm in 1861, persuaded by friends that the land high on the southeastern slope of Neabaeck Hill was an ideal location for a cemetery.

According to historical accounts, the Reuben Shipleys agreed to donate the land with the understanding that African Americans could be buried there along with whites.[1] This represented a significant breakthrough in racial relations in the region, as another nearby cemetery barred non-white burials. It wasn't unusual for minorities to be denied burials in Caucasian cemeteries. The deed

The Mt. Union Cemetery near Philomath. Former slaves Reuben and Mary Jane Shipley donated land for the cemetery with the understanding it would be open to burials of both blacks and whites. Large granite marker in foreground was installed in 1981 to recognize the Shipleys for their donation. (Photo by author)

for the cemetery land, dated May 1, 1861, doesn't mention the understanding, which must have been implied. The deed does specify "the tract of land be used only as a cemetery" and transferred the property from the Shipleys to the care of three trustees: E. Hartless, William Wyatt, and A. Newton. Hartless was Eldridge Hartless, who gave Shipley a job after he gained his freedom. In the space on the deed for their signatures, both Shipleys signed their name with X's.

One reason the Shipleys were encouraged to set aside the land for a cemetery might have been that Hartless buried three of his young children there in 1854, three years before Shipley bought the property. While no cause of death is given, the children quite possibly died during one of the epidemics of diphtheria or typhoid fever that periodically devastated pioneer families.

Above the cemetery, near the top of the hill, once stood the Union School, built about 1850, and attended by the children of the Reuben Shipleys and other families in the area. According to historical accounts, the school was named Union "to denote the strong patriotic sentiments" of the region. A new school was built in 1870, a half mile to the east.[2] The Reverend Conner, who owned property near the Shipleys, held services in the first Union School until the Beulah Chapel was built in 1857. The black Shipleys, and possibly the white Shipleys, were members.

Mt. Union Cemetery has served both whites and blacks in the Philomath area for nearly a hundred and fifty years. It has expanded from its original three acres to seven acres, and counts nearly two thousand graves. On an early summer morning, standing amidst the headstones—many worn smooth with age—one may look down the gentle, grassy slope of Neabaeck Hill, out over mist-shrouded fields in the valley below and toward grey-green forests on distant mountains. It is as spiritual a setting as can be found in the area.

⸱⸱⸱

Reuben Shipley died in 1872 after contracting smallpox while visiting Mary Jane's sister, Roxanna, in Salem. One of the Shipley daughters, Martha, also fell victim to smallpox.

Family members are listed on a four-by-four-foot granite headstone in the original northwest corner of the cemetery. These include Mary Jane and four Shipley children, Wallace, Martha, Ella and William—William was a son who died in infancy in 1860. The headstone was placed sometime in the 1940s by the Shipleys' last surviving son, Edward Ficklin. Also engraved on the headstone is the name R. E. Ficklin, a name unknown to a cemetery researcher, who complained in writing that someone had made a mistake. "This researcher does not believe that R. E. Ficklin is buried in Mt. Union Cemetery."[3] The unnamed researcher said the person buried there had to be Reuben Shipley.

A separate notation said Shipley's son, Edward Ficklin, must have had "a temporary lapse of memory" when he donated the headstone. A 1981 article in the *Corvallis Gazette-Times* laments that the marker over the Shipley grave "bears another's name." There was, however, no mistake. Shipley and Ficklin were the same person. Typical of the slave experience, Reuben had used the surname of his most recent owner, Robert Shipley. Ficklin may have been the name of a previous owner. Both Robert Shipley and Reuben Shipley were born in Kentucky—Robert in Barren County. At least nine persons named Ficklin were listed as slave owners in Kentucky in 1850, one of whom possibly was a previous owner of Reuben.[4]

While researchers and others thought there had been a mix-up in names, the author had the advantage of a family genealogy, compiled by his grandparents, the late Minnie Wyatt Junkin and William "Will" Junkin of Tigard. They wrote of the circumstances of Shipley's coming to Oregon as a slave, and of his burial in the Mt. Union Cemetery "probably under his true name R. E. Ficklin together with his own family." Minnie Junkin had correctly predicted in a letter written in 1965 that confusion would result if the name Shipley didn't also appear on the headstone. She wrote of attending a meeting years earlier where the issue was raised.

Some years ago in the meeting of the historical society, the question was brought up regarding the Reuben Ficklin family (the old negro) and the fact that his name, Uncle Reuben Shipley was left off the cemetery stone erected by his son Eddie. As old uncle Reuben gave the land for Mt. Union Cemetery to the county for cemetery purposes it looks only right that some note should be made of it. No one knows the name Ficklin, but all old timers were familiar with Uncle Reuben Shipley, and we feel that something should be done about it. Otherwise in another generation no one will know that Reuben Ficklin and Reuben Shipley were one and the same.[5]

It remains unknown why the son, Edward, preferred the name Ficklin over Shipley, as he would himself have never known the Kentucky Ficklins. Perhaps the rest of the explanation is found in the following comment by Minnie Junkin, who wrote that Shipley's son, Eddie, "was a very proud young man, and would do most anything to conceal that he was colored."[6]

·ᴗ ᴗ·

Benton County honored the Reuben Shipleys in 1981 with a large marker of pink granite, placed at the cemetery entrance. People entering the cemetery can't miss it. Among the approximately forty people at the dedication ceremony were state and county officials, clergy, historians, officers of the Benton County Historical Society, and the Corvallis Chapter of the National Association for the Advancement of Colored People. The inscription reads:

On May 11, 1861 Reuben and Mary Jane Holmes Shipley, former negro slaves, deeded from their farm purchased from Charles Bales' donation land claim, the original plot for this cemetery. Buried in Lot 10 are Reuben Shipley, Mary Jane Shipley Drake, Alfred Drake, and the Shipley Children: Ella, Wallace, Martha, William.

Three years after Reuben's death, Mary Jane married Alfred Drake, another African American from Missouri. But more tragedy had already befallen the family. Leonidas, or Lon, the youngest son of Robin and Polly, "apparently" was lynched—"apparently" because there is some confusion about whether it was actually the same Lon.

Leonidas Holmes had lived for a time with the Shipleys in Benton County, probably helping with the farm work, but had returned to Salem to live with his mother. His father, Robin, was by then deceased. Pauline Burch gave one version of what happened to Lon in her family history:

> *After the death of Robin, Polly and Lon lived alone. One day early in 1864 [?], Polly came running to the Boyle home and said: "Some men are hanging my Lon". . . Dr. Boyle hastened to the spot and stopped the hanging. B. E. (sic) and other gamblers had lost money and tried to accuse Lon of a theft. They had gone to Polly's home, ripped open the feather beds and upset her belongings. They found no money and the boy Lon declared he was innocent.*[1]

Lon "died not long afterward from the injuries received." However, burial records at the Salem Pioneer Cemetery list his cause of death as consumption, or tuberculosis. They also record a different year for his death, 1877. Lon apparently had pursued a career as a barber, as the 1870 census listed an L. Holmes, age nineteen, as a barber in Salem. He was unmarried and living alone.[2]

There is no way to reconcile Pauline Burch's recollection with the cemetery records. However, it is possible that writing years later, she confused Leonidas with Mary Jane's stepson, also named Lon, one of Alfred Drake's children. It needs to be said that Burch wrote portions of her family history to correct what she claimed were exaggerated and fictionalized accounts of the Ford family relationship with the Holmes family. And given the fragmentary records left behind, absolute certainty is impossible concerning many of the events in the lives of the Fords, Holmeses, and Shipleys. Burch's family history is itself replete with misstatements of fact, including her unequivocal declaration that "Reuben [Shipley] never was the slave of Mr. [Robert] Shipley." Nevertheless, there is no reason to think she made up the story of Lon's death, even though she may have confused important details.

Alfred Drake died in December 1875, just months following his marriage to Mary Jane on August 15, leaving her once again a widow. He was forty-nine, or fifty-three; records vary. Drake, like Reuben Shipley, was born in Kentucky and probably followed the same path, taken to Missouri by a slave owner, with a second migration to Oregon. He brought four children of his own to the marriage. His first wife, Elizabeth, who was born in Missouri, died in 1869 at age thirty-two. Drake's children in 1870 were Joseph (fourteen) and Lon (eleven), both born in Missouri, and George (five), James (three), and Elizabeth (one), all born in the Oregon Territory. Elizabeth died in March 1870 at age two.

Two burial locations are given for Alfred Drake, one at the Salem Pioneer Cemetery and the other in the Mt. Union Cemetery.[3] His first wife, Elizabeth, his daughter, Elizabeth, and a son, Joseph, are buried in the Salem cemetery. The family had lived in Independence in Polk County.

During their brief marriage, Mary Jane and Alfred Drake lived on the Shipley farm. Following Drake's death, Mary Jane was left with his children, although it's not clear how many remained at home. The 1880 census listed James Drake and George Drake as living in Salem with Albert Bayless, said to be a fugitive slave from Tennessee, who fled to California during the gold rush, and then to Salem, where he worked as a blacksmith.

Joseph Drake, the eldest of the Drake children, met a tragic death, hanged on the grounds of the Marion County Courthouse on March 20, 1885, for a murder he insisted he didn't commit. The victim was a Salem-area farmer, Dave Swartz, who, according to statements, had angered many around him, including his own wife and son, who were initially arrested for the crime.

The Oregon Supreme Court rejected Drake's final appeal. Justice Reuben Boise set the date of his execution. An article in the *Statesman* said "numerous jurists and the majority of public opinion felt the young black man had been falsely convicted . . . he was simply in the wrong place at the wrong time and took the fall for the real murderer." The newspaper's article said there was a large community turnout for the procession to Drake's burial at the Salem cemetery.[4]

The funeral of Joseph Drake, who was executed last Friday, took place on Sunday. The colored people of the city were all in attendance and a number of carriages containing white ladies and gentlemen were in the procession. Religious services were held at the grave and the last act of the tragedy closed decently, leaving only the record of its ghastly debate on the memory of those conversant with the facts and circumstances by which it was surrounded.

Mary Jane sold the Neabaeck Hill farm on March 14, 1889. The price was $2,900, more than four times the amount Reuben Shipley had paid to purchase it thirty years earlier.[5] Mary Jane signed the deed of sale with an "X" over the name Mary J. Drake. Others listed as sellers were an unmarried daughter, Nettie Shipley, and a married couple, R. F. Baker and Nettie Baker. The relationship of the Bakers, who were white, to Mary Jane is unknown. The 1880 census listed Baker as a saloonkeeper in Corvallis. After selling the farm, Mary Jane moved to Portland. The 1920 census showed her residing with her son, Edward Ficklin, and a daughter, Alice Williams. Edward worked as a janitor for the Southern Pacific Railroad.

Most of the Shipley children died at relatively young ages. By the time Mary Jane moved to Portland, apparently all except Edward and Alice were deceased.[6] Martha died of smallpox in 1873. Thomas, a herdsman, drowned in 1879 somewhere along the Klamath River in southern Oregon or northern California. He was twenty. Circumstances of the deaths of the other children are unknown.

Mary Jane apparently had lived for a time in east Salem in 1880 with her daughter, Nellie, or Nettie, and a man identified as Charles. A Charles Miller was married to Mary Jane's deceased sister, Roxanna. For Mary Jane, living in Salem was a temporary absence from her farm. Possibly she was in Salem to help during a family illness. Returning to her farm, she would later help neighbors in Benton County during a typhoid epidemic in the 1880s.[7] That same epidemic may have claimed some of her children and stepchildren.

The Ford family's last contact with Mary Jane came shortly before her death when Caroline Burch visited her in a Portland nursing home "during her last illness."[8] Mary Jane Holmes Shipley Drake died in the nursing home in 1926 at age seventy-two. Edward Ficklin, very much the doting son, arranged to bury his mother at Mt. Union Cemetery. He visited her grave once a year until the early 1940s when he stopped visiting, probably because of age or infirmity. He purchased the headstone listing those buried in the Shipley plot, including Alfred Drake. Whether Drake is actually buried there is unknown.

Edward Ficklin died in Portland on March 13, 1946, at age seventy-four. When he moved into the Edgefield Manor in Portland a few years before his death, he said he was divorced and had no living relatives. A letter from the Caldwell Colonial Mortuary listed Edward's father's name as "Reuben Edward Ficklin." For reasons probably only Ficklin could explain, he apparently decided against being buried with the rest of his family in Philomath and is instead interred at Lincoln Memorial Park in Portland. If Minnie Junkin was correct in saying he wanted to escape his color, perhaps that was the explanation. Ficklin was not a pauper; he left behind a life insurance policy in the amount of $500.[9]

It is a sad irony that after their struggles to win their freedom, the Shipleys— Reuben and Mary Jane—did not have direct living descendants who could long enjoy that freedom. But at a time of great racial division in Oregon, they did leave behind a lasting legacy to racial cooperation and understanding: the Mt. Union Cemetery.

The Shipley home on Neabaeck Hill collapsed in a snowstorm in 1918. The lumber was used to build a small smokehouse under the locust tree planted years earlier by Shipley to provide shade to the home.[10]

Slaveholders' Last Stand

Last-ditch attempts to protect "slave property" in Oregon embroiled the territorial legislature in absurdities in its final pre-statehood session in December 1858 and January 1859.

The first state legislature, which met in July 1858 to elect Lane and Smith as Oregon's first two U.S. senators, adjourned after four days.[1] Congress hadn't yet approved Oregon as a state, so the constitution with its anti-slavery clause wasn't yet in effect. Die-hard slavery advocates sought to take advantage when the territorial legislature met in December.

Two legislators submitted petitions on January 4 seeking legal protection for slave property, another way of saying slave ownership. These new petitions followed the petitions submitted the previous January by William Allen of Yamhill County. Representative W. W. Chapman of Lane County presented a petition from "certain citizens" asking lawmakers to "recognize the right of citizens of the Oregon Territory to the protection of slave property." William T'Vault of Jackson County—the editor/owner of the *Sentinel* newspaper in Jacksonville—presented two petitions, also from "certain citizens," also "praying the enactment of a law to protect slave property."[2]

T'Vault said it wasn't enough that the Supreme Court ruled in the Dred Scott case that neither Congress nor a territorial legislature had the right to prohibit citizens from holding slaves in the territories. He said slave owners still needed a fugitive slave law to compel runaway slaves in Oregon "to return to the service of said master."[3] T'Vault, from Kentucky, was once quoted as saying if he had "one drop" of abolitionist blood in his veins, he would "cut it out."[4]

Chapman delivered his petition on behalf of James Southworth, the former Tennessee and Missouri slave owner, who brought Louis Southworth and his mother to Oregon in the mid-1850s as slaves. Southworth had nearly fifty signatures on his petition asking the legislature "to acknowledge by legislative act the right of citizens of the United States to emigrate to and settle in the Territory with all their property (slaves included), and the consequential right to ask and receive protection from the Territorial government." The petition, along with others, was referred to the House Judiciary committee.[5] The significance of the petitions was not so much in the two hundred or so signatures of support, but that the signers, at least some of them slaveholders, were emboldened enough by the Dred Scott decision to go public with their pro-slavery views, apparently without concern that doing so would damage anyone's reputation.

Chapman followed up his petitions with a bill on January 10, 1859, to protect slaves as property, and also to make it a crime to harbor a slave without the owner's consent—a fugitive slave law for Oregon. The measure passed the House by a vote of thirteen to nine on the last day of the session.[6] It didn't come before the Council where Nathaniel Ford was a member—we can only speculate Ford would have voted in favor.

Looking back from today's perspective, it seems both nonsensical and inconceivable that Oregon's Territorial House of Representatives actually approved a local version of a fugitive' slave law. Indeed, it made no sense either to an Oregon historian writing over a century ago. Mused Walter Carleton Woodward: "it is an interesting fact that such a bill was actually introduced and rather heartily supported. And that too, after the people of Oregon, in accordance with the Democratic doctrine of popular sovereignty, had decided against slavery by a vote of approximately five to one."[7]

Also before the legislature was a resolution introduced by N. H. Craner of Linn County on January 12, urging the lawmakers to go on record as saying protection of slave property "needs no special legislation." Because of the Dred Scott decision, Craner argued, slave property was entitled to the same protections as any other property.

[I]t is believed by the undersigned [Craner] that neither Congress nor the Territories, under the Dred Scott decision, have the power to legislate upon the question of slavery within the Territories. And if Congress cannot, under the Constitution of the United States, legislate upon the question of slavery in the Territories, according to the decision of the Supreme Court, known as the Dred Scott decision, and which decision is now recognized by all portions of the Union as a fair and just exposition of the Constitution of the United States, then it is certainly clear that it could delegate no such power to the Territorial Government thereof to legislate upon the question of slavery.[8]

Craner's argument was rebutted by another representative, Erasmus Shattuck, representing Washington and Multnomah counties, who said the Dred Scott decision was irrelevant to circumstances in Oregon.

The slavery question should be regarded as settled here, by a most emphatic expression of public sentiment, in the vote upon the State Constitution; and no legislation on this subject can be regarded as consonant with public sentiment . . . the passage of the bill. . . or any similar act, would be regarded by a majority of the people of this territory as an outrage to public sentiment, and would arouse, in all their fury, the elements of strife and discord, which have proved the curse of other Territories, and from which we cannot claim to be exempt. It will distract and confuse the powers of our State organization and prove a lasting curse of vexation and trouble.[9]

Craner's resolution was tabled.

The following month, on February 14, 1859, President Buchanan signed a bill approving Oregon as a state—along with its new constitution prohibiting slavery and excluding blacks.

·~·

With inhabitants of the new state of Oregon watching from a distance, events moved quickly toward disunion and war. Abraham Lincoln was elected on November 6, 1860, and inaugurated four months later on March 3, 1861. In the interim, secessionist states formed the Confederate States of America on February 4, 1861. Civil War descended on the nation when Confederate forces fired on Fort Sumter on April 12, 1861.

The war came and went, tearing the country apart, but having little direct military impact in Oregon, although regular Army troops were withdrawn from Oregon to join the fighting in the East. Prominent casualties from the Pacific Northwest during the war included U.S. Senator Edward R. Baker of Oregon, killed at the battle of Ball's Bluff in northern Virginia on October 21, 1861, and Isaac Stevens, former governor of the Washington Territory, killed in 1862 while leading his troops at the Second Battle of Bull Run. Despite Stevens' support for the Breckinridge-Lane ticket in 1860, he had joined the Union Army, serving as a major general and division commander.

The late journalist and historian, Alvin Josephy Jr., wrote that the attack on Fort Sumter helped "set off a burst of pro-Union patriotism" in both Oregon and California, whose loyalty had previously been somewhat suspect.[10] Forced to choose, many of Oregon's pro-slavery advocates, Judge Deady among them, took the Union side, as did Asahel Bush, whose views on slavery had long been ambiguous. Supporters of the Union coalesced into a new Union Party, which dominated Oregon's war-time legislature. Joseph Lane, however, never wavered in his sympathy for the South. In a letter to Deady on the eve of the Thirty-Seventh Congress, the last before the South broke away, Lane predicted the Southern states would "go out of the Union into one of their own; forming a great, homogeneous and glorious southern confederacy."[11] That didn't happen. The 1860 election and the outbreak of the war effectively ended Lane's career in Oregon politics.

According to one report, the defeated U.S. senator and vice presidential candidate arrived back in Oregon by ship from Washington, D.C., bringing several boxes of munitions, ostensibly to mount a revolt.[12] However, there was nothing in Lane's subsequent behavior that suggested he was involved in a plot. Apparently the rumor of munitions started with a bystander, who pointed to several boxes and "with mock gravity pronounced them full of Sharpe's rifles."[13] Lane did return with two hunting rifles, one each for himself and his son, Lafayette.[14]

Unlike Lane's previous homecomings from Washington, D. C., there was no dockside band, no dignitaries, no excited crowd to greet him. One account of his return said, "Spurned even by his former friends [Lane] made his way unaccompanied and unheralded to his southern Oregon home by a devious trail, fearing the mob justice of the justly enraged citizens of the leading valley towns."[15] Lane apparently was shot in the chest along the way under circumstances that have never been clear. An Applegate family history said he was taken to Jesse Applegate's home near Yoncalla in Douglas County to recover.[16] While the incident appeared highly suspicious—an assassination attempt, perhaps—Applegate evidently accepted the explanation that Lane shot himself when he dropped his gun while climbing out of his wagon.[17]

⌣⌣

The Confederacy was not without supporters in Oregon. Southern sympathizers organized themselves as the "Knights of the Golden Circle," a local branch of a national movement that sought to create a separate slave territory, called the Pacific Republic, extending into Mexico. Oregon counted as many as twenty-three hundred members, organized in ten so-called "circles," including two in Portland, two in Salem, and one each in Scio, Albany, Jacksonville, and Yamhill County.[18] While the Knights occasionally threatened resistance, there was little actual violence, in part because then-Governor Addison C. Gibbs, a Republican, organized a militia to confront them.[19]

There were rumors that the Knights planned to attack and seize Fort Vancouver, although if there were such plans, they weren't carried out. Also, when pro-Confederate partisans "raised their flag in Jacksonville, they faced opposition and backed down."[20] The movement had been predicated on a southern victory, but after it became clear the North was winning the war, it faded away.[21]

The *Statesman* reported on May 12, 1866, that a "treasonable secret society" called the "Jones Family" had stockpiled weapons, brought into Oregon from Canada "preparatory to aggressive operations," of which there were none. The newspaper said the weapons, probably rifles, came aboard a schooner from Victoria, B. C. "in long boxes marked 'shovels', which were distributed in Polk County." Possibly this group was the same as the Knights, as the newspaper projected the membership at about twenty-five hundred, nearly the same membership estimated for the Knights. The *Statesman* offered no sourcing for its report.[22]

⌣⌣

Oregon's major newspapers, the *Statesman* in Salem and the *Oregonian* in Portland, were solidly pro-Union. But a number of smaller newspapers voiced strong southern sympathies, and a half-dozen were shut down by General George Wright, the military commander for Oregon and California. Wright denied the offending newspapers the use of the U.S. Mail, on which they depended for circulation. In addition to suppressing newspapers, Wright also ignored writs of *habeas corpus* and infringed on other rights "in his determination to crush any sign of disloyalty or treason."[23]

Among the newspapers was the *Messenger*, also known as "Avery's Ox," established in Corvallis in 1857 by J. C. Avery. Described as a "vehement and defiant advocate of slavery," the *Messenger* supported Breckinridge and Lane in the 1860 election, and urged that Oregon remain neutral in the event of war. After war broke out, it "grew more outspoken for the secessionists" before finally being shut down in 1863 for its pro-South stand.[24] Two newspapers in Jacksonville were suppressed, the *Intelligencer*, "a seccession newspaper" edited by William T'Vault, and the *Southern Oregon Gazette*, described as "an intensely Democratic sheet . . . bitter and disloyal to the government."[25]

In Eugene, the *Democratic Herald,* edited by Oregon poet Joaquin Miller, who "espoused the cause of the confederacy," was suppressed. When it resumed publishing as the *Register,* it was suppressed again "on account of treasonable utterances," after which Miller left the paper.[26] The *Register* carried this closing notice on September 20, 1862:

> *Subscribers of the Register will be furnished the Review in its place as the circulation of the paper is prohibited by order of General Wright, military ruler of the coast.*[27]

Also out of business by military order were the *Oregon Democrat* of Albany, founded by Delazon Smith, and the pro-slavery *Daily Advertiser* of Portland, established by Alonzo Leland.[28]

᛫᛫᛫

The war ended on April 9, 1865, with General Robert E. Lee's surrender at Appomattox. The outcome settled once and for all that slavery would henceforth be illegal throughout the land. Slaves, all slaves, were freed.

The Oregon Legislative Assembly on December 5, 1865, ratified the Thirteenth Amendment to the federal Constitution abolishing slavery. The following September, the legislature ratified the Fourteenth Amendment, extending citizenship and equal protection of the law to African Americans. The two amendments rendered irrelevant Oregon's exclusion clause, although it would remain in the constitution.

While the slavery issue was settled and exclusion acts were voided, racism nevertheless remained deep-seated in Oregon in this period and beyond. The 1862 legislature imposed an annual poll tax of five dollars on "each and every negro, Chinaman, Kanaka [Hawaiian] and mulatto."[29] The 1866 legislature outlawed intermarriage between whites and blacks, or whites and other minorities.

In 1868, with the Democrats back in power in Salem, and amid controversy over Reconstruction, the legislature passed a resolution withdrawing Oregon's ratification of the Fourteenth Amendment.[30] Although the withdrawal of Oregon's approval made no difference to the implementation of the amendment, it reflected the stubborn refusal of white Oregonians to consider African Americans worthy of equal rights. A senator from Lane County, H. C. Huston, had argued in 1866 that by granting citizenship to blacks, the Fourteenth Amendment would circumvent the Oregon Constitution and "place the inferior races upon an equality with the superior."[31]

It took the Oregon Legislature nearly a century to re-ratify the Fourteenth Amendment. The *Oregonian*, evidently oblivious to Oregon's history in this period, commented in an editorial that most Oregonians were unaware that the amendment had been de-ratified.[32] However, members of the black community were aware, and reversing the historical embarrassment was a top priority for Representative William McCoy, the first African American to serve in the Oregon legislature.[33] McCoy, elected in 1971, said Oregon "should set the record straight."[34] Re-ratification passed overwhelmingly, but quietly, on May 21, 1973.

Oregon's re-ratification of black citizenship—more than a century after it was guaranteed in the U.S. Constitution—merited a mere three paragraphs in the *Oregonian*. The article was so obscurely placed on page thirty that many readers probably didn't notice.[35] And that may have been the point. In spite of McCoy's wish, there was little record-straightening. Wrote one scholar. "Politicians got their wish—hardly anyone found out about Oregon's embarrassing oversight."[36]

It wasn't until February 24, 1959, that the Oregon legislature approved the Fifteenth Amendment extending voting rights to African Americans, ninety years after it was submitted to the states for ratification. In 1870, Governor LaFayette Grover had refused even to call a special session to consider the amendment, saying giving the vote to blacks would do "violence to the inherent and reserved rights of the several States."[37] The 1870 legislature agreed, declaring the amendment "an infringement on popular rights."[38] The California legislature, which had also declined to ratify the Fifteenth Amendment, finally approved it on October 15, 1962.

Withholding approval had no impact on the amendment, however. U.S. Secretary of State Hamilton Fish certified on March 30, 1870, that the necessary number of states had ratified the amendment. Undeterred by Oregon's failure to ratify, local African Americans held a formal celebration of the amendment in Portland on April 6, 1870.[39] That same year, the Oregon Supreme Court upheld voting rights for blacks on the grounds that the Fifteenth Amendment was part of the U.S. Constitution. An 1866 anti-miscegenation law, barring marriage between whites and non-whites, remained a law in Oregon until revoked in 1951.

The exclusion clause in Oregon's constitution was never enforced, although there were several unsuccessful attempts, including in the 1864 legislature. A measure was introduced to require a county-by-county census of blacks, giving the sheriff authority to deport blacks living illegally.[40] The measure failed. One last attempt at enforcement in 1866 was sent to a Senate committee that recommended indefinite postponement.[41] However, the clause remained in the constitution for decades. Efforts to repeal the clause over the next seventy-five years were likewise unsuccessful. A proposed repeal failed in the November 2, 1900, election by a two-to-one margin. The *Oregonian* attributed the outcome partly to other proposed changes on the ballot, all rejected by voters. But the newspaper editorialized that it didn't really matter.

> *The vote on repeal of the clause that forbids negroes to come to Oregon would have been affirmative, had there been any need of it, but that clause of the Constitution is obsolete, never indeed was operative, and long since was wholly superseded by amendments to the Constitution of the United States. To strike it out of the Constitution of Oregon would be merely a perfunctory act, and the votes cast against it were thrown (sic) simply as a protest against the eagerness of agitators to amend the Constitution.*[42]

The clause came before voters again on November 2, 1926, when it was condemned in the Oregon voters pamphlet as "a constant reminder of intolerance and hatred, a reproach to the people of this commonwealth, a slur upon those whom it sought to proscribe."[43] The vote to remove the clause was decisive—91,129 in favor to 55,042 against. In a one-paragraph mention of the election outcome, the *Oregonian* said the clause was "objectionable and obsolete."[44]

Oregon's long flirtation with exclusion laws had finally ended. But while the exclusion laws were rarely enforced in Oregon, the tragic legacy of the laws was that they discouraged blacks from coming at all.

Moving On

ROBERT AND MARY HOLMES

Robert and Mary Holmes—Robin and Polly—lived out their lives in Salem. In the 1860 census, three of their children resided with them, Roxanna, James, and Leonidas. The Holmeses were not poor. The census listed Holmes' wealth at $500 in real estate and $200 in personal property. His occupation was given as "day laborer." There is no record of what happened to the Holmeses' nursery, whether it was sold, went out of business, or was still in their possession.

On February 1, 1862, Holmes—then "of failing health and body"—drew up a will naming as executor Reuben Boise, the Supreme Court justice and former prosecuting attorney who represented him during his case against Nathaniel Ford. Holmes left his money and property "to my wife, Polly," and his four surviving children: Mary Jane, Leonidas, Roxanna, and James. Each was to receive five dollars. The date of Robert Holmes' death is uncertain, but it is thought he died in 1863, at about age fifty-three. He had purchased Lot 202 in what is now the Salem Pioneer Cemetery, and is presumed buried there with his son, James, and daughter, Roxanna Miller. There is no headstone, but the names of the Holmeses—Robert, James and Roxanna—are among those engraved on a headstone installed in 2007 by the Oregon Northwest Black Pioneers.[1]

James Holmes died in December 1862 just ten months after his father drew up his will. Roxanna died on July 22, 1873, of tuberculosis. She was twenty-six and lived in Salem with her Kentucky-born husband, Charles Miller, whom she married in 1865. They had three children.

Leonidas, the youngest of the Holmes children, died in Salem in March 10, 1877, at age twenty-four, also of consumption—or, according to Pauline Burch, of a lynching and beating—whichever version is to be believed.

Sadly, Mary—or Polly Holmes—was listed in the 1870 census as an inmate at the then so-named Oregon Hospital for the Insane in east Portland. Her date of death is unknown.

NATHANIEL FORD

Ford's term in the 1857-1858 Oregon Territorial Legislature was his last significant elected office. After an earlier near-meteoric rise in Oregon politics, his alliance with the dissident national Democrats seems to have doomed any hopes of further advancement. Ford regained some status in the Democratic Party, as he was listed in 1859 as a member of its central committee, part of the Lane purge of Bush-dominated party leaders.[2] In one of Ford's final actions in the territorial legislature, he cast the lone negative vote on January 22, 1859, in the legislative council against a measure to pay the expenses of Oregon's 1857 Constitutional Convention. There is no explanation for his vote, although it's possible it was out of personal pique at Democratic leaders for not making him a convention delegate. Or, perhaps, he objected to the clause prohibiting slavery.

Ford was chairman of the council's military committee, charged with preparing a report on the identity and number of whites killed during "peacetime" by Native Americans. Ford reported back that two hundred and seventy-three whites were killed during the period from 1834 to 1857. Among the victims were George LeBreton and Sterling Rogers, both killed in the Cockstock incident.[3]

As age crept up on them, Ford and his wife, Lucinda, sold half of their donation land claim—three hundred and twenty acres—in 1865 to a Charles Claggett, who was said to be another former slave owner.[4] Nathaniel Ford died in 1870 at age seventy-five. Following her husband's death, Lucinda sold a large portion of her remaining property to a daughter, Sarah Burch, for $4,360. Lucinda, who lived out her life on the original donation land claim, died in 1874 at age seventy-four. She is buried with her husband in the Burch Pioneer Cemetery near Rickreall. Sarah Burch is also buried there.

JOHN THORP FORD

Nathaniel Ford's grandson, John Thorp Ford—whose father, Marcus, died on the Northwest coast in 1850—lived most of his life in Polk County. He was elected to two terms as county sheriff, serving from 1902 to 1906, and, in 1917, was elected city auditor and police judge, serving seven consecutive terms. Ford, who had lived with Nathaniel Ford until age twenty-two, told Fred Lockley in a 1922 interview that his grandfather was "a man of great decision and character." John Ford died in 1930 at age eighty-three.

JUDGE GEORGE H. WILLIAMS

Following his service on the Territorial Supreme Court, Judge Williams went on to national prominence. He was nominated by President James Buchanan to a second term as chief territorial judge in 1857, but resigned soon after.[5] In 1865, he finally achieved his goal of becoming a U.S. senator, elected by the Oregon Legislature, serving one term. While in the Senate, Williams was a member of the Joint Committee on Reconstruction, which drafted the Fourteenth Amendment. President Ulysses S. Grant appointed him U.S. Attorney General in 1871 and nominated him for chief justice of the U.S. Supreme Court in 1873.

The 1868 Oregon Legislature voted to recall Williams as senator—and also Oregon's second senator, Henry Corbett. Williams' chief offense seems to have been his support of Reconstruction and his help in managing the impeachment of President Andrew Johnson. Democrats had regained a majority in the legislature and tilted back toward overt sympathy for the defeated South. They accused Williams and Corbett of "plain and palpable violations" of the Constitution in their support of the Reconstruction laws, which "in their enforcement have overthrown and subverted civil liberty in eleven [southern] states of the union and consigned the citizens thereof to odious and despotic military dictatorship."[6] The U.S. Senate ignored the attempted recall.

Williams served out his term. However, his national career was soon to collapse. There were unproved but damaging accusations regarding a bribe, and also controversy caused by what some saw as the exorbitant lifestyle of his second wife, Kate Hughes George, whom he married in 1867. She was described in one account as "a curious compound of social elegance, loose language and 'unvictorian' behavior."[7]

Contributing to Williams' political difficulties were the enemies he made along the way. The U.S. Senate refused to confirm his nomination to the Supreme Court, and Grant withdrew it. Williams returned to Portland to practice law. He was elected mayor in 1902 at age seventy-nine, serving a single term. But even as mayor, Williams' career continued to crumble. He was indicted by a grand jury in connection with a sewer construction scandal, although the charge, possibly trumped up, was later dropped. He also faced criticism for failing to crack down on illicit gambling and other criminal activity.[8] U.S. Senator John Gearin was quoted as saying of Williams: "He has not been a bad mayor; he's not been a mayor at all."[9]

Timothy Davenport wrote that Williams' greatest contribution to the anti-slavery movement in Oregon was his Free State Letter. However, Davenport lamented that it was his only contribution. In an article following Williams' death, Davenport said Williams was constrained by his political ambitions.

Doubtless Judge Williams preferred free institutions among which he was born, reared and schooled; but, like most persons in the Northern states, having a strong desire for political promotion, never permitted his anti-slavery sentiments and preferences to interfere with his political aspirations. . . . He was not even a protester against the errors and perverse tendencies of his party, though he had the intellectual ability and oratorical force, if he had been of more heroic mould, to have exerted a modifying influence favorable to republican institutions.[10]

Davenport conspicuously overlooked the significance of Williams' 1853 decision in Holmes vs. Ford, in which Williams effectively ruled slavery unlawful in Oregon. He did have staunch defenders, among them Harvey Scott, publisher of the *Oregonian*, who, following Williams' death in 1910, wrote that his "services, throughout a long and eventful life, both to the State of Oregon and to our common country, the United States, have been of highest distinction and value." Of Williams' near-miss at becoming chief justice of the Supreme Court, Scott blamed it on "sectional and social jealousies."[11]

Williams died April 4, 1910. He is buried in Portland's Riverview Cemetery.

REUBEN P. BOISE

As far as is now known, Reuben Boise left just a single public comment on the Holmes vs. Ford case, in which he played a major role. This was a letter sent to Timothy Davenport on June 4, 1906—a year before Boise's death—rebutting what was described as a careless statement by Davenport that there had never been slaves in Oregon.[12] Boise wrote:

Colonel Nathaniel Ford came to Oregon from Missouri in 1844 and brought with him three slaves—two men and one woman. The woman was married to one of these men and had some small children. Ford claimed these children as slaves and continued to claim them until 1853. One of these children—a girl—had, prior to that time, been given to Mrs. (Dr.) Boyle, a daughter of Ford. Prior to 1853 the parents of these children (Robbin and Polly) had claimed their freedom and left Ford and in 1852 were living at Nesmith's Mills. But Ford had kept the children. In 1853, Robbin, the father of the children, brought a suit by habeas corpus to get possession of the children. The case was heard by Judge George

H. Williams in the summer of 1853, and he held that these children being then (by the voluntary act of Ford) in Oregon where slavery could not legally exist, were free from the bonds of slavery and awarded their custody to their father.[13]

Boise had a distinguished judicial career. He was one of three men named to a code commission to rewrite and update the territorial laws into a Code of Oregon in 1854. It was this code that resulted, either mistakenly or purposely, in repeal of the 1849 exclusion law. Boise served on the Oregon Supreme Court from 1858 to 1870 and from 1876 to 1880. He was chief justice from 1862 to 1864 and from 1867 to 1870. He served in the territorial legislature in 1854 and as a delegate to the 1857 Oregon Constitutional Convention, where he played a moderating role amidst heated debate over racial issues.

Following the death of his first wife, Ellen Lyon, in 1865, Boise married Emily Pratt in 1867. He died in 1907 at age eighty-seven. Judge Williams delivered the eulogy at Boise's funeral, saying, "As a judge, he has been absolutely impartial and upright; his private life irreproachable, and in public, above suspicion."

JUDGE MATTHEW P. DEADY

The most favorable view of Matthew Deady is through the prism of his life after the outbreak of the Civil War.

President Buchanan appointed Deady to the U.S. District Court in Portland in 1859, where he served until his death in 1893 at age sixty-eight. During his long career as a jurist, Deady helped establish the University of Oregon law school and served as president of the university's board of regents. Deady Hall bears his name.

As a judge, Deady established a deserved reputation as an opponent of discriminatory legislation. Northwest author Barry Lopez credited Deady for important rulings that in later years "reinforced principles of fair treatment and equal rights" in a hostile political climate, especially toward immigrant Chinese. But according to one biographer, Malcom Clark Jr., Judge Deady could never completely shake his past as a pro-slavery apologist.

His earlier support of slavery plagued him throughout the war years, when his loyalty was openly questioned, and it continued to embarrass him in later years. . . . But despite his troubled conscience, he never once faced up to the fact that the institution [slavery] itself was inherently evil.[14]

Deady was in later years forgiven for his pro-slavery views by many of those who opposed him. One of these was John McBride, who clashed with Deady in the 1857 Constitutional Convention. McBride would later say Deady deserved credit for opposing secession during the Civil War. "He believed in a government that had force behind it, and when the rebellion began in 1861 he became as ardent a champion of the government as any Unionist in the land."

Jesse Applegate, who, like McBride, had his differences with Deady in the convention, later would count him as a close friend. Following the outbreak of the Civil War, Applegate opposed an attempt to remove Deady as a U.S. district judge on grounds of disloyalty. In a letter to U.S. Attorney General Edward Bates in 1861, Applegate insisted Deady was not a secessionist:

> *While he has no faith in the capacity of the masses to govern themselves, I think it quite probable had the south continued to fight her battles in the Union and with the ballot box, she would still have had his political support. But these opinions I believe are not inconsistent with loyalty to Union and opposition to rebellion and treason, for if the government were to refuse the services of all who hold them it would lose the support of some of its most earnest and able defenders.*[15]

Yet Applegate later broke off all contact, feeling betrayed by a Deady ruling that hurt him financially.[16]

Deady died in Portland in 1893 at age sixty-eight.

JOSEPH LANE

Joseph Lane was described by Judge George Williams as "a born politician" who "knew how to flatter and please people."[17] However, Lane's engaging personality was not sufficient for him to survive the nation's schism over slavery. He chose the losing side and his career plunged like a spent rocket.

After the Breckinridge-Lane ticket lost to Abraham Lincoln in the 1860 presidential election, Lane returned to Oregon an "embittered and broken man," unheralded for his many past achievements on behalf of Oregon.[18] He lived out his life on a farm near Roseburg in Douglas County.

One former adversary who tried to help Lane was Jesse Applegate, who in 1878—the war long ended—sought to get him elected to the U.S. Senate, a highly improbable outcome. Applegate was dissatisfied with the slate of candidates then running for office. He wrote the following to Matthew Deady on June 7, 1878:

*Lane is the man of all others to be selected for senator in this emergency.
. . . I have lately spent the best part of two days with the old general and
freely conversed with him upon the past struggles and present dangers
that threaten our institutions. Tho' he has been a Democrat of the "States
Rights" school, he accepts the results of the war as settling the questions
embodied in the amendments of the Constitution finally and forever, and
thinks the preservation of the Union the greatest good to all sections—in
short, he is a true patriot and always has been.*[19]

Lane was then seventy-six. The election to the Senate didn't happen. It is
doubtful it was seriously considered.

Lane's wife, Polly, died in 1870. Afterward, Lane lived as a hermit, his only
companion an African American boy, named Peter Waldo, said to have been
"committed to his care" by a Josephine County court in 1864.[20] It seemed
poetic justice that after a career spent defending slavery, Lane's lone companion
in the last years of his life would be an African American.

Interestingly, Lane was given a Native American slave, a Modoc boy, in
1850 as a gift from a chief of the Rogue River tribe, although it's not clear Lane
considered the boy a slave. According to Lane's biographer, the boy showed
signs of malnutrition and beatings. Lane "took him, bathed and clothed him,
named him John and within a few weeks became quite attached to him."[21]

Following Lane's death in 1881, at age seventy-nine, Judge Williams would
write of him:

*[H]e had all the essential qualifications of a successful politician, and if he
had not been so imbued with a desire to extend slavery, might in all human
probability have represented Oregon in the Senate as long as he lived.
He was intensely southern in all his feelings and sympathies, a devoted
friend of Jefferson Davis, and opposed to coercive measures to preserve
the Union. It is due to his memory to say that he had what many shifty
politicians have not, the courage of his convictions, and he stood by them
to the bitter end.*[22]

PETER BURNETT

If Peter Burnett is remembered at all in California, it is for the racist positions
he took, both as governor and as a Supreme Court justice. In Oregon he is
remembered for his contributions to settlement of the Oregon Country, but
also as the architect of Oregon's 1844 exclusion law, known as the "lash law."

Burnett, who seemed not to remain in one occupation for very long, had a stormy experience as California's first governor, repeatedly at odds with the legislature. He advocated an exclusion law, which the California legislature declined to enact. He resigned in 1851, after a little more than a year in office.

In 1857, Burnett was appointed to a year-long term on the California Supreme Court, where he and two other justices returned a free black, eighteen-year-old Archy Lee, to his former slave owner, who wanted to return Lee to Mississippi. The owner, Charles Stovall, had brought Lee to Sacramento in 1857. Lee escaped, which should have been enough to insure his freedom in free state California.

But Stovall had Lee arrested. He argued that the Dred Scott decision protected slavery not only in the federal territories, but also in free states where the legislature had not explicitly banned slavery, even though the Constitution of California prohibited the practice.[23] Burnett, who wrote the court's opinion, rejected those arguments, but nevertheless held that Stovall had reason to be unaware of the expiration of California's Fugitive Slave Act, and therefore could assume his slave property was safe. Burnett said Stovall could return Lee to Mississippi. Burnett's ruling was widely seen as "a judicial absurdity."[24] Leading Lee's defense at several stages of the proceedings was Edward Baker, the future U.S. senator for Oregon. Lee was not returned to Mississippi. Widespread outrage greeted the decision, and a lower court overruled Burnett and dismissed the case, allowing Lee to go free. The case has been called "the dying gasp of slaveholding rights in California."[25]

Burnett suffered the posthumous indignity in 2011 of having his name removed from a San Francisco preschool after local activists became aware of his racist history. The name of the Burnett Child Development Center was changed to the Leola M. Havard Early Education School after the city's first female African American principal.[26] "Through the change of this name, we're getting away from a vestige of our dark past," said The Reverend Amos Brown, head of the local chapter of the NAACP.[27]

In memoirs written years later, Burnett acknowledged making a mistake in his support for Oregon's 1844 lash law, a mistake he claimed he corrected by supporting a new non-corporal punishment.[28] He said he hadn't thought it possible for African Americans, after years of subjugation as slaves, to achieve anything positive in their lives, and believed Oregon and California would be better off without them. "Had I foreseen the civil war, and the changes it has produced, I would not have supported such a measure. But at the time I did not suppose such changes could be brought about."[29]

Burnett finally achieved his goal of paying off his Missouri debts. He had become wealthy as a land speculator even before being elected California's governor.

He died May 17, 1895, in San Francisco.

MOSES "BLACK" HARRIS

As guide to some of the earliest emigrant wagon trains, Moses Harris played a key role in helping to settle Oregon. He was described by one author as "a black man of medium height with black hair, black whiskers and dark brown eyes."[30] Harris was an experienced and skilled guide, reflected in the confidence placed in him to lead the Ford-Gilliam wagon train of 1844. A former fur trapper, Harris also was known for leading the successful rescue of the famous lost wagon train led by Stephen Meek in 1846.

Harris was fluent in the language of the Snake tribe, making him "of great service to us on the Plains," wrote Lindsay Applegate.[31] Harris was a key member of the 1846 expedition that developed the southern route into Oregon known as the Applegate Trail and later wrote letters to newspapers defending it from criticism.

After arriving in Oregon in 1844 with the Ford-Gilliam wagon train, Harris lived for several years in Yamhill County. He returned to Missouri in 1847, hoping to continue his work as a trail guide. He was hired to lead a wagon train of would-be gold miners to California, but fell ill with cholera. His death was reported in the *Independence [Missouri] Daily Union* on May 14, 1849.[32]

Harris was known for the tall tales he would tell around camp fires, one of the most popular of which concerned a petrified forest. As Harris told the story, the forest had become so quickly petrified that the leaves, and the birds in the branches, were petrified as well. Harris' biographer, Verne Bright, wrote:

> *He spent practically all the years of his adult life on the frontier as trapper and guide, ranging over every section of the region from Canada to Mexico and from the Missouri River to the Pacific Ocean. It was said of him as early as 1823 that he was an 'experienced mountaineer . . . [known] for his knowledge of the country and his familiarity with Indian life.' This Harris was reputed to be a man of 'great leg' and capable from his long sojourning in the mountains, of enduring extreme privation and fatigue.*

Bright also quoted an epitaph written by James Clyman, a friend of Harris.

Here lies the bones of old Black Harris
Who often traveled beyond the far west
And for the freedom of equal rights'
He crossed the snowy mountain heights
He was a free and easy kind of soul
Especially with a belly full.[33]

CORNELIUS GILLIAM

Cornelius Gilliam, whose wagon train from Missouri joined Nathaniel Ford's in 1844, was killed during the Cayuse War in 1848. He served as a colonel in the militia formed following the massacre of Marcus and Narcissa Whitman and eleven others in 1847. Gilliam's death was considered accidental. He was returning from present-day eastern Washington to The Dalles for supplies, when he somehow entangled a rope with a gun, which went off and shot him dead.[34]

JESSE APPLEGATE

Although Jesse Applegate was a member of the Oregon Constitutional Convention, he neither signed nor endorsed the constitution, not then, not ever. Indeed, in a letter to Matthew Deady on November 15, 1868, he called the constitution "a disgrace" to those who authored it, especially because of the exclusion clause. Applegate's letter was in response to a request from Deady to join a celebration for the constitution. He rejected the invitation, reminding Deady he had voted against it.

It would be dishonest for me to seek honor as one of the framers of Constitution in which I took no part, and as I consider it a disgrace to those who did frame it, I hope you will not insist in making me a share of it.[35]

In this same letter, he told Deady he could not send him a photograph, as Deady requested, because he had never had his picture taken "nor is it likely it ever will be." And it wasn't.

Applegate lived out his life at his home at Yoncalla in Douglas County. He had several serious financial setbacks, one resulting from an unwise investment that left him without resources. He wrote extensively, and impressively, and became known as "The Sage of Yoncalla." He died on April 22, 1888, at age seventy-seven.

FORD'S DONATION LAND CLAIM

The original Ford donation land claim has been divided over the years among multiple owners. Half of the town of Rickreall, plus the highway intersection of Oregon Routes 22 and 223, fit easily onto the old claim, with much of it still remaining as farmland.

Gus Quiring knew the old Ford property probably better than anyone else alive in 2010. For twenty years, he farmed one hundred and fifty acres while working for the Cadle family—Albert R. and Porter N. Cadle, both now deceased, acquired a large portion of the Ford claim in 1920. "It's some of the best soil in Polk County," said Quiring, then eighty-seven and retired. "It's not the easiest to farm—it's heavy, mucky soil, but it's the best producer."[36]

Quiring knew nothing about the Fords. He said the Cadles used to grow grain and peas, but later switched to grass seed, then much in demand nationwide for new lawns. But the market had since declined. "Warehouses around here are all full of grass seed, but no one is buying."

Quiring, a Nebraska-born World War II veteran, lived in a double-wide on a sloping hill at the south end of the property. He and his wife owned the home, but not the land under it. Quiring said the Cadle family rewarded his years of service by allowing him to live out his life on the property.

Until recently, Quiring enjoyed an unbroken view from his front porch, looking north down the gentle slope and the grass-covered fields, once farmed by Ford, and out across Highway 22 to the Baskett Slough National Wildlife Refuge. To the west are the foothills of the Coast Range. The view had lately been scarred by a thirty-foot wide gravel road winding across the property from east to west. The road was built by the current owners, who proposed to develop a subdivision.

Epilogue

The late Alvin M. Josephy Jr. faulted history books, which—at the time he wrote, although less so in later years—offered to American school children a distorted view of the settlement of the United States, wherein white men who protected their property were called patriots, while Native Americans doing the same were called murderers. In an article entitled "The Forked Tongue in U.S. History Books," Josephy wrote:

> *The writing of history, done by the white intruders, conquerors and dispossessors, has been self-serving from the start—meeting the needs, generation after generation, of the people who were pouring in from Europe, first erecting colonies and then building a new nation. Little attempt was made to understand—and much less explain—the different and unfamiliar Indian cultures against which the newcomers rubbed. Because they were different, they were deemed inferior and dangerous.*[1]

While Josephy was addressing the portrayal of Native Americans, his comments could just as easily apply to African Americans and other minorities. General interest history books have had little to say about the slaves, exclusion laws, or other discriminatory legislation during Oregon's early years.

Isn't it about time we catch up?

Acknowledgments

Many people deserve my heartfelt thanks for their help, encouragement, and understanding as I worked on this book. Especially deserving is my wife, Candise, who read the manuscript and encouraged me every step of the way while patiently enduring my need for solitude to write. A special thanks also goes to my brother, Bill Nokes, who started me on this journey when he asked one afternoon, "Why don't you write about Reuben Shipley?" and pointed me to a page about the former slave in a family genealogy. Bill lives his dream sailing the Pacific in his ketch, *Someday*.

My deepest thanks goes, too, to my son Jeffrey Nokes and my sisters, Gail Hulden and Kathy Nokes, all of whom read early versions of the manuscript and offered their suggestions, and to my other son, Deston Nokes, whose work on my websites and advice on marketing is invaluable. I am also much beholden to Darrell Millner, professor of black studies at Portland State University, who offered direction and suggestions, and steered me away from several errors of interpretation. The same for Stacey Smith, assistant professor of history at Oregon State University, who expanded my reading list and pushed me to give greater weight to Oregon's place in the national debate over slavery. And where would I be without the tireless help of the good people at the Oregon Historical Society Library, most notably Research Librarian Scott Daniels, and reference assistants Hannah Allan and Jennifer Keyser.

Any listing of those who helped me is risky because of deserving people I may overlook. But the list must include Harold H. Kerr II, president of the Howard County Missouri Genealogical Society; Gary Gene Fuenfhausen, a cultural historian in Arrow Rock, Missouri; Diane Knutson of the Miller County (Missouri) Museum; Mary Gallagher of the Benton County (Oregon) Historical Museum; Nita Wilson of the Polk County (Oregon) Museum; Lee Merklin, historian for the Henkle Family Association; Brian Waldo Johnson of Monmouth, Oregon; Renita Bogle-Byrd of Decatur, Georgia; Greg Shine, chief ranger and historian at the Fort Vancouver National Historic Site; Walter Bachman of New York City; Amy Everetts and Donna Postma of the Cartography Department in the Polk County Assessor's Office; Michael Ramirez of the Benton County records and licenses office; David Malone, land surveyor in the Benton County Public Works Department; Peggy Smith of the Independence (Oregon) Heritage Museum; Kylie Pine of the Willamette Heritage Center in Salem; Willie Richardson and Gwen Carr of Oregon

Northwest Black Pioneers; and Andrew Needham and Austin Schulz of the Oregon State Archives in Salem. Also, Stephenie Flora, whose comprehensive list of early emigrants on oregonpioneers.com is invaluable. And, not least, my appreciation to Tom Booth and Jo Alexander of Oregon State University Press, who, respectively, guided this book through the selection and publishing process, and to my editor, Tara Rae Miner, whose attention to detail made this a better book.

Lastly, one more word about the Oregon Historical Society Library. It is a treasure trove without parallel for researchers of Oregon and Northwest history. Found on its shelves are the journals and biographies of early settlers, newspapers dating to the 1850s, early photographs, and more than a century of *Oregon Historical Quarterlies*. Among the quarterly articles most helpful to me were several written in the early twentieth century by the late Fred Lockley, an *Oregon Journal* columnist whose indefatigable interest in the early history of our region, including interviews and sketches of former slaves, made a major contribution to this book.

This author alone is responsible for any errors of commission or omission.

APPENDIX I

Henkles and Wyatts

The author is a direct descendant of two pioneer families, the Henkles and Wyatts, who play a part in the preceding account of early slavery in Oregon. Members of both families knew Reuben Shipley and his wife, the former Mary Jane Holmes. As mentioned in the prologue, the author is also a shirt-tail relative of Robert N. Shipley, who brought Reuben to Oregon as a slave in 1853.

The Henkles, Wyatts, and Shipleys all settled in the Philomath area of Benton County and were later linked by marriage. Rachel Ann Henkle married John L. Shipley, the son of Robert N. Shipley, on November 20, 1862. As a young boy, I remember meeting Rachel Ann at the Tigard home of my maternal grandparents, Minnie Wyatt Junkin and William "Will" Junkin. I recall little about Rachel Ann other than her advanced age. When I last saw her, she was over one hundred—an astounding and nearly impossible age to a young boy, and it made me afraid of her. I vaguely remember her sitting on a sofa near my grandmother, hunched over some dark material, cross-stitching or knitting. I can't say she ever spoke a word to me.

Rachel Ann died September 5, 1949, at age one hundred and two. She has the distinction of having lived the longest of all the direct descendants of the Henkles, a family "where an advanced age is fairly common," in the words of the family genealogy. As the reader will have noted, the name Henkle is spelled in several ways by different branches of the family.

Rachel Ann was born in 1846 in Lee County, Iowa, the daughter of Jacob and Elizabeth Wood Henkle Jr. Rachel Ann and John L. Shipley had six children. John died in 1877, and Rachel Ann married John M. Kittson, also in Philomath, in 1882. Kitson also predeceased her.

The pioneering Henkles, Wyatts, and Shipleys followed different paths to Oregon, but all arrived by wagon train. William Wyatt, and his wife, Mary Theodosia End, arrived in Philomath in 1847. They came to America from England in 1836, married in 1838, and lived in both New York and Lenox, Illinois, before setting out for Oregon. Robert N. Shipley left from Miller

County, Missouri, travelling the Oregon Trail in 1853. He was accompanied by his first wife and their seven children, including John L. Shipley, who was born in Miller County in 1840.

Jacob Henkle, Sr., the grandson of German immigrant The Rev. Anthony Jacob Henckel, and Jacob's wife, Anna Gragg, began their westward journey from Pendleton County, Virginia, now West Virginia. They moved with their extended family, first to Ohio and later to Iowa, with some family members stopping in Lee County and others in Appanoose County. In recalling the family's decision to continue on to Oregon in 1853, Jacob Henkle Jr. and Elizabeth Conger Henkle said in a 1908 interview that the promise of free land through the donation land claim law was an important lure. The Henkle wagon train of twenty-one wagons left from the "little town of Cincinnati" in Appanoose County in 1853, arriving in Oregon that September. Nearly all of the seventy-nine people in the Henkle train were related. They settled in Benton County. The difficulties they faced during the two thousand-mile journey were typical of other wagon trains. The Henkles told an interviewer:

> *Down the Rockies and on until we reach the Snake River, through sage brush and sand, alkali and cactus. Cattle giving out and dying. Indians driving off our stock. Having to leave some of our wagons, cutting some of them in two, to make them as light as possible, and throwing much of the luggage away we thought necessary when we started. Some standing guard while others slept, to watch the stock from being driven away.*[1]

Once in Oregon, they faced the additional difficulty of finding a place to settle. Wherever they stopped, they were told by earlier settlers that the land was already taken, and they should move on. The interviewer continued:

> *They did move on and about Christmas time in the year 1853 they landed in Benton County on the south fork of Mary's River in the foothills of Mary's Peak, a mountain towering high above the surrounding hills, and covered with snow a great part of the year.*
>
> *The Indian name for this mountain was Mt. Chintiminy and the old legend was that no white man ever going to the top of the Peak ever came home.*
>
> *There this pioneer couple (Jacob Sr. and wife, Anna) took up their donation claim of 320 acres, each of their children doing the same, settling again around them, while perhaps not so close to them as formerly (in Virginia and Iowa) yet all in Benton County. Here again they began to build up for themselves a home, undergoing many hardships and privations common to a pioneer life.*[2]

The Wyatt and Henkle families merged when John End Wyatt, son of William and Mary Wyatt, married Mary Melissa Henkle in 1870 in Philomath. Mary Henkle was born in Appanoose County, Iowa, and crossed the plains with her parents at age two. John was born in Benton County. They had nine children.

The Reverend Thomas Jefferson Connor, or T. J., settled in Philomath in 1852, having led a group of United Brethren Church members to Oregon. Connor adopted a two-year-old boy whose mother died on the trek west. The Reverend James E. Connor, the adopted son, married Nancy Caroline Henkle in Philomath in 1872, uniting the Connor family with the Henkles.

T. J. Connor is credited with giving the town the name of Philomath, said to mean "lover of learning." T. J. Connor and William Wyatt were prime movers in establishing Philomath College in 1865. The college no longer exists; the building now houses the Benton County Historical Museum. The annual Henkle family reunion was for many years held both at the old college building and the church next door.

I am deeply indebted to my grandparents for their decades of work in compiling the genealogy of the Henckel family, where I first learned there had been slaves in Oregon, and which made possible this book. A history of the Henkle wagon train, *Wagons to Oregon, Stories of the Henkle train of 1853*, was compiled from family memories in 1986 by my late mother, Evelyn Junkin Nokes.

APPENDIX II

Slaves in Oregon

Known Slaves	County	Year Arrived
Rachel Belden	Marion	1843
Girl (name unknown)*	n/a	1843
Robin Holmes	Polk	1844
Polly Holmes	Polk	1844
Harriett Holmes	Polk	1844
Celi Ann Holmes	Polk	1844
Mary Jane Holmes	Polk	1844
James Holmes	Polk	---
Roxanna Holmes	Polk	---
Scott	Polk	1844
Hannah Gorman	Polk	1844
Eliza Gorman	Polk	1844
Luteshia Carson	Benton	1845
Carson (infant)	Benton	1845
Maria Scott	Polk	1846
Johnson	Polk	1846
Ame or Annie	Benton	1847
Travis Johnson	Marion	1849
Cora Cox	Linn	1850
Adeline Cox (infant)	Linn	---
Louis Southworth	Benton**	1853
Louis' mother	unknown	1853
Amanda Johnson	Linn	1853
Benjamin Johnson	Linn	1853
Tom Davis	Marion	1853
Tom's sister	Marion	1853
Alice	Linn	unknown
Reuben Shipley	Benton	1853

Probable Slaves	County	Year Arrived
America Waldo	Marion	1846***
America's mother	Marion	1846
Tilly	Polk	unknown

Possible Slaves	County	Year Arrived
Caesar Taylor	Benton	unknown
Alfred Drake	Polk	unknown
Lon Drake	Polk	unknown
Joseph Drake	Polk	unknown

Known Slaves, Washington	County	Year Arrived
Monimia Travers	Clark****	1850
Charles Mitchell	Thurston	1855

List compiled from miscellaneous sources, including census and court records, emigrant accounts, newspaper articles, and family histories. It is by no means comprehensive, as the author found references to slaves who were not named, and some African Americans listed as servants in census records may have been slaves, but are not listed here. The author counted children who came to Oregon as slaves, but, in most cases, not those born in Oregon to a slave parent. Exceptions were James and Roxanna Holmes, who were named in a court case, and Adeline Cox, listed as a slave in the 1860 Census. Some slaves were freed soon after arriving in Oregon; others held longer.

*   The unidentified girl drowned near The Dalles during the 1843 emigration.
**   Southworth lived in several counties. Others were Polk, Jackson and Lincoln.
***   The year America and mother arrived in Oregon is uncertain.
**** Clark County was part of the Oregon Territory in 1850; the Washington
          Territory was established in 1853.

NOTES

PROLOGUE

1 Lopez, "A Dark Light in the West: Racism and Reconciliation," *The Georgia Review*, Fall 2010, 368.

2 Ibid., 369.

FIRST SLAVES

1 The first known African American in the Oregon Country was believed to be Marcus Lopez, a native of the Cape Verde Islands and a cabin boy on Robert Gray's Lady Washington. According to Elizabeth McLagan in *A Peculiar Paradise*, the ship dropped anchor on August 14, 1788, near Tillamook. While ashore on August 16 to get provisions, Lopez was killed in a dispute with Native Americans. The second African American was believed to be York, a black slave who traveled with the Lewis and Clark Expedition in 1805. Others had come too, including several with the Peter Burnett wagon train in 1843.

2 An 1847 Missouri law was typical. It assessed a penalty of up to $500 and six months imprisonment for anyone who would "teach or keep any school for the instruction of any negroes or mulattoes in reading or writing . . . ." Trexler, *Slaves in Missouri, 1804-1865*, 83-84.

3 Woodward, "Rise and Early History of Political Parties in Oregon III." *Oregon Historical Quarterly*, 145. (Hereafter *OH Quarterly.*)

4 Schneider, *Black Laws of Oregon*, 31. Schneider based his judgment in part on editorials in newspapers throughout the country as reported in the *Oregon Statesman* (hereafter *Statesman*) on June 8, 1857, 2-3. The *New-York Tribune*, described by the *Statesman* as a "frantic abolitionist sheet," said in an undated editorial: "We have a number of letters from Oregon, by the last mail, containing the startling information that this Territory hitherto sat down as a certain for Freedom, will, in all probability, present herself to the next Congress for admission into the Union with a constitution legalizing slavery."

5 Trexler, *Slaves in Missouri*, 4. Also the 1860 U.S. Census, which listed no slaves in Oregon, overlooking local census takers who officially listed at least three slaves; other known slaves were identified as laborers or servants, or not listed at all.

6 Carey, *History of Oregon*, 571.

7 "Oregon City Once a Slave Mart in a Small Way," *Oregon Journal* (hereafter *Journal*), January 8, 1920, 10.

8 Junkin, *The Henckel Genealogy*, 359.

THE GOOD LIFE IN MISSOURI

1 Burke, *On Slavery's Borders*, 310. Lafayette County had the greatest number of slaves: 6,374.

2 Slave couples were seldom officially married, and the status of the Holmeses' marriage is unknown.

3 Affidavit, April 6, 1853, Robin Holmes vs. Nathaniel Ford, *habeas corpus* suit Polk County Circuit Court, case No. 21, filed April 16, 1852. Original transcript in office of Polk County Clerk, Dallas, Oregon. (Hereafter Holmes vs. Ford). Also, copy of transcript in Lockley, "The Case of Robin Holmes vs. Nathaniel Ford," *OH Quarterly*, June, 1922, 112-37.

4 Ibid.

5 List of Howard County, Missouri, sheriffs, *History of Howard and Cooper Counties*, 354.

6 Stone, *Little Dixie, Missouri*, 73.

7 Lockley, interview with Ford's grandson, John Thorp Ford, "Observations and Impressions of the Journal Man," *Journal*, March 24, 1922.

8 Pauline Burch, affidavit of family history, filed in Linn County, Oregon, March 16, 1953, copy in possession of author.

9 U.S. Slave Census.

10 Burke, *On Slavery's Borders*, 310.

11 *History of Howard and Cooper Counties*, 353.

12 *Missouri Intelligencer*, Fayette, Missouri, August 29, 1818.

13 Lockley, interview with John Thorp Ford.

14 John Thorp Ford, undated biography of Nathaniel Ford by his grandson, from Benton County Historical Museum (hereafter Benton Museum), Philomath, Oregon. The conflict resulted from clashes over land between Mormons and non-Mormons after Mormons moved into western Missouri in large numbers, beginning in 1831. Jackson County, Missouri, had great religious importance for the Mormons because founder Joseph Smith predicted Jesus would reappear there. Non-Mormons feared being overwhelmed by Mormons and skirmishes broke out, the worst of which was in October 30, 1838, at a place called Haun's Mill, in which seventeen Mormons were massacred. The massacre followed an order issued by Governor Lilburn Boggs on October 27, 1838, declaring that "Mormons must be treated as enemies, and must be exterminated or driven from the State, if necessary, for the public good." Ostling, *Mormon America*, 30-37. Smith and other church leaders were arrested and jailed on charges of treason. A general refused to carry out an order to execute Smith and the others, and Smith was allowed to escape. The Mormons left Missouri and moved to Illinois. Smith was murdered in 1844 in Carthage, Illinois, by a mob which attacked the jail where he was being held following a subsequent arrest. Krakauer, *Under the Banner of Heaven*, 103-104.

15 Caroline Burch, *Ford Family of Rickreall*, Benton Museum, 5-6.

16 *Holmes vs. Ford*, April 6, 1853.

17 Office of County Clerk, Howard County, Missouri, Deed Book T, 297-99. (Hereafter Missouri Deed Book.)

18 Copy of page from Ford family Bible, Polk County Museum (hereafter: Polk Museum), Rickreall, Oregon. Also Burch affidavit.

19 Missouri Deed Book T, 607.

20 Ibid. U, 237-40.

21 Ibid.

22 Ibid., 3, 255-56.

23 Ibid. U, 266.

24 Ford to Shirley, June 22, 1852, reprinted in *Missouri Historical Review*, January 1931, 285-87.

25 Coffman, *Blazing a Wagon Trail to Oregon*, 1.

26 Stone, *Little Dixie, Missouri*, 24.

27 Trexler, *Slavery in Missouri*, 18.

28 Burke, *On Slavery's Borders: Missouri's Small-Slaveholding Households, 1815-1865*, 6.

29 Trexler, *Slavery in Missouri*, 39.

30 Ibid., 24.

31 Gary Fuenfhausen to author.

32 State Historical Society of Missouri: http://shs.umsystem.edu/index.shtml

THE LURE OF OREGON

1 Nokes, *Wagons to Oregon*, 7.

2 Bancroft and Victor, *History of Oregon*, 419.

3 There were earlier wagon trains to Oregon, including an expedition organized by John Bidwell and led by Thomas Fitzpatrick that left from Sapling Grove, Missouri, on May 19, 1841, and considered by some as the first emigrant wagon train. It comprised about seventy people in five missionary carts and thirteen wagons. About thirty people and eight wagons, known as the Bidwell-Bartleson party, separated at Soda Springs and headed for California. Other earlier emigrants traveled to Oregon by ship, including George Abernethy, destined to be Oregon's first provisional governor, who arrived in 1840 on the ship *Lausanne*, via Cape Horn. with a party of Methodist missionaries. Dary, *The Oregon Trail*, 74-75, and http://www.oregonpioneers.com/1840.htm

4 Carey, *General History of Oregon*, 327.

5 O'Hara, *Pioneer Catholic History of Oregon*, 93.

6 Dary, *The Oregon Trail*, 79. An estimate from 1842 gave a higher population figure—eight hundred and twenty-five men, women, and children. The informal census was conducted by Elijah White, who arrived in Oregon in 1842 from Missouri at the head of a party of one hundred and twelve people and eighteen wagons.

7 Unruh, *The Plains Across*, 119-120.

8 *Columbian Missourian*, Columbia, Missouri, January 23, 1926. John Minto wrote that anti-Mormon feeling was so high that during court appearances Burnett sat "with a loaded pistol in hand." Minto, "Antecedents of the Oregon Pioneers and the Light These Throw on Their Motives," *OH Quarterly*, March 1904. 56.

9 California didn't become a state until September 1850, although Burnett was inaugurated in November 1849. He resigned in 1851 after clashing repeatedly with the legislature.

10 Minto, "Antecedents," 56.

11 Ibid., 46.

12 Burnett, "Recollections and Opinions of an Old Pioneer," *OH Quarterly*, March 1904, 65.

13 Johnson, *Founding the Far West*, 42.

14 Coffman, *Wagon Trail*, 3.

15 Burnett, "Recollections," 99.

16 Ibid.

17 Dary, *The Oregon Trail*, 85.

18 Minto, "Antecedents," 46.

19 Neiderheiser, *Dialogue with Destiny*, 82.

20 *Northwest Magazine, The Oregonian*, September 20, 1970.

21 Coffman, *Wagon Trail*, 11.

22 Dary, *The Oregon Trail*, 110-11.

23 Burnett, "Recollections," 92.

24 Carey, *History of Oregon*, 394.

25 Applegate, *Memoirs of Jesse A. Applegate*, 97-100. Also Bancroft, *History of Oregon*, 408.

26 Ibid.

27 Ibid., 105.

28 Applegate, Shannon, *Skookum: an Oregon Pioneer Family's History and Lore*, 388-89.

29 Bancroft, *History of Oregon*, 409.

30 Renita Bogle-Byrd, e-mail to author, November 26, 2012. America's name in the 1870 census was America Bogle, although mistakenly listed as America Boyle.

31 Brian Waldo Johnson, interview with author, October 24, 2012.

32 Bell, "Marion County's Claim to First Black Settlers," *Historic Marion*, 6.

33 Minto, "Antecedents," 49.

34 *Perseverance*, 72-74. Also, *The Hanging of Uncle George*, a collection of articles on the murder of Daniel Delaney Sr., oregonpioneers.com. Also Bell, "Marion County's Claim," 6.

35 Davenport, "Slavery Question in Oregon, Part I," *OH Quarterly*, September 1908, 195.

36 Minto, "Reminiscences of Honorable John Minto Pioneer of 1844," *OH Quarterly*, June 1901, 130.

37 The Northwest Territory would become the states of Ohio (1803), Indiana (1816), Illinois (1818), Michigan (1837), and Wisconsin (1848).

38 The act was part of the 1850 Compromise that admitted California as a free state.

39 The Dred Scott ruling was more narrowly focused on whether Dred Scott, a slave who had lived temporarily in a free state, was still a slave when returned to Missouri. The court ruled it had no jurisdiction in the case, and, as a slave, Scott was not a citizen, and could not sue in federal court. Seven of the nine justices, all Democrats, offered their opinions that the Missouri Compromise was unconstitutional and slavery could not be prohibited in the territories. Although the two other justices, both Republicans, argued that these opinions were outside the scope of the case before the court, the significance of the ruling was nonetheless devastating for African Americans.

ON THE TRAIL

1 "The Oregon Expedition," *Maine Cultivator and Hallowell Gazette*," July 6, 1844, partial reprint from the *Western Expositor*, Independence, Missouri.

2 Dary, *Oregon Trail*, 120.

3 OregonPioneers.com

4 Bright, "Black Harris, Mountain Man, Teller of Tales" *OH Quarterly*, 7. Some contemporary writers and historians refer to Harris as a black, or African American. The *Dictionary of Oregon History* refers to him as black. Among others who identified him as black is McLagan, *Peculiar Paradise*,

14-15. References to Harris in the nineteenth century, including by people who knew him, generally do not identify him by race, although Jesse Applegate was quoted once as saying of Harris that "tho (sic) a white man, his face was the color of his coat." Applegate, "Wearing Buckskin in the Forties, Stories of First Settlement of Polk Councy," *Polk County Observer*, March 13, 1903. Birth and census records that might confirm Harris' race have not been located, if they exist.

5 Corning, *Dictionary of Oregon History*, 107.

6 Bright, "Black Harris," 9.

7 Ibid., 8.

8 Lockley, *The Lockley Files: Voices of The Oregon Territory*, 138.

9 Ibid., 112.

10 *Maine Cultivator*. Also, OregonPioneers.com

11 Ibid.

12 Bancroft and Victor, *History of Oregon*, 425.

13 Ibid., 448-49.

14 Ibid., 450.

15 Taylor, "Slaves and Free Men: Blacks in the Oregon Country, 1840-1860," *OH Quarterly*, Summer 1982, 160. Taylor wrote that Bush traveled separately with six families led by Michael Simmons. Researcher Stephenie Flora says that the Simmons group traveled as part of the Cornelius Gilliam wagon train, with Gilliam as "general" and Simmons as "colonel."oregonpioneers.com

16 Minto, *Reminiscences*, 150.

17 Burch, *Ford Family*, 6.

18 Ibid.

19 Ibid., 7.

20 Pauline Burch, *Pioneer Nathaniel Ford and the Negro Family*, 1.

21 Holmes vs. Ford, June 23, 1853.

22 Ibid., April 6, 1853.

23 Burch, *Negro Family*, 1.

24 Ibid.

25 Burch, *Ford Family*, 11-12.

26 Dary, *Oregon Trail*, 120.

27 Minto, *Reminiscenses*, 155.

28 Dary, *Oregon Trail*, 120.

29 Hafen, *Trappers of the Far West*, 157.

30 Ibid., 156.

31 Minto quoted in Bancroft, *History of Oregon*, 454.

32 Burch, *Negro Family*, 2.

33 Ibid.

34 Dary, *Oregon Trail*, 234. He cited estimates by Merrill J. Mattes in *Platte River Road Narratives*, University of Nebraska Press, 1988, 3.

35 Burch, *Ford Family*, 1-2.

36 Ibid., 12.

37 Ibid.

38 Burch, *Negro Family*, 3.

39 Ibid.

40 The Applegates would later relocate to the Umpqua Valley.

41 Ibid. Also Carey, *History of Oregon*, 705.

42 Glen, "John Lyle and the Lyle Farm," *OH Quarterly*, June 1925, 134-35.

43 See the photograph on page 27. It seems possible this was not the Ford home, but was instead the Nesmith Mills boarding house. However, this is pure speculation by the author and would contradict the notation on the photograph.

44 Phinney, *WPA Historical Records*.

FREEDOM DELAYED

1 Carey, *History of Oregon*, 336.

2 O'Hara, *Catholic History*, 95. At an earlier meeting on February 17, 1841, "some of the inhabitants of the Willamette Valley" decided they wanted a code of laws for the government of settlements south of the Columbia River. Settlers north of the river, "not connected with the Hudson's Bay Company," could apply to also be covered by the laws. Grover, *Oregon Archives*.

3 Deady, *General Laws of Oregon, 1845-1864*, 83.

4 Carey, *History of Oregon*, 336.

5 Grover, *Oregon Archives*, 29.

6 Prior to the end of its slave trade, British ships carried an estimated 3 million captive Africans into slavery in the Western Hemisphere. Hochschild, *Bury the Chains*, 307.

7 Darrell Millner to author, August 2, 2011. Millner also said that because

of the region's tiny population base, "in any given year the makeup of the latest wagon train—often totaling hundreds of people—could dramatically change the local politics of the area and usually did." The prevailing attitude toward slavery and exclusion at any given time "was simply a reflection of the dominant 'power' in residence."

8 Carey, *History of Oregon*, 342-43.

9 Ibid.

10 Grover, *Oregon Archives*, 49-50.

OREGON'S DIXIE

1 Lewis A. McArthur wrote that Rickreall may be derived from the French *La Creole,* which, in turn, had its origin in the drowning of a Native American at a ford near the present-day town of Dallas. McArthur noted that others contend it's a Native American name. *Oregon Geographic Names*, 5th edition, 621-622.

2 Ibid.

3 Burch, *Ford Family*, 2.

4 Ford to Lowery, *Jefferson City (MO) Inquirer*, July 25, 1845.

5 This was probably the Billy Doke mentioned in Jesse A. Applegate's *Memoirs* as a member of the Burnett wagon train who survived the tragedy on the Columbia River that claimed two of the Applegate boys.

6 Fenton, "Winning of the Oregon Country," *OH Quarterly*, December, 1905, 363.

7 Abernethy letter to Legislature, August 18, 1845, Grover, *Oregon Archives*, 122.

8 *Oregon Blue Book 2011-2012*, 318.

9 Grover, *Oregon Archives*, 122.

10 *Oregon Spectator*, February 4, 1847. (Hereafter: *Spectator*.)

11 Carey, *History of Oregon*, 357.

12 *Oregon Spectator*, May 16, 1850, 3.

13 Edwards, *List of Oregon Legislatures*, 3-48. In 1856 and 1858, the Polk County legislative district was combined with Tillamook County. Ford represented both counties at those sessions.

14 It is significant that none of the family accounts mentioned Nathaniel Ford as a state senator. John Terry, former history columnist for the *Oregonian*, told the author that confusion may have partly resulted from Nineveh Ford's obituary in the *Oregonian* of March 9, 1887, which said he represented "the state of Oregon three terms in congress." Said Terry: "The Congress part is obviously wrong. I think probably the writer likely saw a reference to his serving in the House of Representatives and thought it meant Congress, not the state House . . ." The confusion is further compounded by editorial references in *The Oregonian* of May 28, 1940, and January 19, 1948, to "Nineveh Ford, of Yamhill County, who was elected judge of Oregon in 1844, an office which he declined to accept, and Nineveh Ford came to the Yamhill region in early pioneer times." The editorialist surely meant Nathaniel Ford, who turned down the judicial appointment. Nineveh Ford lived for many years in the Pendleton-Walla Walla region.

15 H.N.V. Holmes vs. Nathaniel Ford, Contested Election in the Council of the Oregon Territory, files in Oregon State Archives (hereafter: State Archives), Salem. H.N.V. Holmes subsequently was elected to the 1858 Territorial House.

16 Ford, undated biography, 37.

17 Ford letter, *Jefferson City Inquirer*.

18 Zenk, *Handbook of North American Indians*, 551. Also, Ruby, *Indians of the Northwest*, 24. Neither author suggested how the Kalapuyans caught the illness.

19 Ruby, *Indians of the Northwest*, 93. The last known fluent speaker of the Kalapuyan language, John B. Hudson, died at Grand Ronde in 1954. Mackey, *The Kalapuyans*, 179.

20 Burnett, "Recollections," 97.

21 Grover, *Oregon Archives*, 70.

22 O'Donnell, *Arrow in the Earth*, 43.

23 Burnett letter, *Jefferson City Inquirer*, August 8, 1845.

24 Burnett letter, October 23, 1843.

25 Burnett, "Recollections," 187.

26 Ibid., 141.

27 Pickett letter, *Spectator*, June 10, 1847, newspaper on microfilm at the Oregon Historical Library (hereafter: OHS Library). Pickett would later move to Oregon and become a "zealous slavery apostate." Woodward, "Political Parties," 157.

LAND AND MORE LAND

1 Lincoln to John Addison, *Collected Works of Abraham Lincoln, Volume I*, 65. Lincoln, who had also turned down an appointment as territorial secretary, recommended Simeon Francis, a close friend and newspaper editor in Springfield, Illinois, as territorial secretary. Francis didn't receive the appointment, but later moved to Oregon where he became editor of the *Oregonian*.

2 Richard, "Unwelcome Settlers: Black and Mulatto Oregon Pioneers, Part I," *OH Quarterly*, Spring 1983," 36. The African American population figures are estimates only. The figures for both 1850 and 1860 were adjusted by Richard and others to discount Hawaiians and persons of Indian blood counted in the census as mulattoes.

3 Bergquist, "Oregon Donation Act," *OH Quarterly*, March 1957, 23.

4 *Spectator*, August 22, 1850, 1.

5 Carey, *History of Oregon*, 481-82.

6 Ibid.

7 Bergquist, "Oregon Donation Act," 33.

8 O'Donnell, *Arrow in the Earth*, 167-68.

9 Ibid. Palmer to the Tualatin chiefs, March 21, 1854.

10 Zenk, *Handbook*, 551.

11 Ibid., 547. Also, Juntunen et al, *World of the Kalapuya*, 25-26.

12 Johnson, *Founding the Far West*, 44.

13 Metsker's Atlas of Polk County, 1929.

14 Indenture from Ford to Dempsey and Thorp, February 25, 1865, Office of County Recorder, Polk County, Deed Book, 712.

15 Burch family file, Polk County Museum.

16 Bergquist, "Donation Act," 29.

THE APPLEGATE TRAIL

1 Burch, *Negro Family*, 3.

2 Fort George was established as Fort Astoria by John Jacob Astor's Pacific Fur Company in 1811. It was sold to British interests after only two years.

3 Carey, *History of Oregon*, 262, 265. Carey said McLoughlin "ruled by might of his dominating personality and by virtue of a far-reaching policy which disarmed oppositions in advance."

4 O'Hara, *Catholic History*, 47.

5 Carey, *History of Oregon*, 444.

6 Ibid.

7 Lockley, *Lockley Files*, 137. Lockley attributed the recollection to Richard Watson Helms, who was sixteen at the time.

8 Unruh, *Plains Across*, 361.

9 Lockley, *The Lockley Files*, 138.

10 Unruh, *The Plains Across*, 361.

11 Ford letter, *Spectator*, April 15, 1846.

12 Ibid., June 25, 1846.

13 Ibid., April 15, 1846.

14 Typewritten Applegate letter, September 10, 1846, from Fort Hall, addressed to *Independence (MO) Expositor*. Applegate file, OHS Library.

15 Haines, *Southern Emigrant Route*, 13.

16 Emerson, *The Applegate Trail of 1846*, 33-34, 80.

17 Ibid., 74.

18 *Spectator*, December 10, 1846.

19 It's worth noting that the wagon train in which Thornton traveled initially included California-bound emigrants who fared even worse. They became stranded in the Sierra Nevada and are known in history as the Donner Party.

20 Unruh, *Plains Across*, 349.

21 Burnett letter, *Liberty (MO) Weekly Tribune*, August 21, 1847.

22 Lindsay Applegate, "Notes and Reminiscences of Laying Out and Establishing the Old Emigrant Road into Southern Oregon in the Year 1846," *OH Quarterly*, March 1921, 41.

23 Burch, *Negro Family*, 3.
24 Ibid.

OREGON'S "LASH LAW"
1 Berwanger, *Frontier Against Slavery*, 81. Also, *Crafting the Oregon Constitution,* exhibit of State Archives, 2009
2 Ibid.
3 Grover, *Oregon Archives*, 58. Executive Committee members were Osborn Russell and P.G. Stewart. Their recommendation, in full, was as follows: "We would recommend that the act passed by the assembly, in June last, relative to Negroes and mulattoes, be so amended as to exclude corporal punishment and require bonds for good behavior in its stead."
4 Burnett, "Recollections," 218.
5 "Amendment of act passed June 2, 1844 regarding slavery," Grover, *Oregon Archives,* 82.
6 Berwanger, *Frontier Against Slavery*, 32.
7 Darrell Millner to author.
8 Millner, *Blacks in Oregon*, 13.
9 Berwanger, *Frontier Against Slavery*, 33.
10 Ibid., 1.
11 Dodds, *American Northwest*, 75.
12 Grover, *Oregon Archives*, 82.
13 Ibid., 81.
14 Carey, *History of Oregon*, 349-50.
15 Ibid, 346.
16 Deady. *General Laws of Oregon,* 71-88.
17 Ibid.
18 Woodward, "Political Parties," 342-43.
19 Ibid.
20 Johannsen, *Frontier Politics and the Sectional Conflict*, 17.
21 Potter, *Impending Crisis,* 24-25.
22 Ibid., 26.
23 The Treaty of Guadelupe Hidalgo was signed May 30, 1848.
24 Potter, *Impending Crisis*, 65.
25 Letter from Senator Benton to the People of Oregon, March 1847, reprinted in *Spectator*, October 24, 1850, 3. Mexico abolished slavery in 1829.

26 Ibid.
27 Potter, *Impending Crisis*, 75-76.
28 Deady, *General Laws*, 71-88.

THE COCKSTOCK AFFAIR
1 The first *USS Peacock* served in the war of 1812 and was credited with capturing 120 ships.
2 McLagan, *Peculiar Paradise*, 10-11.
3 Anderson worked with a white trapper, Tennessee-born Ewing Young, whose death in 1841 created the need for a legal procedure to settle his estate, setting in motion the events leading to Oregon's first provisional government.
4 Taylor, *Slaves and Free Men*, 156.
5 Dodds, *American Northwest,* 83.
6 White to Porter, May 1, 1844, in Gray, *A History of Oregon*, 396.
7 Berwanger, *Frontier Against Slavery*, 81-83.
8 Taylor, *Slaves and Free Men*, 157.
9 "An Act to prevent Negroes and Mulattoes from coming to, or residing in Oregon," *Statutes of a General Nature passed by the Legislative Assembly of the Territory of Oregon, December 2, 1850.* State Archives, 181.
10 *Journal of Legislative Assembly of Territory of Oregon During First Regular Session*, State Archives, 94.
11 "An Act to prevent Negroes and Mulattoes," 11.
12 *Spectator*, December 24, 1846, 2.
13 Taylor, *Slaves and Free Men*, 164.
14 *Oregon Blue Book, 2011-2012*, 215.
15 Magruder vs. Vanderpool, 1851, MSS 996, OHS Library.
16 Ibid.
17 *Spectator*, September 2, 1851.
18 "Blacks File," Polk County Museum.
19 *Statesman*, September 3, 1851, 3. Researchers find the lack of local reporting in newspapers of this period frustrating. The Vanderpool case seemed important enough to merit a detailed account of the defense attorney's arguments and the reasons behind the ruling that the law was constitutional. But there was none of that. Moreover,

newspapers almost never offered any attribution for the few facts in news account. Newspapers of the period were more interested in political commentary than local news. They were frequently shoestring operations with a staff of one or two employees.

20 Lapp, *Blacks in Gold Rush California*, 213.

21 Ripley, *The Black Abolitionist Papers, 1830 to 1865, Volume IV*, 103-4.

22 Ibid.

23 Provisional, Territorial and Government papers, Nos. 621 and 3864, microfilm, OHS Library.

24 McLagan, *A Peculiar Paradise*, 88-90. Also Lapp, *Blacks in Gold Rush California*, 242 and 252. Lapp cited estimates that between four hundred to eight hundred blacks left California for Victoria over a period of several years, beginning in 1858. The exodus was partly for jobs and economic opportunity, but also because California's legislature was debating an exclusion law. It seems Abner Francis joined them from Portland.

25 Laws and Journals of Oregon, 1853-1856, Journals of the Legislative Assembly, 5th annual session, *Oregon Archives*.

26 Taylor, *Slaves and Free Men*, 165. Records in Oregon Territorial Government Records, Reel No. 55, files 5696 and 6024, OHS Library.

27 Minto, "Reminiscences," 125.

28 Ibid., 212.

29 Schneider, *Black Laws of Oregon*, 11-12.

30 Lockley, *"Some Documentary Records of Slavery in Oregon," OH Quarterly*, March 1916, 112.

31 Tobie, "Contributions of Virginians in Oregon," *OH Quarterly*, June 1951, 76.

32 Taylor, *Slaves and Free Men*, 159-60.

33 Quintard Taylor wrote that although slavery was banned in California, the ban wasn't enforced, with the result that the state's attitude was interpreted by slaveholders as giving

"tacit support" to slavery, *In Search of the Racial Frontier*, 77. Taylor said there about three hundred slaves working in the gold fields in 1852, 78.

34 Berwanger, *Frontier Against Slavery*, 84.

35 Ibid., 71.

36 Potter, *Impending Crisis*, 112.

37 Lapp, *Blacks in Gold Rush California*, 14. Lapp wrote that "the anti-Negro laws of these Western free states were no secret to the free blacks of the North. They had read about the constitutions which denied to blacks the rights of suffrage, and testimony rights in the courts, and education for black children."

38 Ibid.

39 As quoted in the *Statesman*, August 2, 1853, 3. The *Statesman* said it was reprinting the *Baltimore Sun* article "merely for the purpose of correcting a mistaken notion which seems to have been permitted to run wild in these days of slavery excitement." Also, Section 12 of "An Act to Establish the Terriotial Government of Washington," March 2, 1853.

40 For story of James Tilton, See McConaghy and Bentley, *Free Boy, A True Story of Slave and Master*.

41 Avery, *Washington: A History of the Evergreen State*, 189.

42 McConaghy, *Washington Territory's Confederate Governor*, 9.

43 Lapp, *Blacks in Gold Rush California*, 5.

44 Ibid., 22.

45 U.S. Census.

46 *Statesman*, January 13, 1857, 4.

47 Kelly, "History of the Preparation of the First Code of Oregon," *OH Quarterly*, 1903, 191-192. Kelly also wrote that there was considerable confusion because the legislature worked from two separate printings of the proposed code, which weren't identical. Most of the first printing, done in New York City, was lost at sea during a voyage around South America. Kelly said the process for submitting individual pieces of the code to the

House and Council for approval proved cumbersome. The third member of the Code Commission was Daniel R. Bigelow of Thurston County, who stepped down after Congress created the Washington Territory, in 1853.

48 *Statesman,* January 13, 1857, 4.
49 Ibid.
50 Ibid., January 20, 1857, 1.
51 Ibid., January 13, 1857, 4.
52 Ibid.

GOLD MINERS AND SLAVES

1 It's not clear what impact the three-year grace period enacted by the provisional government in 1844 would have had on Ford, were it ever enforced, which it wasn't. A rewriting of the laws in 1845 had dropped the grace period, and simply declared slavery unlawful. However, the grace period was in effect at the time Ford arrived in Oregon with his slaves, and he might well have claimed it should still apply to his situation. The same case could have been made by others who brought slaves in this period.

2 Burch, *Negro Family,* 5.
3 Holmes vs. Ford, June 23, 1853.
4 Ibid., April 6, 1853.
5 Burch, *Negro Family,* 3.
6 Holmes v. Ford, April 6, 1853.
7 Dary, *The Oregon Trail,* 194.
8 Edwards, Oregon Legislatures, 16. The others who resigned their seats were Asa L. Lovejoy, Robert Newell, James W. Nesmith, Osborne Russell, J.L. Snook, and Ralph Wilcox. Those from Oregon didn't just mine gold. A family account said Benjamin Simpson, owner of an Oregon City sawmill who would become a prominent Oregon legislator, left for California in 1849 with a cargo of lumber to build sluice boxes for gold mining. He also shipped a kind of pre-fab house which sold in San Francisco for $1,000. "In short order he amassed quite a fortune." www.bdhhfamily.com/benjamin_simpson.htm
9 Smith, "Remaking Slavery in a Free State: Masters and Slaves in Gold Rush California," *Pacific Historical Review,* October 2011, 28, 49. Relying on

various sources, Smith estimated no more than "a few hundred" slaveholders were in California at any one time, bringing possibly a thousand slaves, including at least two hundred slaves from just two counties in North Carolina, Burke and McDowell counties, 37.

10 Ibid., 36.
11 Lapp, *Blacks in Gold Rush California,* 130-31.
12 Ibid., 38.
13 Ibid., 21.
14 Ibid., 69-70.
15 Lapp, *Blacks in Gold Rush California,* 131-32. Lapp wrote that the unidentified buyer bought the woman and child because he couldn't find a servant to work for him. The *Daily Picayune* of New Orleans carried the Newark newspaper's article on the front page on June 30, 1849.
16 *Holmes vs. Ford,* April 6, 1853.
17 Burch, *Negro Family,* 4.
18 Ibid. Shoalwater Bay is now Willapa Bay on the Washington coast, north of the entrance to the Columbia River, and known for its oyster beds. At the time of the western migration, it was inhabited by the Shoalwater Tribe, which now has a reservation west of Tokeland, Washington. The 2000 U.S. Census listed the reservation's population at seventy.
19 From an unattributed account in the Ford Family file, Polk County Museum.
20 *Spectator,* January 24, 1850, 3.
21 Matthews, *American Merchant Ships, 1850-1900,* 117.
22 Burch, *Negro Family,* 4.
23 Lockley, "Observations and Impressions of the Journal Man," *Journal,* March 24, 1922.
24 Burch, *Ford Family,* 3-4.
25 Ibid.
26 Shaw, "The Story of Ellendale." *Historically Speaking,* September 1990, 6.
27 Burch, *Negro Family,* 3.
28 Ibid. 5.

"MY CHILDREN HELD AS SLAVES"

1 While blacks were prevented from voting in Oregon, there were no

restrictions at the time against African Americans filing lawsuits or testifying in territorial courts until 1855 when the territorial legislature acted to deny blacks the right to go to court against whites, in what was a possible reprisal for Holmes' suit. Oregon's 1857 statehood constitution barred blacks and Chinese from filing suits or testifying in court, although there were instances where the restriction was overlooked. California imposed similar restrictions on African American's legal rights when it became a state in 1850.

2 Quintard Taylor wrote that slaves in Oregon in this period were generally unaware "they could claim freedom in this new region." "Slaves and Free Men," 166-67.

3 Dallas was named in 1850 for George M. Dallas, vice president under President Polk. Dallas was relocated in 1856 a mile south from its original location on Rickreall Creek. The 2010 U.S. Census put Dallas' population at 14,583.

4 Holmes vs. Ford. Fred Lockley transcribed the entire record—forty hand-written pages—for an article in the *OH Quarterly* in June 1922. When Lockley's transcriptions are compared with the originals, there are very few differences, none of them significant.

HOLMES VS. FORD

1 Section 4 of "An Act Concerning Minors, Orphans and Guardians," Grover, *Oregon Archives*, 168-69. The act was one of a number of laws adopted by the territorial legislature in 1849 from the Revised Laws of Iowa.

2 Hendrickson, *Joe Lane*, 74. Douglas argued that because Pratt once represented the Hudson's Bay Company, he could be biased in favor of the British.

3 Franklin, or Old Franklin, was across the Missouri River from Boonville, Missouri. Franklin was washed away by the floods of the 1820s. The town is gone, but a couple of the original houses on the bluffs still stand. The town was moved about a mile north on the Missouri bluff and is now New Franklin.

The county seat was also moved from the washed-away Franklin in the 1820s and became Fayette. Boonville was settled in the 1830s and survived as the county seat of Cooper County.

4 "Public Meeting in Fayette," *Daily Commercial Bulletin,* St. Louis, February 26, 1836.

5 U.S. 1840 Slave Census.

6 *Alphonso Wetmore vs. United States,* 35 US 647, United States Supreme Court, January term, 1836.

7 Holmes vs. Ford, April 16, 1853.

8 Ibid.

9 Ibid.

10 Hendrickson, *Joe Lane of Oregon,* 235.

FORD'S SECRET STRATEGY

1 Smith, "Remaking Slavery in a Free State," 56-57.

2 Ibid.

3 Ibid.

4 Ford to Shirley, *Missouri Historical Review.*

5 Burch, *Negro Family,* 2.

6 *Missouri Historical Review.*

ENTER JUDGE WILLIAMS

1 Teiser, *Almost Chief Justice,* 5-7.

2 Williams, *Political History of Oregon,* 1853-1865, 1. The *Statesman* of June 4, 1853, was less than thrilled. Editor Asahel Bush supported Pratt and wrote after Williams' appointment that "the federal curs who yelp after Judge Pratt's heels will have a season for rejoicing . . . and in due time be found laughing out of the other side of their mouth."

3 Holmes vs. Ford, July 13, 1853.

4 *Statesman,* July 19, 1853, 2.

5 Ibid., July 25, 1853, 2.

6 *Statesman,* July 12, 1853, 2.

7 Williams, "Political History of Oregon, 1853-65," *OH Quarterly,* March 1901, 6.

8 Unattributed news clipping in files of Benton Museum.

9 The Oregon Territory was divided into three judicial districts; the justices decided among themselves which districts to take. Deady took the first district

comprising the southern Oregon counties of Jackson, Douglas, and Umpqua. Olney took the third district counties of Clatsop, Clackamas, Columbia, and Washington, which then included a major portion of present-day Multnomah. Williams took the second district counties of Marion, Linn, Lane, Benton, Polk, and Yamhill.

10 Carey, *The Oregon Constitution and Proceedings and Debates of the Constitutional Convention of 1857*, 485.

11 Reuben Boise's photograph is also on the wall.

12 Interviews with Darrell Millner, December 7, 2010, and April 12, 2011.

13 Demaratus, *Force of a Feather*, 77. Because African Americans in California were barred by California's Constitution from bringing suits or testifying against whites, the suit was brought on behalf of the former slaves by a third party, whose name was never made public. Judge Hayes took testimony from the former slaves in his chambers. A complete account of this case and the trial is found in *The Force of a Feather*.

14 Ibid., 112.

15 House Journal for 1853, 33, and Council Journal for 1853-1854, OHS Library, 74.

16 Revised Statutes of the Territory of Oregon, Enacted by the Legislative Assembly Fifth and Sixth Regular Sessions, State Archives, 130.

REUBEN SHIPLEY

1 *Henckel Genealogy*, 359.

2 Ibid.

3 Lurwell interview, *WPA Historical Records*, Benton Museum.

4 Eighth U.S. Census, 1860, NARA Film M652.

5 *Henckel Genealogy*, 359.

6 Ibid. The precise date Reuben Shipley gained his freedom isn't known, but he was a free man by 1857.

7 Henkle interview, *WPA Historical Records*.

8 Benton County Deed Book, County Clerk's office, Book C, Page 452 and Book G, Page 295.

9 Dasch, *Early Black Women in Benton County*, 7.

THEY WEREN'T ALONE

1 *Journal of the House of Representatives of the Territory of Oregon*, 9th Regular Session, 1857-1858, 58. Records at OHS Library. Also, Woodward, "Political Parties," 158-160.

2 Richard, "Unwelcome Settlers," Part II, 192. Richard wrote that holding slaves in Oregon had little practical value and was "an expensive luxury rather than an important capital investment."

3 Woodward, "Political Parties," 160.

4 Ibid.

5 Carey , *Oregon Constitution*, 38.

6 Woodward, "Political Parties," 158.

7 In 1860, there were 3,572 free blacks in Missouri, while the slave population was 114,931.

8 Healthy, young slaves would presumably welcome their freedom, but it might be more problematic for aging and infirm slaves if they were turned out by white owners with few options to make a living. See discussion in Chapter 15.

9 Mariah Scott document, Blacks file, Polk Museum.

10 Richard, "Unwelcome Settlers," Part II, 191. National census figures did not list Oregon with any slaves. Richard said the census changed the "slave" designation to "servant." Also, U.S. and state censuses.

11 Luteshia Carson vs. Granbury Smith, February 28, 1854, copy of complaint in Blacks file, Benton Museum.

12 Seventh U.S. Census, 1850. NARA film, roll 742, State Archives. Additional information from letter regarding "Uncle Davy" Carson from Louisa DuBosch April 27, 1981, Blacks file, Benton Museum.

13 *Statesman*, October 17, 1854, 3.

14 Brownell, *Negroes in Oregon*. Also unsourced document in files of Benton Museum.

15 *Statesman*, October 17, 1854, 3.

16 Ibid., December 5, 1854, 3.

17 Martha Anderson, *Black Pioneers*, 58.

18 McLagan, *A Peculiar Paradise*, 84.

19 Ibid.

20 Anderson, *Black Pioneers*. Those interviewed were not identified.

21 Dasch, *Early Black Women*.

22 Patricia Baldwin, "Louis Southworth," *Oregon Encyclopedia*.

23 Lockley, "Facts Pertaining to Ex-Slaves in Oregon and Documentary Record of the Case of Robin Holmes vs. Nathaniel Ford," *OH Quarterly*, March 1916, 111.

24 The additional information from Lockley interview in Standish-Carey, "Black Pioneers, Part III," *The Brownsville (OR) Times*, February 19, 1951, 2.

25 Eighth U.S. Census, 1860, NARA film M652.

26 Renita Bogle-Byrd, email to author, Nov. 26, 2012.

27 The 1830 slave census lists Daniel Waldo of Gasconade, Missouri, with four slaves, all male.

28 Brian Waldo Johnson, e-mail to author, November 24, 2012.

29 *Oregonian*, January 31, 1863.

30 Kathryn Bogle, Black Oral History interview, Washington State University Libraries, September 10, 1974. Can be heard at http://kaga.wsulibs.wsu.edu/flash/?aud=bogle&img=bla She was married to Richard Waldo Bogle Sr., grandson of Richard and America Waldo Bogle, and who preceded her in death.

31 R. J. Hendricks, "Bits for Breakfast" column, the *Statesman*, December 26, 1930, 4.

32 The 1840 slave Census lists John B. Waldo of Rives, Missouri, with three female slaves.

33 Waldo Lincoln, *Genealogy of the Waldo Family*, 432-33.

34 Maude Cauthorn Keady interview, *WPA Historical Records*.

35 Ibid.

36 Dasch, "Hannah Gorman & Eliza J. Gorman," unpublished paper in Black file, Benton Museum.

37 Ibid. Also, Eighth U.S. Census for 1860, NARA film, reel 1, roll M652.

38 Obituary, *Corvallis Gazette*, July 17, 1869, 3.

39 Eighth U.S. Census, NARA film, roll M652.

40 Taylor, "Slaves and Free Men," 163.

41 Ibid., 160, 162.

42 Richard, "Unwelcome Settlers" *OH Quarterly*, 1983, 38. Also, "Black Pioneers, Part II," Margaret Standish-Carey, *Brownsville (OR) Times*, February 5, 1981, 2.

43 Eighth U.S. Census, NARA roll M652.

44 Brownell, *Negroes in Oregon*. Also, Susan Bell, "Marion County's Claim to First Black Settlers," *Historic Marion*, Marion County Historical Society, Summer 1999, 6-7.

45 Taylor, "Slaves and Free Men," 165.

46 Berwanger, in *Frontier Against Slavery*, found it suspicious that census takers in 1850 "conveniently listed all negroes as free," 82.

47 Oregon's county census data, OHS Library.

48 Brownell, *Negroes in Oregon*.

49 Burch, *Ford Family*, 13.

50 Blacks file, Benton Museum.

51 Burch, *Negro Family*, 5.

AN ARMY SLAVE

1 Lockley, *Slavery in Oregon*, 108. Lockley didn't say where he found the documents. Greg Shine, historian at the Fort Vancouver National Historic Site, said they no longer exist and may have been destroyed in a fire. There was no explanation why the documents were dated six years apart. Possibly the second date was when it was officially recorded. Also Lockley's quotation from the document giving Monimia Travers her freedom is the only specific reference to a document freeing a slave so far located in the Pacific Northwest.

2 After the settlement of the Oregon boundary dispute with Great Britain in 1846, the United States established a military post called Columbia Barracks, adjacent to the Hudson's Bay Company's Fort Vancouver. Members of Jones' unit were housed both in Oregon City and Fort Vancouver.

3 Shine, "A Slave Freed at Fort Vancouver," National Park Service website http://www.nps.gov/fova/historyculture/a-slave-freed-at-fort-vancouver.htm, 1-5. Trexler, in *Slaves in Missouri*, said Isaac B. Burbbayge (cq) was an agent in St. Louis. He advertised in the *Daily Missourian* as "proprietor of the old established Real Estate, Negro, Slave, Money Agency and Intelligence Office," 51.

4 Settle, *March of the Mounted Riflemen*, 17. By the time the Oregon expedition finally got under way, it's possible fewer companies may have made the trip.

5 Ibid., 15.

6 Ibid., 129.

7 Unruh, *The Plains Across*, 207.

8 Settle, *Mounted Riflemen*, 281.

9 Shine, *A Slave Freed*, 1-5.

10 Settle, *Mounted Riflemen*, 22.

11 Johnson, *Founding the Far West*, 153.

12 Clark, *Pharisee Among Philistines*, xxiv.

13 Settle, *Mounted Riflemen*, 166. Whatever Simonson's offense, however, it did not end his career, as he was promoted to colonel in 1861, and to brigadier-general in 1865 "for long and meritorious service in the army." 276.

14 The 2nd Dragoons were involved in attempts in the late 1840s and 1850s to subdue the Comanche tribes menacing the settlers moving onto tribal lands in Texas and the Southwest. The 1st Dragoons were also involved in struggles against the tribes, including the Comanches, but mostly engaged tribes in combat in California and southern Oregon. Depending on the author writing about them, the Dragoons met with varying degrees of success. S.C. Gwynne, in *Empire of the Summer Moon*, wrote of the war-fighting capability of the 2nd Dragoons against Comanches: "They were a heavily mounted infantry who rode horses to the scene of battle, but fought dismounted. They were undoubtedly effective against comparably mounted and armed opponents, but on the Texas frontier they were a shocking anachronism. . . . The only way the Indians could ever be in danger from these soldiers, observed one Texas Ranger, was if their ridiculous appearance and ungainly horsemanship caused the Indians to laugh themselves to death." 160-161.

15 Trexler, *Slaves in Missouri*, 209. Missouri law also forbade working a slave on Sundays, except for housework, 27.

16 Obituary information from the *Corvallis Gazette*, July 6, 1906. Sarcastic account from Lone Fir Cemetery records, copied in Blacks file at Benton Museum.

17 Bell, "Marion County's Claim," 7-8.

18 Root, "A Family History of the Oregon Pioneer Families of Philip Glover and John H. Palmer," 47. OHS Library.

THE FREE STATE LETTER

1 Carey, *Oregon Constitution*, 507.

2 Ibid., 509.

3 Johnson, *Founding the Far West*, 156.

4 Clark, *Pharisee Among Philistines*, xxxv.

5 Deady to Benjamin Simpson, July 28, 1857, Deady letters, MSS dd44, OHS Library.

6 Hendrickson, *Joe Lane of Oregon*, 10.

7 Ibid., 2.

8 Woodward, "Political Parties," 159.

9 "Why Oregon Should Be a Non-Slave State," *Statesman*, July 28, 1857, 1. Also, "The Free State Letter of Judge George H. Williams," *OH Quarterly*, September, 1908, 255-73.

10 Williams, *Political History*, 16.

11 Deady to Simpson.

12 Williams, *Political History*, 16.

13 Ludington, *Oregon Newspapers*, 256. Hendrickson, *Joe Lane of Oregon*, viii, wrote that "despite the high-handed tactics Bush pursued, the Clique gave Oregon efficient and responsible government, remarkably free of the graft and corruption so commonly associated with political machines."

14 Ibid.

15 Turnbull, *Oregon Newspapers*, 75.

16 Johnson, *Founding the Far West*, 47. Thurston died April 9, 1851, aboard a ship west of Acapulco, Mexico. Turnbull, *Oregon Newspapers*, 75.

17 Johnson, *Founding the Far West*, 53. The *Statesman* was initially located in Oregon City, the territorial capital, but Bush moved it to Salem, the new territorial capital, in 1853. It also was briefly in Corvallis, which also was briefly the capital.

18 Davenport, "Slavery Question," 223. Known as "the Sage of Silverton," the New-York-born Davenport arrived in Oregon in 1851. He was also a physician, surveyor, and Indian agent in the Umatilla agency. He was elected to the Oregon Senate in 1882.

19 Barbara Mahoney said "Bush consistently opposed slavery in Oregon, "Asahel Bush, Slavery, and the Statehood Debate,"*OH Quarterly*, Summer, 2009, 213.

20 Woodward, "Political Parties," 152. Woodward said he spoke with Williams on July 28, 1909. Members of the newly organized Republican Party were branded Black Republicans by Asahel Bush and other opponents because of their anti-slavery positions.

21 Ibid, 153.

LET VOTERS DECIDE

1 Carey, *Oregon Constitution*, 12, 18.

2 Carey, *General History*, 504-5.

3 *Oregon Argus*, December 1, 1855, 1.

4 Carey, *Oregon Constitution*, 176.

5 Johannsen, "The Kansas-Nebraska Act and the Pacific Northwest," *Pacific Historical Review*, 138.

6 Joint Resolution, House Journal, 1854, 51-54.

7 *Statesman*, January 20, 1857, Lovejoy, from Massachusetts, was involved in the famous 1845 coin toss with Francis Pettygrove that gave the name of Portland—Pettygrove's choice— to the new city. Lovejoy served as the first speaker of the Oregon Territorial House of Representatives in 1849.

8 *Scott v. Sanford*, U.S. Supreme Court, 1856. John Sanford was the owner when Scott appealed a lower court ruling to the Supreme Court. The case was heard in 1856, and the decision rendered on March 6, 1857.

9 Ibid.

10 The Missouri Compromise had already been negated by the Kansas-Nebraska Act.

11 Potter, *Impending Crisis*, 291.

12 Ibid., 337.

13 Ibid., 328.

14 Ibid., 331.

15 It was during Douglas' Senate campaign that Douglas and Lincoln engaged in their historic debates, in which they disagreed over popular sovereignty, also referred to as "squatter rights." Douglas' theory was known as "The Freeport Doctrine."

16 Potter, *Impending Crisis*, 328.

17 *The Oregonian*, November 1, 1856, 3.

18 Carey, *History of Oregon*, 506.

19 Carey, *Oregon Constitution*, 24-25.

20 Ibid., 29.

21 Johnson, *Founding the Far West*, 57.

22 Woodward, "Political Parties," 141.

23 Ibid., 154.

24 The territorial capital building, which would have been a more appropriate venue for the convention, had burned to the ground in 1855 and was yet to be replaced.

25 The courthouse was the first of three county courthouses on the same block. The 1854 courthouse was moved in 1871 to make way for its successor. At its new location, the building housed various businesses before ending its usefulness as a livery stable at the turn of the twentieth century.

26 Woodward, "Political Parties," 154.

THE SLAVERY NON-DEBATE

1 Excerpts of debate from Carey, *Oregon Constitution*, 65-399.

2 Davenport, "The Late George Williams." *OH Quarterly*, 280.

3 Sutton, "A Profile of Oregon's Past," *Oregonian*, September 20, 1970, 9. The

author was unable to locate the primary source for Applegate's statement, but has no reason to doubt its authenticity.

4 Excerpts, *Oregon Constitution*, 65-399.

5 Ibid.

6 Excerpts of newspaper coverage from Carey, *Oregon Constitution*, 65-399.

7 Ibid., 98.

8 Ibid., 99.

9 Ibid., 122.

10 Ibid., 126.

11 Ibid., 129.

12 Ibid., 173-74.

13 Johnson, *Founding the Far West*, 425.

14 Carey, *Oregon Constitution*, 266.

15 Ibid., 318.

16 Ibid., 321.

17 Ibid., 328.

18 Ibid., 361.

19 Henrickson, *Joe Lane*, 95-96. Also, *Statesman*, December 12, 1894. The 1854 legislature stipulated that each voter should announce his vote in a loud, clear voice, or hand his ballot to the precinct judge, who would announce it in the same manner. The idea behind it was to expose members of the secretive Know Nothing party. But it also was useful for Democratic Party leaders to make sure party members voted the party way. The *Statesman* editorialized in 1854 that the leading Know Nothing members were "doomed men . . . There is not a man of prominence or influence belonging to the damning conspiracy in Oregon whose connection with it will not be known in less than six months." The Know Nothings, among other things, sought to exclude the foreign-born and Roman Catholics from public office.

"CONSECRATE!!!" OREGON FOR WHITES

1 Carey, *Oregon Constitution*, 361-62.

VOTERS DO DECIDE

1 Carey, *Oregon Constitution*, 383.

2 Ibid., 493.

3 Carey, *Oregon Constitution*, 385.

4 Carey, *Oregon Constitution*, 393.

5 Carey, *History of Oregon*, 511.

6 Davenport, "Slavery Question," 195.

7 Ibid.

8 Ibid.

9 Applegate to Deady, Nov. 15, 1868, in Carey, *Oregon Constitution*, 31.

10 Williams, *Political History*, 18.

11 Woodward, "Political Parties," 139.

12 Ibid., 226.

13 *Statesman*, April 13, 1858, 3.

14 Ibid.

15 Woodward, "Political Parties," 233. In the nomenclature of the day, the state Democrats were "the hards," and the national Democrats were "the softs."

16 *Statesman*, May 18, 1858.

17 Ibid.

18 *Sentinel*, June 12, 1858, 3. Dowell, said to be a distant relation of Benjamin Franklin, was a Whig, but not opposed to slavery. An attorney in Jacksonville, he became a self-made expert on collecting war claims against Native American tribes following the Rogue River wars. He purchased the *Sentinel*, a Republican newspaper, in 1864.

19 Carey, *Oregon Constitution*, 42.

20 Josephy, *The Civil War in the American West*, 233.

21 Johnson, *Founding the Far West*, 280.

22 *Sentinel*, January 29, 1859, 3.

23 Johannsen, *Frontier Politics*, 127.

24 Hendrickson, *Joe Lane of Oregon*, 226. The regular delegate who attended was Lansing Stout, Oregon's congressional representative. Lane monitored events from Washington, D.C., from where he encouraged the delegation's walkout.

25 Johannsen, *Frontier Politics*, 129.

26 Ibid., 115. The *Oregonian*'s Dryer was instrumental in persuading Baker to move to Oregon.

27 Johnson, *Founding the Far West*, 281. For a detailed discussion of the party maneuvering in this period, see pp. 279-283.

28 Ibid, 151; also Potter, *Impending Crisis*, 443.

A VOICE FOR EQUALITY

1 Oliver, "Obed Dickinson and the 'Negro Question' in Salem," *OH Quarterly*, Spring 1991, 8.

2 Ibid., 9.

3 Ibid., 15.

4 The Holmeses are mentioned in church documents as members. Evidence that Johnson was the third former slave is circumstantial. The 1850 census listed a William Johnson, age eleven, in Polk County. Possibly he was the W.P. Johnson who helped organize a school for black children in Salem in 1867. *Perserverance*, 42-43 and 20-21. A parishioner recalled Mrs. Holmes referring during a church service to a "Brother Johnson."

5 The Reuben Shipleys by this time were attending the Beulah Chapel of the United Brethren Church near Philomath.

6 Oliver, "Obed Dickinson," 12.

7 Records of the First Congregational Church, Salem, Oregon Territory, 1852-1859, kept by Obed Dickinson.

8 Ibid.

9 McLagan, *Peculiar Paradise*, 84-85.

10 Bush letter to Deady, January 15, 1863, manuscript file, OHS Library. The year is misdated as 1862 in the file.

11 "Letter from Oregon," *San Francisco Bulletin*, February 2, 1863, which in addition to its own commentary reprinted the *Oregonian* article from January 31, 1863.

12 Ibid.

13 Bush letter to Deady, February 24, 1863.

14 Salem *Statesman-Journal*, February 26, 2007. "Obed Dickinson Garden Seeds" was on Commercial Street.

REUBEN AND MARY JANE

1 Ford to Shirley, June 22, 1852.

2 Hazel Waterman, "Twice Under the Cloud of Slavery," *Oregonian*, March 2, 1952, 16-17.

3 Burch, Negro Family, 7.

4 Marion County Marriage Book No. 2, Salem.

5 Horner, "Woman Who Came to Oregon as Slave Spends Last Days in Home for the Aged," *Oregonian*, January 27, 1924, sec. 4, p. 8. Dr. Horner was a professor of history at Oregon Agricultural College, now Oregon State University. Although Horner wrote that Mary Jane Holmes Shipley Drake had a "clear mind" during the interview, he did not directly quote her.

6 Henkle interview, *WPA Historical Records*.

7 Horner interview.

8 Henkle interview.

9 Horner interview.

10 Bethers interview, *WPA Historical Records*.

11 Ibid.

12 *Statesman*, June 19, 1857, 4. The "Avery" mentioned in the letter was most probably Joseph Avery, who served in the territorial House in 1854, representing Benton County. He was one of the dissident Democrats who, along with Nathaniel Ford, broke with the Salem Clique and thus earned Asahel Bush's enmity. Avery also in 1851 platted the town of Marysville, today's Corvallis. The reference to "Jim" was possibly to James Slater, who had just been elected to the territorial House from Benton County on an opposition ticket. Slater would later become a U.S. senator.

13 Burch, *Negro Family*, 6.

14 Judge Boise's letter is a footnote in Davenport, "Slavery Question," 196.

WHO WAS REUBEN FICKLIN?

1 McLagan, *A Peculiar Paradise*, 81.

2 Shipley file, Benton Museum.

3 Note found in cemetery records at the Benton Museum.

4 1850 U.S. Census.

5 Letter from Minnie Wyatt Junkin to the Benton County Historical Society, cemetery file, Benton Museum.

6 Ibid.

MARY JANE'S LAST TRIAL

1 Burch, *Negro Family*, 6.

2 1870 U.S. Census for Marion County, OHS Library.

3 It seems highly unlikely there were two different Alfred Drakes, as the same children were named.

4 "Murderer Hanged—The Death Scene," *Statesman*, March 27, 1885.

5 Benton County Deed Book, County Clerk's Office, Book W, 348.

6 Waterman, "Under the Cloud of Slavery," *Oregonian*.

7 McLagan, *Peculiar Paradise*, 82.

8 Burch, *Negro Family*, 6.

9 Letter from Multnomah County Home and Farm in Troutdale, February 25, 1953, sent to Oregon State Library in Salem. Copy in Shipley file at Benton Museum.

10 Waterman, *Oregonian*, 1952.

SLAVEHOLDERS' LAST STAND

1 Carey, *Oregon Constitution*, 516.

2 Journal of the House of Representatives of the Territory of Oregon 10ᵗʰ Regular session, 1858-1859, 111, OHS Library.

3 T'Vault petititon, Oregon Provisional and Territorial Government Records, Reel No. 73, Item 10964, OHS Library.

4 Turnbull, *Oregon Newspapers*, 103.

5 Southworth petition, Oregon Provisional and Territorial Government Records, Reel No. 73, Item 10974, OHS Library.

6 Woodward, *"Political Parties,"* 239.

7 Ibid.

8 Journal of the House of Representatives, 174-75.

9 Ibid., 175-79.

10 Josephy, *Civil War*, 236.

11 Carey, *Oregon Constitution*, 776.

12 Platt, "Oregon and Its Share in the Civil War," *OH Quarterly*, June 1903, 96.

13 Hendrickson, *Joe Lane*, 250.

14 Ibid.

15 Platt, "Civil War," 96.

16 Neiderheisen, *Dialogue with Destiny*, 225.

17 Ibid.

18 Carey, *History of Oregon*, 666.

19 Platt, "Civil War," 108.

20 Beckham, *Oregon Blue Book*, 353-54.

21 McLagan, *Peculiar Paradise*, 68.

22 *Statesman*, 13, 1866.

23 Josephy, *Civil War*, 240-41.

24 Turnbull, *Oregon Newspapers*, 143.

25 Ludington, *Newspapers of Oregon*, 237. T'Vault was the first editor of Oregon's first newspaper, the *Spectator* of Oregon City, but was fired for voicing his political views.

26 Turnbull, *Oregon Newspapers*, 274.

27 Ludington, *Newspapers of Oregon*, 237-38.

28 Ibid.

29 "An Act to Provide for Taxing Negroes, Chinamen, Kanakas, and Mulattoes," *The Code of Civil Procedure and Other Laws of Oregon, 1862*, 76-77.The tax had nothing to do with voting, but was for "the use of the county in which such negro, chinaman, mulatto or kanaka may reside." The equal protection clause of the Fourteenth Amendment put an end to such laws.

30 Two who voted approval in 1866 were later determined not to be legal members. Democrats were back in control in 1868 and the re-vote was to disapprove. For a more complete discussion of the ratification issue, see Cheryl A. Brooks, "Race, Politics, and Denial: Why Oregon Forgot to Ratify the Fourteenth Amendment," 2004 *Oregon Law Review*, 731-762.

31 Brooks, "Race, Politics and Denial," 732.

32 Ibid., 753.

33 Ibid., 753.

34 Ibid., 751.

35 Ibid., 753.

36 *Oregonian*, May 18, 1973.

37 Brooks, "Race, Politics and Denial," 754.

38 McLagan, *Peculiar Paradise*, 71.

39 Ibid.

40 Richard, "Unwelcome Settlers," Part II, 183.

41 McLagan, *A Peculiar Paradise*, 71.

42 *Oregonian*, June 26, 1900, 6.

43 *Proposed Constitutional Amendments and Measures To Be Submitted to the Voters of Oregon at the General Election Tuesday, November 2, 1926*, 9. The argument in favor of repeal was signed by Senator Milton R. Klepper and Reps. William F. Woodward and Frank J. Lonergan, all of Multnomah

County. There were no opposing arguments. Pamphlet in the files of the OHS Library.

44*Oregonian*, November 3, 1926, 8.

MOVING ON

1 Records of the Salem Pioneer Cemetery and interview in August, 2012, with Gwen Carr of the Oregon Northwest Black Pioneers.

2 *Sentinel*, December 3, 1859, 3.

3 Military Committee Report, Council Journal for 1858-1859, OHS Library, 27.

4 Oswald West, "Reminiscences and Anecdotes," *OH Quarterly*, September, 1951, 145. Despite owning a slave, Claggett was a founder of the Union Party, which included Republicans and dissident Democrats, and dominated Oregon politics during the Civil War.

5 Williams, *Political History*, 15.

6 Carey, *History of Oregon*, 787.

7 Clark, *Pharisee Among Philistines*, xxix.

8 Johnson, *Founding the Far West*, 299.

9 Jewell Lansing, *Portland: People, Politics and Power, 1851-2001*.

10 Davenport, "The Late George H. Williams," *OH Quarterly*, March 1910, 281.

11 Harvey Scott, "An Estimate of the Character and Services of Judge George H. Williams," *OH Quarterly*, June 1910, 224.

12 Lockley, *Slavery in Oregon*, 108-9.

13 Ibid.

14 Clark, *Pharisee Among the Philistines*, 61

15 Applegate to Bates, December 30, 1861. Deady file, OHS Library.

16 Clark, *Pharisee*, 61.

17 Williams, "Political History," 10.

18 West, "Reminiscences and Anecdotes," 148.

19 Letter from Applegate to Deady, November 15, 1868. Deady file, OHS Library. The two former adversaries frequently corresponded on political and personal matters.

20 Hendrickson, *Joe Lane*, 256. Peter Waldo's relarionship to the Waldo family, if any, is unclear.

21 Hendrickson, *Joe Lane*, 22-23. He cites Lane's "Autobiography," 88-100. The boy apparently lived only a few years.

22 Williams, "Political History," 27.

23 Smith, *Remaking Slavery*, 61-62.

24 Lapp, *Blacks in Gold Rush California*, 148.

25 Smith, *Remaking Slavery*, 61-62.

26 "Preschool strips name of a governor," *San Francisco Chronicle*, May 19, 2011, C-1.

27 "California School Named After Racist Governor Gets New Title," *The Associated Press* on HuffingtonPost.com, July 19, 2011.

28 Burnett, *Recollections*, 218.

29 Ibid.

30 Dary, *Oregon Trail*, 120.

31 Applegate, "Old Emigrant Road," 1921.

32 Bright, "Black Harris," 9.

33 Ibid.

34 O'Donnell, *Arrow in the Earth*, 101.

35 Applegate to Deady, November 15, 1868.

36 Quiring, interview with author, November 2, 2010.

EPILOGUE

1 Josephy, *The Forked Tongue in U.S. History Books*, 3.

APPENDIX

1 Nokes, *Wagons to Oregon*, 10-11.

2 Ibid.

BIBLIOGRAPHY

BOOKS

Anderson, Martha, *Black Pioneers of the Northwest, 1800-1918* (Martha E. Anderson, 1980).

Applegate, Jesse A., *Westward Journeys: Memoirs of Jesse A. Applegate and Lavinia Honeyman Porter Who Traveled the Overland Trail* (Chicago: Lakeside Press, 1989).

Applegate, Shannon, *Skookum: An Oregon Pioneer Family's History and Lore* (New York: Beech Tree Books, 1988).

Avery, Mary W., *Washington: A History of the Evergreen State* (Seattle: University of Washington Press, 1961).

Bancroft, Hubert Howe and Victor, Frances Fuller, *History of Oregon, Volume 1, 1834-1848* (San Francisco: The History Company, 1886).

Basler, Roy P., *Collected Works of Abraham Lincoln, Volume II* (New Brunswick, New Jersey: Rutgers University Press, 1953).

Beckham, Stephen Dow, *Oregon Blue Book, 2011-2012* (Salem, Oregon: Office of the Secretary of State, 2011).

Beckham, Stephen Dow, *The Indians of Western Oregon: This Land was Theirs* (Coos Bay, Oregon: Arago Books, 1977).

Berwanger, Eugene H., *The Frontier Against Slavery: Western Anti-Negro Prejudice and the Slavery Extension Controversy* (Urbana, Illinois: University of Illinois Press, 1967).

Brown, Wilfred H., *This Was a Man: About the Life and Times of Jesse Applegate* (North Hollywood, California: Wilfred H. Brown, 1971).

Brownell, Jean, *Negroes in Oregon before the Civil War* (1962 unpublished manuscript in files of Oregon Historical Museum Library).

Burke, Diane Mutti, *On Slavery's Borders: Missouri's Small Slave-Holding Households, 1815-1865* (Athens, Georgia: University of Georgia Press, 2010).

Burnett, Peter H., *Recollections and Opinions of an Old Pioneer* (New York: D. Appleton & Co., 1880).

Carey, Charles H., *General History of Oregon: Through Early Statehood* (Portland: Binfords & Mort, 1971).

Carey, Charles H., *The Oregon Constitution and Proceedings and Debates of the Constitutional Convention of 1857* (Salem, Oregon: State Printing Department, 1926).

Clark Jr., Malcolm, editor of Matthew Deady's diary, *Pharisee Among Philistines* (Portland, Oregon: Oregon Historical Society, 1975).

Coffman, Lloyd W., *Blazing a Wagon Trail to Oregon: A Weekly Chronicle of the Great Migration of 1843* (Enterprise, Oregon: Echo Books, 1993).

Corning, Howard McKinley, *Dictionary of Oregon History, Second Edition* (Portland, Oregon: Binfords & Mort Publishing, 1956, compiled from Oregon Writers Project).

Dary, David, *The Oregon Trail, an American Saga* (New York: Alfred A, Knopf, 2004).

Deady, M. P., *General Laws of Oregon, 1845-1864,* (Portland, Oregon: A.G. Walling & Co., 1866).

Demaratus, DeEtta, *The Force of a Feather, the Search for a Lost Story of Slavery and Freedom* (Salt Lake City: University of Utah Press, 2002).

Dodds, Gordon B., *The American Northwest: A History of Oregon and Washington* (Arlington Heights, Illinois: The Forum Press, 1986).

Edwards, Cecil L, *Chronological List of Oregon Legislatures* (Salem, Oregon: Legislative Administrative Committee, 1993).

Emerson, William, *The Applegate Trail of 1846* (Ashland, Oregon: Emerson Ember Enterprises, 1996).

Gray, W. H., *A History of Oregon 1792-1849, Drawn from Personal Observation and Authentic Information* (Portland, Oregon: Harris & Holman, 1870).

Grover, LaFayette, *Oregon Archives, including Journals, Governors' Messages and Public Papers of Oregon* (Salem, Oregon: Asahel Bush Public Printer 1853).

Gwynne, S. C., *Empire of the Summer Moon: Quanah Parker and the Rise and Fall of the Comanches, The Most Powerful Indian Tribe in American History* (New York: Scribner, 2010).

Haines, Francis D., *The Applegate Trail: Southern Emigrant Route 1846* (American Revolution Bicentennial Commission of Oregon: 1976).

Hafen, Le Roy Reuben, *Trappers of the Far West: Sixteen Biographical Sketches* (Lincoln, Nebraska: Bison Books and University of Nebraska Press, 1983).

Hendrickson, James E., *Joe Lane of Oregon: Machine Politics and the Sectional Crisis, 1849-1861* (New Haven, Connecticut: Yale University Press, 1967).

Hochschild, Adam, *Bury the Chains: Prophets and Rebels in the Fight to Free an Empire's Slaves* (New York: Houghton Mifflin Company, 2005).

Johannsen, Robert W., *Frontier Politics and the Sectional Conflict: The Pacific Northwest on the Eve of the Civil War* (Seattle, Washington: University of Washington Press, 1955).

Johnson, David Alan, *Founding the Far West: California, Oregon and Nevada, 1840-1890* (Berkeley, California: University of California Press, 1992).

Junkin, William S. and Minnie Wyatt, *The Henckel Genealogy*, 1500-1960, (C. W. Hill Printing Co: Spokane, Washington, 1964).

Juntunen, Judy Rycraft; Dasch, May D.; Rogers, Ann Bennett, *The World of the Kalapuya: A Native People of Western Oregon* (Philomath, Oregon: Benton County Historical Society and Museum, 2005).

Krakauer, Jon, *Under the Banner of Heaven* (New York: Doubleday, 2003).

Lapp, Rudolph M., *Blacks in Gold Rush California* (New Haven, Connecticut: Yale University Press, 1977).

Lincoln, Waldo, *Genealogy of the Waldo Family: A Record of the Descendants of Cornelius Waldo of Ipswich, Massachusetts from 1647-1900* (Worcester, Massachusetts: Charles Hamilton, 1902).

Lockley, Fred, *The Lockley Files: Voices of the Oregon Territory* (Eugene, Oregon: Rainy Day Press, 1981).

Mackey, Harold, *The Kalapuyans: A Sourcebook on the Indians of the Willamette Valley* (Grand Ronde, Oregon: The Confederated Tribes of Grand Ronde, 2004).

Mattes, Merrill J., *The Great Platte River Road*, (Lincoln, Nebraska: University of Nebraska Press, 1969).

McArthur, Lewis A., *Oregon Geographic Names, Fifth Edition* (Oregon Historical Society Press: 1982).

McLagan, Elizabeth, *A Peculiar Paradise: A History of Blacks in Oregon* (Portland, Oregon: Georgian Press, 1980).

Millner, Darrell, *Blacks in Oregon 1888-1940* (Portland, Oregon: Portland State University, 1978).

Neiderheiser, Leta Lovelace, *Jesse Applegate: Dialogue with Destiny* (Mustang, Oklahoma: Tate Publishing and Enterprises, 2010).

O'Donnell, Terence, *An Arrow in the Earth: General Joel Palmer and the Indians of Oregon* (Portland: Oregon Historical Society Press, 1991).

O'Hara, Edwin V., *Pioneer Catholic History of Oregon* (Portland, Oregon: Glass & Prudhomme Co., 1911).

Ostling, Richard N and Joan K., *Mormon America: The Power and the Promise* (San Francisco, California: HarperCollins, 1999).

Perseverance: A History of African Americans in Oregon's Marion and Polk Counties (Salem, Oregon: Oregon Northwest Black Pioneers, 2011).

Potter, David M., *The Impending Crisis, 1848-1861,* (New York: Harper & Row, 1976).

Ripley, C. Peter. *The Black Abolitionist Papers, 1830-1865, Volume IV,* (Chapel Hill: University of North Carolina Press, 1985-1992).

Ruby, Robert H., and Brown, John A., *Indians of the Pacific Northwest* (Norman, Oklahoma: University of Oklahoma Press, 1981).

Settle, Raymond W., *The March of the Mounted Riflemen: From Fort Leavenworth to Fort Vancouver* (Lincoln, Nebraska: University of Nebraska Press, 1989).

Stone, Jeffrey C., *Slavery, Southern Culture, and Education in Little Dixie, Missouri, 1820-1860* (New York: Routledge, 2006).

Taylor, Quintard, *In Search of the Racial Frontier, African Americans in the American West, 1528-1990* (New York: W.W. Norton & Company, 1998).

Teiser, Sidney, *Almost Chief Justice: George H. Williams,* 1947 (Reprint from *Oregon Historical Quarterly*, September and December, 1946).

Trexler, Harrison Anthony, *Slavery in Missouri, 1804-1865* (Baltimore, Maryland: John Hopkins Press, 1914).

Turnbull, George S., *History of Oregon Newspapers* (Portland, Oregon: Binford & Mort, 1939.

Unruh, John Jr., *The Plains Across* (Urbana, Illinois: University of Illinois, 1979).

Wilkerson, Isabel, *The Warmth of Other Suns,* (New York: Vintage Books, 2011).

Williams, George H., *Occasional Addresses by George H. Williams* (Portland, Oregon: F.W. Bates & Co., 1895).

Wong, Marie Rose, *Sweet Cakes, Long Journey, The Chinatowns of Portland, Oregon* (Seattle, Washington: University of Washington Press, 2004).

Zenk, Henry B., *Kalapuyans* in Sturtevant, William C., *Handbook of North American Indians, Volume 7, Northwest Coast,* (Washington, D.C,: Smithsonian Institution, 1900).

ESSAY, ARTICLES, AND LETTERS

Applegate, Jesse, *Letters from Jesse Applegate, 1867-1875* (Portland, Oregon: Oregon Historical Museum Library MSS48).

Applegate, Lindsay, "Notes and Reminisces of Laying Out and Establishing the Old Emigrant Road into Oregon in the Year 1846" (*Oregon Historical Quarterly*, March 1921).

Baldwin, Peggy, "A Legacy Beyond the Generations," 2006. http://www.family-passages.com/Publications/SouthworthLewis.pdf

Baldwin, Peggy, "Louis Southworth (1829–1917)," *Oregon Encyclopedia*, http://www.oregonencyclopedia.org/entry/view/southworth_louis_1829_1017_/

Bell, Susan N., *Marion County's Claim to First Black Settlers* (Salem, Oregon: Historic Marion, publication of Marion County Historical Society, Summer, 1999).

Bergquist, James M., "Oregon Donation Act and the National Land Policy" (*Oregon Historical Quarterly*, March 1957).

Bogle, Kathryn. Black oral history interview (Washington State University Libraries, September 20, 1974).

Bright, Verne, "Black Harris, Mountain Man, Teller of Tales" (*Oregon Historical Quarterly*, March, 1951).

Brooks, Cheryl A., "Race, Politics, and Denial: Why Oregon Forgot to Ratify the Fourteenth Amendment" (Eugene, Oregon: *Oregon Law Review*, Volume 83, 2004.)

Burch, Caroline, *Ford Family of Rickreall* (typewritten and undated article in files of Benton County Historical Museum).

Burch, Pauline, *Pioneer Nathaniel Ford and the Negro Family* (typewritten article in files of Benton County Historical Museum, 1953).

Clark Jr., Malcolm, "The Bigot Disclosed: 90 Years of Nativism" (*Oregon Historical Society Quarterly*, June 1974).

Crafting the Oregon Constitution (Exhibit of Oregon State Archives, 2009). http://arcweb.sos.state.or.us/exhibits/1857/index.htm

Dasch, May, *Early Black Women in Benton County, Oregon* (essay in the files of Benton County Historical Museum, Philomath, Oregon, 1985).

Davenport, Timothy W., "Slavery Question in Oregon, I, II" (*Oregon Historical Quarterly*, September and December, 1908).

Davenport, Timothy W., "The Late George H. Williams" (*Oregon Historical Quarterly*, March 1910).

Dickinson, Obed, *Records of the First Congregational Church, Territorial Period* (Salem, Oregon: files of First Congregational Church).

Fenton, W.D., "The Winning of the Oregon Country," reprint of an address given June 6, 1897 (*Oregon Historical Quarterly*, December 1905).

Ford, John T., *Colonel Nathaniel Ford*, undated biography (Polk County Museum, Rickreall, Oregon).

Glen, Julia Veazie, "John Lyle and Lyle Farm" (*Oregon Historical Quarterly*, June 1925).

Hendricks, R. J. "Bits for Breakfast" (*Statesman*, December 26, 1930).

Hogue, Theresa, "A Grave History Lesson" (Corvallis, Oregon: *Corvallis Gazette-Times*, August 5, 2002).

Holmes, Frederick V., "A Brief History of the Oregon Provisional Government and What Caused its Formation" (*Oregon Historical Quarterly*, June, 1912).

Horner, John B., "Woman Who Came to Oregon as Slave Spends Last Days in Home for the Aged" (*The Oregonian*, January 27, 1924).

Johannsen, Robert W., "The Kansas-Nebraska Act and the Pacific Northwest Frontier" (Berkeley, California: *Pacific Historical Review*, Volume XXII, May 1953).

Josephy, Jr., Alvin M., "The Forked Tongue in U.S. History Books" (*Learning, the Magazine for Creative Teaching*, January 1973).

Josephy, Jr., Alvin M., *The Civil War in the American West* (New York: Vintage Books, 1991).

Journals of the Legislative Assembly of the Territory of Oregon, 1849, 1851, 1853, 1855, 1857, 1858-1859 (Salem, Oregon: Oregon State Archives).

Kelly, James K., "*History of the Preparation of the First Code of Oregon*" (*Oregon Historical Quarterly*, September 1903).

Kozer, Sam A., secretary of state, *Proposed Constitutional Amendments and Measures To Be Submitted to the Voters of Oregon at the General Election, Tuesday, November 2, 1926.*

Laws of Oregon Passed by the Legislative Committee and Legislative Assembly, 1853 (Salem, Oregon: Oregon State Archives).

Lockley, Fred, "Observations and Impressions of the Journal Man" (*The Oregon Journal*: March 24, 1922, and December 28, 1933).

Lockley, Fred, "Some Documentary Records of Slavery in Oregon" (*Oregon Historical Quarterly*, March 1916).

Lockley, Fred, "Facts Pertaining to Ex-Slaves in Oregon and Documentary Record of the Case of Robin Holmes vs Nathaniel Ford" (*Oregon Historical Quarterly*, June 1922).

Lopez, Barry, "A Dark Light in the West: Racism and Reconciliation" (*The Georgia Review*, Fall 2010).

Lynn, Capi, "Minister braced racist backlash" (Salem, Oregon: *Statesman-Journal*, February 26, 2007).

Ludington, Flora Belle, "Oregon Newspapers 1846-70" (*Oregon Historical Quarterly, September 1925*).

Mahar, Franklin David, *Benjamin Franklin Dowell, 1826-1897, Claims Attorney and Newspaper Publisher in Southern Oregon,* a master's thesis, (University of Oregon, 1964).

Mahoney, Barbara, "Asahel Bush, Slavery, and the Statehood Debate" (*Oregon Historical Quarterly*, Summer 2009).

McArthur, Scott, "The Polk County Slave Case," *Historically Speaking, Volume II* (Monmouth, Oregon: Polk County Historical Society, August 1970).

McConaghy, Lorraine, *Washington Territory's Confederate Governor: Richard Dickerson Gholson,* paper delivered at the 2012 Pacific Northwest History Conference, Tacoma, Washington, October 19, 2012.

Mertz, Sara Jane Bennett, *The Hanging of Uncle George*, a collection of articles on the murder of Daniel Delaney Sr. (OregonPioneers.com).

Metsker, Charles F., *Donation Land Claims, Metsker's Atlas of Polk County, Oregon* (Portland: 1929).

Metsker, Charles F., *Donation Land Claims, Metsker's Atlas of Benton County, Oregon* (Portland: 1929).

Minto, John, "Reminiscences of Honorable John Minto, Pioneer of 1844" (*Oregon Historical Quarterly*, June 1901 and September 1901).

Minto, John, "Motives and Antecedents of the Pioneers" (*Oregon Historical Quarterly*, March 1904).

Minto, John, *Occasional Addresses*, records of Oregon Pioneer Association, 1876 (Oregon Historical Museum Library).

Neabeack Hill, a brief history (Benton County Historical Museum, Philomath, Oregon, undated).

Nokes, Evelyn Junkin, *Wagons to Oregon: Stories of the Henkle Train of 1853* (Henkle Association Western Branch, 1986).

Oliver, Egbert S., "Obed Dickinson and the 'Negro Question' in Salem" (*Oregon Historical Quarterly*, Spring 1991).

Phinney, Mark, *WPA Historical Records Survey*, compiled by Danell Aukerman (Benton County Historical Museum, 2000).

Platt, Robert Treat, "Oregon and its Share in the Civil War" (*Oregon Historical Quarterly*, June, 1903).

Revised Statutes of Territory of Oregon, enacted by the Legislative Assembly, Fifth and Sixth Regular Sessions (Salem, Oregon: Asahel Bush, public printer, 1855).

Richard, K. Keith, "Unwelcome Settlers: Black and Mulatto Oregon Pioneers, Parts I and II" (*Oregon Historical Quarterly*, Spring and Summer 1983).

Robin Holmes vs. Nathaniel Ford, case brought June 22, 1852, original hand-written file in Office of Court Clerk, Polk County Courthouse, Dallas, Oregon. Also *Oregon Historical Quarterly,* June 1922.

Root, Mabel Glover, *Family History of the Oregon Pioneer Families of Philip Glover and John H. Palmer* Oregon Historical Museum Library, 1966.

Schneider, Franz E., *The Black Laws of Oregon* (thesis presented to Department of History, University of Santa Clara, June 1970).

Scott, Harvey W., "An Estimate of the Character and Services of Judge George H. Williams" (*Oregon Historical Quarterly*, June 1901).

Shaw, Claud L., "The Story of Ellendale," *Historically Speaking (*Monmouth, Oregon: Polk County Historical Society, September 1990).

Shine, Greg, *A Slave Freed at Fort Vancouver* (Fort Vancouver National Historic Site, http://www.nps.gov/fova/historyculture/a-slave-freed-at-fort-vancouver.htm).

Slavery in Oregon. Oregon Writers Project, Works Project Administration of Oregon (Corvallis Public Library, October 16, 1940).

Smith, Ross A., *Oregon Overland: Three Roads of Adversity* (www.OregonOverland. com).

Smith, Stacey L., *Remaking Slavery in a Free State: Masters and Slaves in Gold Rush California,* Pacific Historical Review (Berkeley, California: University of California Press: October 2011).

Sutton, Bob, "A Profile of Oregon's Past" (*Northwest Magazine, The Oregonian,* September, 20, 1970).

Taylor, Quintard, "Slaves and Free Men: Blacks in the Oregon Country 1840-1860" (*Oregon Historical Quarterly*, Summer 1982).

Tobie, Harvey E., "Contributions of Virginians in Oregon" (*Oregon Historical Quarterly*, June 1951).

Waterman, Hazel, "Twice Under the Cloud of Slavery" (*The Oregonian Sunday Magazine*, March 2, 1952).

West, Oswald, "Reminiscences and Anecdotes; McNary's and Lane's" (*Oregon Historical Quarterly*, September 1951).

Williams, George H., "Political History of Oregon 1853-65" (*Oregon Historical Quarterly*, March 1901).

Williams, George H., "*The Free State Letter of Judge George H. Williams*" (*Oregon Historical Quarterly,* September 1908).

Woodward, Walter Carleton, "The Kansas-Nebraska Bill in Oregon Politics" (*Oregon Historical Quarterly*, June, 1911)

Woodward, Walter Carleton, "The Rise and Early History of Political Parties in Oregon I-V," reprint of a thesis for a doctorate of philosophy at the University of California, Berkeley (*Oregon Historical Quarterly*, June, 1911).

INDEX